Allegory and Mirror

Tradition and Structure i

PEGASUS  NEW YORK

Allegory and Mirror

Middle English Literature

James I. Wimsatt

This book is one of a series, Pegasus Backgrounds
in English Literature, under the general editorship
of John R. Mulder, New York University.

ACKNOWLEDGMENT

The author and publisher are grateful to Houghton Mifflin Co.
for permission to quote from *The Works,* ed. F. N. Robinson,
2nd. ed. (1957).

For my mother and father

Preface

Though allegory and mirror, as I define them, were never systematically formulated as distinct modes by literary critics, they are nevertheless authentic classifications productive of important insights into Middle English literature. Understanding them can substantially help the reader to recognize meanings and relationships in the imaginative writings of the time which otherwise may appear unrelated and without important significance. Through the exposition of these modes, therefore, I aim to provide the new student of Middle English literature with an approach to it, the more experienced students with one way to organize it, and the specialist perhaps with some additional insights.

The book is in total a definition of the two modes. In the introductory chapter and at various points I attempt explicitly to define and categorize them, but essentially I depend on the analyses of the works themselves to reveal what is of common significance. In each chapter I associate relevant Continental works of seminal influence on Middle English literature with the English works themselves. I relate the *Consolation of Philosophy,* the *Romance of the Rose,* the *Divine Comedy,* the romances of Chrétien de Troyes, and other writings to the works of Chaucer, Langland, the Pearl Poet, Malory, and their fellows, not as sources for individual passages but rather as literary materials which provided the later English writers with forms and methods. The relationships thus presented provide another demonstration of the essential unity of Western culture in the later Middle Ages.

While I hope that this book will be useful to every reader of Middle English literature, I have directed the presentation to those who have but a moderate acquaintanceship with Chaucer, Langland, and other writers of the time. I have supplied translations for the quotations of most writers other than Chaucer; I have normalized spellings, substituting Modern English characters for *eth, thorn,* and *yogh;* and on individual works I have provided background information that the specialist would not need. The Bibliographical Notes which follow the Key to Abbreviations at the end of the book are also largely designed to suit the needs of the nonspecialist.

The Bibliographical Notes actually serve a multiple function. They are not inclusive except in that they represent a complete list of the materials that I have consciously drawn on within the chapters. They also include items which are particularly well known and in some way connected with my discussions, or materials which I think may be of special interest to the reader. Since I do not use footnotes herein, sometimes items quoted are documented in the Notes.

Citations of the *Canterbury Tales* are identified by fragment letter (A, B, etc.) and line number, and of *Troilus and Criseyde* by book number in Roman numerals, then line number. Quotations of *Piers Plowman* are by text version (A, B, or C), passus number in Roman numerals, then line number. Biblical quotations are from the Douay translation of the Latin Vulgate.

For the convenience of the reader, at the beginning of Chapters II through VIII is a list of works which receive important consideration in the chapter. As these lists indicate, I have given *Piers Plowman* a large place in this book. Though teachers and the makers of textbooks have not made students as familiar with *Piers* as with the *Canterbury Tales* and *Troilus,* no work in Middle English is of greater literary worth or is more typically medieval and English. At the same time, some genres have not received the attention here that they merit in a general treatment of Middle English literature; I have in mind particularly the miracle plays and the lyrics.

I am grateful to various people for substantial assistance in the composition of this book. I wish particularly to thank Professor John V. Fleming of Princeton for his careful reading of the manuscript. Though I know that there remains much that he would further change, the book has profited greatly from his numerous helpful suggestions. I must thank my wife Mary Ann not only for her encouragement and moral support, but also for her cogent criticisms from which these essays have profited.

James I. Wimsatt
Greensboro, North Carolina
June, 1969

KEY to ABBREVIATIONS

EETS	Early English Text Society
ELH	*ELH;* formerly *A Journal of English Literary History*
JEGP	*Journal of English and Germanic Philology*
MLN	*MLN;* formerly *Modern Language Notes*
MLQ	*Modern Language Quarterly*
MP	*Modern Philology*
PMLA	*Publications of the Modern Language Association*
RES	*Review of English Studies*
SATF	Société des anciens textes français
SP	*Studies in Philology*

Contents

Preface, vii

Key to Abbreviations, x

List of Illustrations, xiii

Chapter One: The Scholar-Poets, 17

Chapter Two: Personification Allegory, 36

Chapter Three: The Dance of Love, 61

Chapter Four: The Allegory of Reason, 91

Chapter Five: The Allegory of Revelation, 117

Chapter Six: Summas, Manuals, and Mirrors, 137

Chapter Seven: The Mirror of Society
    Chaucer's *Canterbury Tales,* 163

Chapter Eight: The Ideal of Chivalry
    Gawain and Lancelot, 190

Chapter Nine: Conclusion
    The Concurrence of the Modes, 215

Index, 222

List of Illustrations

Figure 1. Jean de Meun at work, 21

Figure 2. The Wheel of Fortune, 38

Figure 3. Personification of Old Age, 41

Figure 4. The carole in the *Romance of the Rose,* 62

Figure 5. The God of Love shoots the Lover with an arrow, 70

Figure 6. Reason instructs the Lover, 96

Figure 7. Natural Understanding and Reason assist Deguilleville's pilgrim, 108

Figure 8. Boethius with Lady Philosophy and the Seven Arts, 111

Figure 9. The *Revelation of St. Bridget,* 119

Figure 10. Gluttony strikes the pilgrim, 138

Figure 11. The Prioress and the Wife of Bath, 164

Figure 12. The Squire and the Knight, 191

Allegory and Mirror

Chapter I

The Scholar-Poets

To open this book by saying that Middle English literature is typically didactic, abstract, allegorical, encyclopedic, and idealistic seems to invite the reader to open another book. Some who have read widely in Middle English literature will feel that such adjectives do not describe the *Canterbury Tales* or *Sir Gawain and the Green Knight,* and that they emphasize only the weaker aspects of the *House of Fame* and *Piers Plowman.* Those who have not read widely in the field perhaps will say that if such adjectives are truly descriptive they have read enough. Nevertheless, I shall stand by the description and simply plead in defense that Middle English literature, though didactic, is worthwhile for its own sake; though abstract, is filled with interesting detail; though allegorical, has many fine stories; though encyclopedic, often ends opportunely; and though idealistic, suffers from few illusions about man or this world.

Because the didactic intent of the writers largely accounts for the other qualities of Middle English literature that I have mentioned, the medieval passion for learning which led to this didacticism provides a good starting point for consideration of the literature. A discussion of this facet of the contemporary mind will conveniently lead into a more comprehensive treatment of the nature and the modes of the writing.

In the Middle Ages to learn about the phenomena of this world was to read God's first book, the book of Creation (His second book was, of course, the Bible), and to find out about the other world was to discover man's permanent home. Chaucer's Clerk, who would gladly learn and gladly teach, is clearly

an admirable man engaged in an exalted occupation. Clergy
(Learning) in *Piers Plowman* states explicitly the elevated notion
of education which prevailed:

> For yf hevene be on this erthe and ese to any soule,
> It is in cloistere or in scole be many skilles I fynde;
> For in cloistre cometh no man to chide ne to fighte,
> But alle is buxumnesse there and bokes to rede and to lerne.
> In scole there is scorne but if a clerke wil lerne,
> And grete love and lykynge for eche of hem loveth other.
>
> B, X, 300-305
>
> [For if there is happiness and solace to any soul on Earth,
> I find for many reasons that it is in school or the cloister.
> For no one comes to the cloister to chide or fight. But
> all is submissiveness there and learning and reading in
> books. In school there is scorn for a clerk who will not
> learn, but at the same time great love and affection
> because each one loves the other.]

Similar statements were commonplace. Gregory the Great
thought nothing dearer than learning except the joys of Heaven
and the hope of eternity. Bede, the first great English scholar,
considered it always a pleasure to "learn or teach or write."
And Alcuin, English nurse of the Carolingian Renaissance,
described the seven arts—the school curriculum—as the seven
pillars of Holy Wisdom and the seven steps to ascend the
heights of Theology.

The great creative writers of the Middle Ages were devotees
of learning. They were typically scholar-poets—not the hedonis-
tic, uncaring scholars that some romantic imaginations picture,
but rather (at their best, anyway) earnest scholars of vision and
insight, inspired to learn about and make visible the forces and
order of God's universe, a universe which encompasses stars and
seas, politics and wars, as well as churls, saints, demons, and
noble, sinful lovers. Because their interests were so inclusive,
many of the creative writers produced important expository
works: Chaucer, for instance, wrote a treatise on an astronomi-
cal instrument, the astrolabe; Dante composed a political essay
on monarchy; and Jean de Meun translated, among other
things, the *Military Art* of Vegetius.

These writers indeed would not have drawn a sharp distinction between their expository and imaginative writings. Both types, as they would have viewed the matter, were grounded in truth and aimed to exhibit it, though one type employed the veil of a "pleasing fiction." It is not surprising, then, that modes in which their fictions are expressed, notably the allegory and the mirror, have counterparts in nonfictional approaches.

The medieval concept of literature clearly was quite different from ours; we establish a domain for the poet separate from that inhabited by the teacher and the expository writer. Because of this difference, medieval criticism did not interest itself in such concepts as *organic form, point of view, episode, denouement, realism, romanticism,* and the like. Modern critics nevertheless profitably discuss medieval works in these terms and often find them by the most sophisticated criteria to be admirably organized and executed. Though different from ours, the premises from which the writers worked—and it is clear that they were conscious artists—obviously had substantial artistic merit.

Where did the medieval writer of imaginative literature learn his art? Medieval critical writings are not plentiful, and they are not to us impressive: there were no Aristotles, Coleridges, or Eliots who dealt extensively with creative writings on their own terms. On the other hand, medieval writers had as guides the examples of some of the very best poets, notably the classical Latin writers whom they studied in school. In addition, they received extensive education in grammatical and rhetorical theory which was particularly relevant to literature, and it is also significant that they learned from the study of logic an intensively analytical approach to all subjects. It will be helpful to consider briefly these aspects of their education.

Though schools were not plentiful in the Middle Ages as compared with our time, most Middle English writers evidently received substantial formal education. The school system in Western Europe had gradually expanded following the reign of Charlemagne (d. 814), and by the twelfth century there were grammar schools throughout England, some connected with the great monasteries and churches, and others maintained by individual priests under special endowments. Schools of advanced study were connected with cathedral centers, and the first great English university grew up at Oxford in the twelfth century.

The student, after entering grammar school, took up in order grammar, rhetoric, and logic, these three forming the trivium. Further studies in the trivium, plus the quadrivium—the mathematical subjects of arithmetic, geometry, music, and astronomy—augmented by the professional curriculums of law, medicine, and theology, provided the subject matter of higher education.

Grammar, the first course, is sometimes identified by contemporaries as "the study of literature." It was Latin grammar, of course. The texts contained discussions of literary style, meter, and figures of speech; and illustrations were drawn from such classical writers as Virgil, Ovid, Horace, and Cicero. Thus every fledgling scholar was weaned on literature, albeit a literature cut up and adulterated by (as we see it) a separate discipline. Nor was the student isolated from literary materials when he progressed to rhetoric, through which he was to learn to make his compositions eloquent. In rhetoric the great authors again provided the primary materials for analysis, and the writing of narrative verse was taught. A certain amount of literary theory was of course innate in the texts which assisted the exercises in versification. In England the best-known of the versifiers' handbooks was the thirteenth-century *Poetria Nova* of Geoffrey of Vinsauf, a Norman English writer.

As a statement of a poetic, both ancients and moderns would certainly find Geoffrey's treatise deficient. Geoffrey deals primarily with the mechanics of openings and conclusions for narrative, and with the various rhetorical devices by which one may dilate or abbreviate the body of his work. While he does not attend to matters like character or plot, nor discuss genres like epic or tragedy, such works as his had an influence on (and were helpful to) many writers. Chaucer seems to have read *Poetria Nova*; he quotes from it and alludes to Geoffrey by name. Certainly, he makes liberal use of the devices and "colors" of rhetoric which are discussed in Geoffrey's work. Almost every other writer of the age comparably shows clear marks of training in rhetoric. The enormously influential *Romance of the Rose*, for example, may be seen as wholly made up of the structures of rhetoric, as Alan Gunn demonstrates in his study of the poem.

If literature came into the medieval curriculum through the side door, then it was the big double door of grammar and rhetoric. Study of these subjects gave the nascent writer contact with great literature and practice in the devices of language with the best of writers as models. On the other hand, the concerns of grammar and rhetoric were confined to individual parts of works; they did not deal in any depth with the literary structure as a whole. On the matter of the whole structure, which to us seems primary and paramount, the medieval writer had little theory to guide him. Here, the third subject of the trivium made up for some of the lack; logic probably was an important force in the creation of forms that made whole coherent works.

Jean de Meun is one of the famous scholar-poets of the Middle Ages. Here he is at work on the second part of the *Romance of the Rose,* in which the allegorical story served as a vehicle for Jean's encyclopedic learning. Pierpont Morgan Library Ms. 324, f. 29. By permission.

The methods of logic, together with the writer's interest in the world, led him to analyze rigorously each of the major aspects of existence. Then his artistic and didactic impulses stimulated him to find ways to express his analyses imaginatively. Since he had a great respect for precedent, he looked particularly to the works of his predecessors and contemporaries for models, and there he found the bases of the two modes, allegory and mirror, that are the subject of this study. These were developed and utilized throughout the medieval period. In numerous classical and early medieval works the writer discovered the materials for *allegory,* a term which I usually limit here to personification allegory and its near relatives. Encyclopedic and didactic writings from the same time similarly provided the origins of the *mirror,* a word popularly applied in medieval titles to an assortment of writings that seems rather disparate but nevertheless forms a reasonably coherent class.

Both modes may be thought of as ways to analyze and organize integral aspects of existence in imaginative literature. They thus are admirably adapted to the purposes of the teacher-poet. These modes account for the important relationships which exist between such works as the *Consolation of Philosophy* and *Piers Plowman,* the *Romance of the Rose* and *Troilus and Criseyde,* and the *Speculum Maius* and the *Canterbury Tales,* though these relationships gained virtually no recognition from medieval theorists, nor has the presence of these relationships been adequately recognized or dealt with by later theoreticians. Consideration of them, nevertheless, can lead one very near the center of Middle English literature.

Allegory is a word that we have inherited from ancient Greek. As used by Greek writers (including St. Paul) and by medieval commentators, the word has a broad application, signifying any statement in which one thing is said and another is understood. But modern critical terminology often restricts *allegory* to developed and continued metaphors, that is, to complex systematic arrangements of events, objects, and characters to convey a double (or multiple) significance. A mere reference to the Ship of the Soul is a simple figure of speech—not an allegory. But if the Ship of the Soul is made to sail across the Sea of Life from the Port of Birth to the Harbor of Death, and encounters on

the way the Winds of Misfortune after a stop at the Isles of Delight, then the metaphor has certainly grown into an allegory.

Modern critics have found at least three varieties of allegory,
thus defined, in medieval literature: topical allegory, in which
fictional characters and a fictional story represent in some
manner the real actions of historical people; scriptural allegory,
written in imitation of the allegory found by medieval exegetes
throughout the Bible; and personification allegory and its relatives, in which the actions of persons representing abstract concepts portray events of general human significance. It is the last
kind with which we will be mostly concerned, but it will be
well to examine at least briefly the nature of all three.

Topical allegory seems to have more historical than literary
interest; it portrays "under a veil" contemporary people and
events. Recent critics, who have been mostly occupied with
showing the literary values that works have for all ages, have
not pursued with diligence identification of topical allegories.
Whether or not the characterizations of Chanticleer and the fox
mask real fourteenth-century people has little direct bearing on
the literary values of the Nun's Priest's Tale. Nevertheless, allegory of this kind would have had a certain stature for the medieval writer if only because one important book of the Bible
provided a model for it: the Song of Songs is a highly figurative
dialogue between unnamed lovers who according to tradition
represent Solomon and his Queen. This is at least an important precedent for Chaucer's *Book of the Duchess,* in which
the fictional lovers seem to be counterparts of John of Gaunt
and his wife Blanche. Other important examples of topical allegory come readily to mind. The Fable of the Mice in *Piers Plowman* is generally accepted as a representation of political events
in Richard II's time. Some of the Canterbury pilgrims, moreover, evidently had historical counterparts. Though such matters have a trivial direct bearing on aesthetic values, they may
yet clarify questions that have a more important relationship to
these values. But in any event this kind of allegory is not of
widespread fundamental importance in Middle English literature, and we will not deal with it further in this book.

We will consider Scriptural allegory only in the *Divine Comedy*
and *Pearl* and in these for the most part in an aspect which re-

lates it to personification allegory. Whether it exists in other compositions is an important but unresolved question. Dante is the most-quoted authority on Scriptural allegory, the "allegory of theologians." His central statement on the matter is contained in the letter to Can Grande della Scala which accompanied his dedication of the *Paradise,* the third canticle of the *Divine Comedy.* His poem, he states, has several meanings:

> There is one meaning that is derived from the letter, and another that is derived from the things indicated by the letter. The first is called *literal,* but the second *allegorical* or *mystical.* That this method of expounding may be more clearly set forth, we can consider it in these lines: "When Israel went out of Egypt, the house of Jacob from a people of strange language, Judah was his sanctuary and Israel his dominion." For if we consider the *letter* alone, the departure of the children of Israel in the time of Moses is signified; if the *allegory,* our redemption accomplished in Christ is signified; if the *moral meaning,* the conversion of the soul from the sorrow and misery of sin to a state of grace is signified; if the *anagogical,* the departure of the sanctified soul from the slavery of this corruption to the liberty of everlasting glory is signified. And although these mystical meanings are called by various names, they can in general all be said to be allegorical, since they differ from the literal or historic.

Dante allies his *Comedy* with Scriptural allegory. The distinguishing feature of this kind of allegory is that the literal narrative is not simply a pleasing story that exists for the sake of its allegorical meanings; rather, the literal narrative has in itself substantial significance apart from any other levels of meaning. Furthermore, the presence of more than two levels of meaning is more common in Scriptural allegory than other varieties. When Beatrice appears to Dante in *Purgatory,* one may find that she has a fourfold meaning. She is first of all literally herself, sent by the Virgin to assist her servant Dante to his salvation. Beyond that, one may say that on the Christological (or allegorical) level she represents Christ incarnate come to save mankind; that tropologically or morally she is Revelation offering enlightenment to Christian man; and that anagogically (on the heavenly plane) she stands for the risen Christ who delivered the just from Hell.

While   Dante   follows   in   the   *Comedy*   the   system   of theologians—that is, his work contains the same kind of allegory which theologians find in the Bible—in his earlier *Convivio (Banquet)*, he explicitly aims to follow the "custom of poets," which he also conveniently explains:

> The first [sense] is called literal, and this is that sense which does not go beyond the strict limits of the letter; the second is called allegorical, and this is disguised under the cloak of such stories, and is a truth hidden under a beautiful fiction. Thus Ovid says that Orpheus with his lyre made beasts tame, and trees and stones move towards himself; that is to say that the wise man by the instrument of his voice makes cruel hearts grow mild and humble, and those who have not the life of Science and of Art move to his will, while they who have no rational life are as it were like stones.

This is a typical medieval moralization of a classical myth: Orpheus is the wise man, the beasts whom he tames are cruel hearts, and the trees and stones are the unlearned. Classical authors, through such allegorical interpretation, are found to be moral teachers who concealed profitable lessons under "pleasing fictions" which are otherwise without significance. All of Ovid's *Metamorphoses* were thought to hide such lessons. Virgil's *Aeneid* was seen as the progress of a representative man through many trials and setbacks to salvation; each incident—the passage by Scylla and Charybdis, the island of the Sirens, the affair with Dido—has a spiritually edifying allegorization.

Such interpretations make personification allegories out of the classical stories, whether of Orpheus, Hercules, or Jason. Call Orpheus Wisdom, his lyre the Harp of Oratory, the animals the Beasts of Cruelty, and the stones the Rocks of Ignorance, and the meaning is made transparent. One should notice, however, that the two levels of action do not merge when abstract names are assigned. There still exist independently a literal action and an abstract action which the literal action points to. On the literal level, despite the generalizing names, a specific man still plays a specific lyre in the woods. This holds true also of all personification allegories in which the actors are labeled with the names of the abstractions that they represent on the other level; even though the metaphorical meanings are quite clear, there remain the two distinct levels.

Both the personification allegory and the moralized story are versions of the "allegory of poets." In the allegory of poets, unlike Scriptural allegory, the literal level of action exists for the sake of an action implied by the literal story. The literal story does not justify its own existence. Whether Orpheus plays the lyre before beasts and stones, or personified Wisdom plays the Harp of Oratory before Bestiality and Ignorance, a medieval commentator like Dante thinks of the fiction as existing for the sake of the moral lesson, which in this case is that wisdom assisted by eloquence tames savagery and dominates ignorance.

In this type of allegory, where abstract entities are the real participants, there is the strong concern of medieval thought with the identification and analysis of the essence which exists within or beneath the variform appearance of things. Of course the philosophers of the medieval schools, the Scholastic philosophers, had many different ideas about the nature of this essence. At one extreme the realists, Platonic thinkers, found essence or being in ideas or patterns; on the other hand, the nominalists thought that there were no shared forms, that each thing exists singularly. But neither extreme was commonly accepted either by the thinkers or authority; for instance, the nominalism of the Englishman William of Ockham (d. 1347) was a factor leading to his excommunication.

Typically the medieval thinker sought for synthesis, and various syntheses were proposed for the realist-nominalist controversy. One of the most ambitious and influential was that of Thomas Aquinas (d. 1274). Thomas differentiated between *essence* and *existence,* postulating that essence is the same within individual species though it is manifested in differing existences; the same entity is thus both universal and particular. The way of thinking that produced this distinction between essence and existence, and like discriminations, helps to account for allegorical figures and actions which present the most generalized kind of existence; these allow essences to show through most clearly.

Another distinction made by Scholastic philosophy that is relevant to generalizing allegory is the ultimately Aristotelian distinction between substance and accidents. Essence in Thomistic terms is referable both to the substantial and accidental qualities of an entity, but only secondarily to the accidental;

the accidents depend on the substance while the substance exists for itself. Thus on the underlying substantial forms depend *absolute accidents* like size and color and *relative accidents* like location in time and space. Allegory may be said to allow one to look beyond the accidents to the substance, or to make manifest the dependence of the accidents on the substance.

The writers of the time found in personification allegory and allied narrative a natural medium for conveying in a pleasing story the truth which they found in the world. And such allegory can be both incisive and pleasurable, the contrary opinions of the nineteenth and early twentieth centuries notwithstanding. Bertrand Bronson accurately describes its double-edged effectiveness:

> Allegory is the most forthright method that we know of conveying an ethical message in representational form. And, despite current example and authority, I will risk the opinion that allegory is a more advanced form of intellectual-artistic expression than its opposite, naturalism. Just as on the physical level it requires a concentration of will and effort to drive a road through the jungle, so in the world of the mind, it requires a greater intellectual and imaginative *effort* to divine or perceive order within the chaotic multiplicity of consciousness, and to represent that ideality with power and beauty, than to reproduce, even with high fidelity, our chaotic impressions and responses to the phenomenal world.

Allegory can portray imaginatively subtle, complex, and important aspects of truth.

It will be well to recapitulate. In Biblical allegory—allegory of theologians—or in allegory which imitates it, the literal statement has significance on its own account; and there are one or more additional levels of meaning growing out of the literal sense. Dante's interpretation of the crossing of the Red Sea by the Israelites illustrates this variety of allegory, which contrasts with the allegory of poets in which the literal statement lacks truth and significant substance, yet points to truths, generally abstract or ideal, that underlie it. We have noted two forms of the allegory of poets: classical myths or other stories interpreted as allegories, and narratives in which named personifications participate. Through the process of interpretation, the two forms become almost identical; whether the harpist is named Orpheus or Wisdom, the underlying significance of the story is the same. It may be noted in addition that, interpreted on the tropological (or moral) level, Scripture and the *Divine Comedy* become personification allegories. In Dante's interpretation of Exodus quoted above, the Jews on the moral level personify the Soul and their departure from Egypt represents (is an allegory of) the conversion of the soul. In the *Divine Comedy* Virgil personifies Reason, and Dante the generalized Man who rises to Heaven with the aid of Reason. When interpretation on the moral level thus makes personification allegory out of allegory of theologians, both kinds of narrative may be considered on this level as forming a single, cohesive mode.

A consideration of some of the major varieties and examples of personification allegory will occupy the first half of this book. As we will see, versions of such allegory have roots in works of major seminal influence on Middle English literature, were employed in numerous important writings of the period, and exercised a strong influence on more realistic narratives. Clear examples of the mode, such as *Piers Plowman, Everyman,* the *Anticlaudian,* and the *Romance of the Rose* will be discussed and related to works like the *Consolation of Philosophy, Troilus and Criseyde,* the Wife of Bath's Tale, and *Pearl.* In all of these works universal experiences, like the youth's falling in love, the anguished complainer's finding comfort in the process of reasoning, the soul's gaining spiritual insight through God's grace, or simply the process of dying, are submitted to the writer's analysis; even in apparently realistic works like *Troilus and Criseyde,* abstractions inherent in the story are the basis of much of the serious meaning and interest.

The second literary mode to be taken up in this book is the *mirror,* another form that was never defined by the critics but instead grew and developed through successive imitations. The word *mirror* appears ubiquitously in medieval writing, in psychological, theological, political, and literary contexts. The definition of comedy known best to the time, for instance, was that ascribed to Cicero, which states that comedy is an "imitation of life, a *mirror* of custom, and an image of truth." Though we are not concerned at the moment with comedy per se, this formulation is useful for showing the nature of the literary mirror. The three terms of it—imitation of life, mirror of custom, and image of truth—were probably seen as virtually identical. The medieval writer would make an *imitation of life* not by minute description of detail, but rather by depicting the universal and lasting features sometimes obscured by the detail. The *mirror of custom,* too, would to him be a reflector of the true nature of that which is presented to the mirror rather than of the cluttered world which superficially appears. Thus both an imitation of life and a mirror of custom would be *images of truth,* of a truth of ideals.

A literary mirror then is designed to be an image of truth. The writer sets before his audience how things are, which at the same time expresses how things should be. Such an image has two chief features: inclusiveness and the presentation of ideals. In works which may be called mirrors both of these features usually are present, with one or the other generally dominating.

Inclusive, encyclopedic treatments of broad aspects of knowledge, in both imaginative and expository writings, were popular throughout the Middle Ages. Three influential models from the early Christian era for the later encyclopedic works are noted particularly by J. W. H. Atkins: the *Marriage of Mercury and Philology* of Martianus Capella, the *Institutes* of Cassiodorus, and the *Etymologies* of Isidore of Seville. Atkins see these as products of the "encyclopaedic trend in contemporary teaching, a development of the taste for summaries and epitomes which had characterized the Latin-speaking world since the close of the first century." In the twelfth century, the *Sentences* of Peter Lombard, the major textbook of theology for over four hundred years, gave particular impetus to the composition of such encyclopedias. "This example of successful systematization," states Charles H. Haskins, "was followed in a host of *summae* or systematic outlines of theology and related subjects." Perhaps the best-known of these is the *Summa Theologica* of Thomas Aquinas, though it is only one of numerous comparable masterworks in various fields from the thirteenth and fourteenth centuries. These works are like those other great monuments of medieval enterprise: "Contemporary with the great Gothic cathedrals," says Haskins, "these architectonic *summae* have well been called cathedrals of human thought."

Encyclopedic works were organized in accordance with traditional schemata which imposed order on any field susceptible of discussion. Secular knowledge, for instance, was classified according to the Seven Liberal Arts; historical treatises were organized according to a system dividing history into Biblical ages; and in encyclopedias of the natural world creatures were dealt with by carefully devised hierarchies. Such fixed schemata, or combinations of them, gave order to the summas, or, as they were often designated, *mirrors*. Particularly important for Middle English literature were the traditional classifications of vices and virtues, and of the estates of society. Treatments of the seven vices and their concomitant virtues formed major parts of the *Ancrene Riwle* and of confessional manuals like the Parson's Tale; and the vices supplied the organizing principle for collections of stories by Robert Mannyng and John Gower. The categorization of society by estates also contributed to the organization of numerous literary works, most notably the *Canterbury Tales*.

Along with being encyclopedic, mirrors set up models or ideals. The word *mirror* in literary contexts is perhaps most often associated with the courtesy book, a manual of education and instruction which sets ideals before its readers. Courtesy books were written for many classes of people; there were mirrors for princes, for knights, for women, for churchmen. Notable courtesy books for princes were written by three medieval Englishmen: John of Salisbury, Giraldus Cambrensis, and Thomas Hoccleve. Such books characteristically utilize encyclopedic schemes of organization, but the predominant aspect of these books is their setting up of exemplars of good (or sometimes bad) conduct. This aspect is comparably found in contemporary narrative, particularly in the romances, wherein the behavior of principal figures is held up for imitation. The occupation of knight is by definition an ideal life, and the authors presented their heroes as models. This feature of the mirror provides the basis for our discussion of Arthurian romance, which concludes the section of this book on mirrors.

The critic, unable to provide a full explication of even the simplest artistic entity, searches for guides to lead the readers toward the center. In the ensuing discussions my ambitious aim is to point toward a common center of a large part of Middle English literature—of the works of Chaucer, Langland, the Pearl Poet, Malory, and others. Allegory and mirror are at such a center, integral to these works. Important examples of each mode are found both in prose and in poetry, and in several of the traditional genre divisions. Furthermore, the modes are complementary; in a sense they are the two divisions of a narrative—the plot and the expository material, the length and the breadth. Allegories (in the restricted sense I am using) are plots which meaningfully analyze generalized experiences, and mirrors are ordered collections of descriptive materials, characters, or actions which present comprehensive images of experience or knowledge.

Many works dealt with here are both allegories and mirrors, as I will take occasion to discuss in the concluding chapter. Either mode, alone or in combination, is well suited to the pleasurable presentation of significant thought and profitable wisdom. And even if the writers' minds were occupied with pedagogic concerns in their compositions, the best of those who used these modes produced literature comparable in aesthetic quality to that of any other age in England or Western Europe. The more familiar one becomes with their writings, the more impressive they appear.

NOTE TO CHAPTER I

Bibliographies of Middle English Literature

Basic bibliographical tools include the footnotes in Albert C. Baugh's history of Middle English literature in the updated *Literary History of England* (2nd ed., 1967); the Middle English sections of the *Cambridge Bibliography of English Literature*, Volume I (1941), and Supplement (1957); and John E. Wells, *A Manual of the Writings in Middle English, 1050–1400* with Supplements (1916–1952). The Wells Manual is undergoing a complete revision under the general editorship of J. Burke Severs; the first fascicle, on the romances, has appeared (1967). Several highly selective bibliographies should be mentioned. The most important of these is Robert Ackerman's review of recent scholarship (1930–1960), "Middle English Literature to 1400," in John H. Fisher, ed., *Medieval Literature of Western Europe* (1966). An annotated selection of items is supplied by Stanley Greenfield's bibliography in David M. Zesmer, *Guide to English Literature from Beowulf through Chaucer and Medieval Drama* (1961). William Matthews, *Old and Middle English Literature* (1968), in the Goldentree series of bibliographies, provides a very helpful listing designed for the student's use.

The most important periodic bibliography of Middle English is that which appears in the *PMLA* annual bibliography (since 1922; international since issue for 1956). Medieval items appearing in American periodicals are listed quarterly in *Speculum* (from 1926). The *Chaucer Review* publishes an annual bibliography (since 1966) of Chaucer studies. And the International Arthurian Society issues yearly a *Bibliographical Bulletin* of work on the "Matter of Britain" (since 1949).

The student of Chaucer is fortunate in having available a series of three bibliographies which provide a relatively complete listing of Chaucerian materials: the period to 1908 is covered by Eleanor P. Hammond, *Chaucer: A Bibliographical Manual* (1908); from 1908 to 1953 by Dudley D. Griffith, *Bibliography of Chaucer* (1955); and from 1954 to 1963 by William R. Crawford, *Bibliography of Chaucer* (1967). Albert C. Baugh's bibliography *Chaucer* (1968) for the Goldentree Series, having a less broad topic than Mattews' compilation for the same series mentioned above, is more inclusive and therefore more satisfactory for research. Twenty-two useful essays, which review the major areas of Chaucer scholarship, are contained in Beryl Rowland's *Companion to Chaucer Studies* (1968). Allan H. MacLaine, *The Student's Comprehensive Guide to the Canterbury Tales* (1964), is especially helpful for its references and summaries of scholarship for the various divisions and particular passages of the *Tales*.

History, Background, Inclusive Treatments, and Anthologies

The best history of Middle English literature is Albert C. Baugh's section of the *Literary History of England.* Two volumes of the *Oxford His-*

tory of English Literature deal with broad aspects of literary activity at the end of the period: Edmund K. Chambers, *English Literature at the Close of the Middle Ages* (1945); and H. S. Bennett, *Chaucer and the Fifteenth Century* (1947). A most suggestive introduction to the cultural background of the age, focussing on religious factors, is found in Christopher Dawson, *Medieval Essays* (1954); some of his literary analyses are outdated. C. S. Lewis in *The Discarded Image* (1964) shows how outgrowths of classical concepts were central in medieval and Renaissance literature. Robert W. Ackerman's brief but useful *Backgrounds to Medieval English Literature* (1966) shows the literary importance of a broad range of contemporary social, scientific and religious ideas.

Short discussions of the individual works of Middle English literature are contained in the Wells Manual and David Zesmer's *Guide to English Literature* (both cited above). Inclusive treatments of the literature of the period outside of Chaucer's work are not plentiful. George Kane, *Middle English Literature* (1951) deals interestingly with a range of the writings, including romances, lyrics, and *Piers Plowman.* A good series of essays on important works, along with a brief anthology, is contained in Boris Ford, ed., *The Age of Chaucer* (rev. ed., 1963). A larger collection of essays, drawn mostly from periodicals, is edited by Edward Vasta, *Middle English Survey* (1965). Several collections of Chaucer criticism have also appeared in recent years, among them Beryl Rowland's *Companion to Chaucer,* mentioned earlier, and the two-volume selection of *Chaucer Criticism* edited by Richard J. Schoeck and Jerome Taylor (1960–1961).

The most popular anthology of Middle English texts is Fernand Mossé, *A Handbook of Middle English* (1952); it has an excellent introduction to the language and valuable notes on the works represented. A more specialized collection, consisting of pre-fourteenth-century texts, is J. A. W. Bennett and G. V. Smithers, eds., *Early Middle English Verse and Prose* (1966). The only broad and inclusive anthology of translations available is Roger S. Loomis and Rudolph Willard, eds., *Medieval English Verse and Prose* (1948), though one by D. W. Robertson is forthcoming.

Medieval Education and Philosophy

A comprehensive discussion of education in medieval times is provided by A. F. Leach, *The Schools of Medieval England* (1915). George G. Coulton, *Medieval Panorama* (1955), pp. 385–432, supplies a briefer, more up-to-date treatment of the same subject. The story of the rise of the universities is vividly told by Charles H. Haskins in *The Renaissance of the Twelfth Century* (1927), and by Henry O. Taylor, *The Medieval Mind* (4th ed., 1925), II, 408–431. For the role of literature in education see particularly Louis J. Paetow, *The Arts Course of Medieval Universities with Special Reference to Grammar and Rhetoric* (1910); and Ernst R. Curtius, *European Literature and the Latin Middle Ages,* translated by Willard R. Trask (1953), pp. 36–78. Richard of Bury's *Philobiblon,* translated by Ernest C. Thomas (1888), witnesses one influential book-lover's belief in the educative value of literature. Enlightening suggestions about Chaucer's education are found in Edith Rickert, "Chaucer at School," *MP*, 29 (1932), 257–274.

For inquiry into the enormous field of medieval philosophy, I will mention only two works of particular usefulness. The *New Catholic Encyclopedia* (1967) supplies convenient, objective entries on most problems of Scholastic philosophy. Etienne Gilson, *History of Christian Philosophy in the Middle Ages* (1955), provides a comprehensive introduction to the subject, and supplies extensive bibliographies and notes.

Literary Criticism

Though medieval critics neglected aspects of literature which we find central, there is a substantial body of important criticism from the time. The most systematic treatment of medieval English theory is J. W. H. Atkins, *English Literary Criticism: the Medieval Phase* (1943). Charles S. Baldwin's *Medieval Rhetoric and Poetic to 1400* (1928) covers a broader geographical area with a more restricted topic. More sympathetic than the preceding to the contributions of rhetorical theory are Ernst R. Curtius, *European Literature* (cited above), especially pp. 145–166, and Robert O. Payne's study of Chaucer's poetics, *The Key of Remembrance* (1963). In his various discussions of medieval aesthetics, D. W. Robertson makes imaginative and relevant use of varied medieval materials, notably religious writings and art; see particularly his *Preface to Chaucer* (1963). In another treatment of Chaucer's aesthetics, Robert M. Jordan, *Chaucer and the Shape of Creation* (1967), the author suggestively and properly asserts some aspects of "Inorganic Structure" in Chaucer's writings, but rejects, I think unnecessarily, other structural values as illusory.

The texts of several rhetoricians' handbooks for poets, including Geoffrey de Vinsauf's *Poetria Nova,* are contained in Edmond Faral, ed., *Les Arts poétiques du xiie et du xiiie siècle* (1924). The most extensive medieval defense of poetry is formed by the last two books of Boccaccio's *Genealogy of the Pagan Gods,* which are translated by Charles G. Osgood as *Boccaccio on Poetry* (1930); these contain especially interesting remarks on hidden, or allegorical, meanings. Dante's *Convivio,* which contains his discussion of the *allegory of poets,* is translated by William W. Jackson (1909); his letter to Can Grande appears in Charles S. Latham, *A Translation of Dante's Eleven Letters* (1891), and is often quoted and excerpted elsewhere. For explicit allegorizations of narrative in the fourteenth century, see, for example, Francis Petrarch, *Familiari,* ed. Vittorio Rossi (1934), II, x.4; and Coluccio Salutti, *De Laboribus Herculis,* ed. B. L. Ullman (1951). Further medieval explanations of allegory are referred to by D. W. Robertson throughout his discussions of allegory and humanism, *Preface to Chaucer,* pp. 286–365.

Charles S. Singleton explains the mode of allegory used in the *Divine*

Comedy in an appendix to his *Dante Studies:* I (1954), "The Two Kinds of Allegory," pp. 84–98. A lucid explanation of the *allegory of theologians* is provided by Joseph A. Bryant in Chapter I of his study of Shakespeare's plays, *Hippolyta's View* (1961). The best guide to medieval exegesis of Scripture is Henri de Lubac, *Exégèse médiévale* (2 volumes in 4 parts, 1959–1964). The relevance to literature of Biblical interpretation is sensibly explained by Robert E. Kaske in *Critical Approaches to Medieval Literature,* ed. Dorothy Bethurum (1960), pp. 27–60. Some dangers in relating Biblical materials to literature are pointed out by Morton W. Bloomfield, "Symbolism in Medieval Literature," *MP,* 56 (1958), pp. 73–81. Important discussions of personification allegory are listed in the Note to Chapter II; I have quoted in this chapter from Bertrand H. Bronson's discussion of Neoclassic allegory, "Personification Reconsidered," *ELH,* 14 (1947), 163–177.

Chapter II

Personification Allegory

Important Works: *Romance of the Rose, Everyman, House of Fame* (Book III), *Piers Plowman* (Passus I–VII).

Personification is a figure of speech which confers particular human form on an abstraction, a thing which by nature does not have a particular embodiment. Among the abstractions which are commonly personified are personal traits (Beauty, Candor), cosmic forces (Fate, Love), states of mind (Melancholy), mental powers (Reason, Memory), and ethical concepts (Pride, Humility). Also rightly classed as personification is the process of giving particular form to abstractions which are persons conceptually though not in actuality; familiar examples are Everyman, Lover, and Friend. Everyman is an abstraction because he represents every man but is no one man and so lacks particularity until endowed with a unique body by the poet.

Since all personifications possess the attributes of particular persons, they may be involved in stories with individuals who are not personifications. Thus, Satan deals with Sin and Death in *Paradise Lost*, and Will and Conscience sit down to dinner with an important theologian in *Piers Plowman*. Such mixing has been criticized and can undoubtedly impair the allegorical representation; but it can also add variety. Personifications naturally coordinate with what may be called objectifications, abstractions embodied in nonhuman form: a tower called Pride, a Rock of Faith, or a whale identified as Evil. It is quite appropriate that Mr. Faithful should acquire the enmity of Mr. Envy at Vanity Fair, the Fair being an objectification of the pleasures of the world. *Pilgrim's Progress,* which has its origins in medieval allegories, has many such figures: the Hill Difficulty, the Valley of Salvation, the City of Destruction, and Doubting Castle. Bunyan's hero Christian, it may be noted, is a personification in that he is the generalized Christian man given a particular form.

Personification may be used for a simple metaphor, as when Chaucer's Black Knight says, recounting his early days, *"Yow the* governed me in ydelnesse," or when the modern ballad relates, *"Love* walked right in and stole my troubles away." Such casual use of personification fills the pages of medieval writings. The preacher of the time could hardly speak of a sin or a virtue without personifying it. In the devil's furnace, says Chaucer's Parson—to cite a random example—there are three "shrewes": "Pride, that ay bloweth and encreesseth the fir by chidynge and wikked wordes; thanne stant Envye, and holdeth the hoote iren upon the herte of man with a peire of longe toonges of long rancour; and thanne stant the synne of Contumelie, or strif and cheeste, and batereth and forgeth by vileyns reprevynges" (I, 554–556). When drawn out to this extent, such a figure virtually forms an allegory. Often casual or undeveloped references to personifications reflect traditional fully developed allegories involving the personifications. The simple reference to Love's entering a heart evokes, and may have been evoked by, numerous allegories in which the familiar character of Love appears.

Any personification or objectification may be described in as much detail as desired. The physical features, adornments, and other accoutrements are made to accord with and bring out the nature of the thing personified or objectified. For example, Old Age in the *Romance of the Rose* is depicted as a feeble old woman with sallow complexion, white hair, and a shriveled, shrunken body (I quote from the Chaucerian translation):

> Al woxen was her body unwelde,
> And drie and dwyned al for elde.
> A foul forwelked thyng was she,
> That whylom round and softe had be.

> Her eeres shoken faste withalle,
> As from her heed they wolde falle;
> Her face frounced and forpyned
> And bothe her hondes lorne, fordwyned.
>
> 359–366

She walks only with the help of a crutch, and to protect herself from the cold which always afflicts old people she wears a furred cope.

The Wheel of Fortune with the Goddess Fortune blindfold and the conventional four figures riding the wheel: Regnabo ascending, Regno on top, Regnavi descending, and Sum Sine Regno cast into the mud naked. Pierpont Morgan Library Ms. 324, f.34v. By permission.

The features of Old Age set forth in the *Romance of the Rose* thus attribute to a person salient characteristics associated with the abstract idea. Some of the features, such as the crutch, the shrunken body, and the hood, so well express the concept of senility and were so often used that they became part of the standard iconography of the abstraction. The iconography which many traditional personifications acquired is very elaborate. Fortune is a prime example; only a part of her traditional iconography is seen in Figures 2 and 6. Her crown and regal dress suggest her high rank and great authority; the blindfold her indiscriminate bestowal of favors. The wheel which she turns objectifies her power to raise a man to the heights of prosperity and thrust him into adversity almost at will. In many standard portrayals, as in these, four characters sit on the wheel, one at each pole and one at each horizontal extremity. These characters commonly are named Regnabo (I will rule), Regno (I rule), Regnavi (I have ruled), and Sum Sine Regno (I am without rule). Such names, while applying most immediately to monarchs, apply figuratively to all men. As Fortune turns the wheel the men change places: Regnabo becomes Regno, Regno becomes Regnavi, and Regnavi is dipped in the mud as he becomes Sum Sine Regno. Fortune deals in this manner with all men, as kings become paupers and paupers kings in the ordinary course of the world.

In the tale of his woes in Chaucer's *Book of the Duchess,* the Black Knight alludes to this "false whel" of Fortune, and also to features not portrayed in our illustrations, such as the goddess' eyes: she is "Ever laughynge/ With oon eye, and that other wepynge" (633–634). The knight also associates her with the scorpion:

> a fals, flaterynge beste;
> For with his hed he maketh feste,
> But al amydde hys flaterynge
> With hys tayle he wol stynge
> And envenyme; and so wole she [i.e., Fortune].
> 637–641

In pictorial representations of Fortune, the scorpion and the clear and weeping eyes often appear. Her whole figure is sometimes divided down the middle: she is attractive, smiling, and well dressed on one side, and ugly, frowning, and shabbily appareled on the other. Or she may be Janus-faced, with one attractive and one forbidding aspect. In either case, her power to look with favor on one man while simultaneously frowning on another is shown (demonstrating graphically how in the world one man will prosper while another fails, without apparent reason). Other attributes, such as a scales and the sea, are also regularly connected with Fortune.

If the representation of a personification involves several significant features, then the representation itself often implies an allegorical action; implicit in Figure 2, for instance, is man's progress on the Wheel of Fortune. Such an allegorical picture might be called an emblem, but perhaps may be better characterized here as a tableau so as to circumvent the narrower connotations of the former term. Sometimes in literature a number of tableaux are strung together to represent an idea or describe a process. In the *Romance of the Rose* the lover sees a series of animated statues outside the garden, including such characters as Old Age (discussed above), Envy, Hypocrisy, and Poverty. Through observing the numerous attributes of these personifications the dreamer learns what one leaves behind before entering the Garden of Mirth, the place of Love. Once inside the garden, he meets such elaborated persons as Idleness, Beauty, Mirth, and Love; from observing their figures he learns what is associated with the practices of love. Thus Courtesy's appearance well represents the manners of the well bred, the only people believed capable of love:

> She was not nyce, ne outrageous,
> But wys, and war, and vertuous,
> Of fair speche, and of fair answere;
> Was never wight mysseid of here;
> She bar no rancour to no wight.
> Clere broun she was, and therto bright
> Of face, of body avenaunt;
> I wot no lady so plesaunt.
> She were worthy for to bene
> An emperesse or crowned quene.
>
> 1257–1266

The action involved in these two series of tableaux is the instruction of the narrator by means of his observations. At this stage of the *Rose*, his interaction with the personifications is of much less importance than what he learns by viewing them.

A more common kind of literary personification allegory than the tableau or series of tableaux is found later in the *Romance of the Rose*. The dreamer, assuming the character of Lover, be-

The Personfication of Old Age as portrayed in a manuscript of the *Romance of the Rose*. Pierpont Morgan Library Ms. 324, f.4. By permission.

comes involved in an affair. He is encouraged by Fair Welcome, repulsed by Danger, and assisted by Friend. The personifications not only act on him but interact with each other: Shame and Fear arouse Danger to repulse the Lover, Candor and Pity urge Fair Welcome to treat him well, and so on. This lengthy story in the *Rose* is an important subject in the next chapter. Narrative allegories can also be quite brief, of course; the Middle English lyric, *Blow, Northren Wind* provides a good example. This early fourteenth-century poem consists of ten stanzas containing a description of the beloved and the lover's complaint about her treatment of him. In connection with the complaint a three-stanza allegory is utilized with a law-process providing the vehicle of the extended metaphor. In the first stanza of the three the lover makes his plea:

> To Love, that lovely is in londe,
> I tolde him as I understonde

How this hende hath hent in honde
An herte that myn was;
And hir knightes me han so soght—
Sikynge, Sorwyng, and Thoght—
Tho three me han in bale broght
Ayeins the power of Pees.

49–56

[I told Love, who is lovely, how this fair lady had
taken my heart in hand; and how her knights, Sighing,
Sorrowing, and Thought, have so pursued me, in defiance
of the power of Peace, that I am brought into woe.]

The allegory here, quite transparent, involves an action in
which the personifications participate much as characters participate in realistic fiction. In this type of allegory, where there is
an integrated action, the central figure (the lover in this case)
may participate along with the personifications, while in a series of tableaux the main character is generally an observer who
is not involved importantly with the personifications.

Whichever type is used, personification allegory is best
adapted to portraying processes of general importance or widespread application: a seduction, the operation of government, a
man's reformation, and similar actions. We will consider how
personification allegory is particularly suitable for presenting
and analyzing such processes by taking up three Middle English works: Chaucer's *House of Fame,* Book III, in which the
cosmic processes of gathering and disseminating information are
analyzed; *Everyman,* which depicts the death of a man; and the
first dream in *Piers Plowman,* wherein the establishment of moral
government is shown.

The *House of Fame* is the second of Chaucer's dream poems,
and Book III contains the best-developed personification allegory in his original work. Here, as in the first part of the *Romance of the Rose,* the allegory is conveyed by a series of tableaux, and the instruction of the narrator is the organizing action. Personifications do not operate importantly in the first two
books. In Book I, after the narrator goes to sleep he sees the
story of Aeneas and Dido depicted on the walls of a Temple of
Venus. How Dido's actions were published throughout the
world and to succeeding ages provides an egregious example of
the ways of Fame. The narrator is taken to Fame's house in

Book II, carried in the claws of an eagle (whose allegorical quality is a subject in Chapter IV); on the way the eagle lectures him about physical laws which enable Fame to operate. In Book III (which though unfinished is longer than the first two parts together) allegorical tableaux show the typical processes by which information and reputation are preserved and published.

The personification of Lady Fame, described in detail, is supplemented by two objectifications of her operations, the Castle of Fame and the House of Rumor, also extensively described. The three tableaux involving these figures combine to present a fairly well-rounded description of the abstraction, Fame. When the narrator is set down by the eagle he sees the Castle above him built on a mountain of ice. On the frozen base are written many names—on the south side in the sun, of people whose fame had been "wide yblowe," but now the ice has melted and the writing has become illegible. On the shaded north side, however, the names are as fresh as if they had just been written (1136–1164). In niches all about the castle stand minstrels and storytellers, all of whom are performing. The castle walls are made of glass, which magnifies everything:

> And made wel more than hit was
> To semen every thing, ywis,
> As kynde thyng of Fames is.
> 1290–1292

The features of this castle thus provide figurative representations of the varying permanence of reputation (the names in ice), the manner in which poetic heroes become known (the minstrels), and the magnifying power of Fame's reports.

Inside the castle the narrator sees the goddess Fame herself. A purveyor of news, true and false, good and bad, she has traditional characteristics as well as features originating with Chaucer. She has varying height: at one time she seems two feet high, the next moment her head touches the heavens. Thus we understand that important and unimportant news falls within her province. She has many eyes, ears, and tongues, the better to record and report information. About her ranged on pillars are famous writers who have recorded Fame's reports—authors such as Homer, Virgil, Ovid, Josephus—each of whom is responsible for a great subject matter—Troy, Rome, Love, the acts of the Jews. Also associated with the goddess is Eolus (Aeolus), the god of the Winds who acts as Fame's trumpeter. Eolus has two trumpets: Clere Laude, which is used for favorable reports, and Sklaundre, which proclaims unfavorable news.

Chaucer sets this allegorical tableau of personified Fame in motion while the dreamer watches and learns. The action is simple and stylized, hardly extending beyond what might take place on a modern parade float (a counterpart to the medieval pageant wagon, which was often used for allegorical representations). Successive groups of people come before Fame and present their petitions; in response to each Fame orders Eolus to sound either Clere Laude or Sklaundre, giving the petitioners good or bad report strictly according to her arbitrary whim. Sklaundre (Ill-Fame) is of course the more interesting trumpet; its noise goes through the world as fast as a shot from a gun:

> And such a smoke gan out wende
> Out of his foule trumpes ende,
> Blak, bloo, grenyssh, swartish red,
> As doth where that men melte led,
> Loo, al on high fro the tuel.
> And therto oo thing saugh I wel,
> That the ferther that hit ran,
> The gretter wexen hit began,
> As dooth the ryver from a welle,
> And hyt stank as the pit of helle.
> 1645–1654

The uncomplicated and repetitive actions do not develop beyond the scope of the tableau, the chief interest residing in the spectacle rather than the narrative which the tableau provides.

The Castle of Fame and its occupants are mostly preoccupied with matters of permanent implications: events of historical import, works of literature, and the establishment of reputation. In order to supplement this one-sided picture, which neglects Fame's role of purveying transient gossip, Chaucer creates an additional edifice to objectify Fame's prowess, the House of Rumor, which the narrator visits after leaving the Castle. The House of Rumor is a tremendous round building, made of twigs, which whirls around very rapidly, and from its many doors and windows and thousands of holes a great volume of noise constantly issues. The reader can readily infer that the flimsy construction represents the insubstantiality of rumor, the rapid movement the speed with which gossip travels, and the many openings emitting loud noises the multiplicity of gossip's manifestations. Inside, the dreamer finds the house filled with people who pass around fledgling *tidings* (rumors) from one to another till they become mature; when full grown, the tidings are ready to fly out the windows. The dreamer notices that often a true and false tiding try to get out the same window at the same time and are stymied. They eventually resolve the difficulty by merging and traveling together; the two declare as they leave:

> "We wil medle us ech with other,
> That no man, be they never so wrothe,
> Shal han on of us two, but bothe
> At ones, al besyde his leve."

2102–2105

Thus truth and falsehood become inextricably mingled in the House of Rumor.

The *House of Fame* breaks off while the narrator is still in the House of Rumor. He notices in a corner of the hall, where men discuss "love-tydynges," a great bustle and clamor. All at once appears a man of "gret auctorite," but since the poem ends here we never find out who the man is, whether another personification, or a person who might impart to the poem topical interest for Chaucer's contemporaries, or perhaps, as B. G. Koonce suggests, Christ. In any event the representation of the nature and processes of Fame through personification and objectification seems virtually complete.

If the reader's understanding of Fame, of processes of building reputation and disseminating information, is not deepened by Chaucer's depictions in this poem, his view of the phenomenon at least may be sharpened and broadened. The first part of the *Romance of the Rose* produces a comparable result; the poet presents an inclusive, if not startlingly revelatory, representation of the elements involved in—and those excluded from—the processes of polite love. In these representations in both poems the interest resides in the justness and ingenuity of the authors' depictions, and in their success in revealing the numerous facets of the phenomena which provide the subjects. The possibilities, then, of this variety of personification allegory are restricted, but this nevertheless is the kind that Chaucer is more interested in. The figures of Fortune in the *Book of the Duchess,* Nature in the *Parliament of Fowls,* and Fame in the *House of Fame* provide his most notable personification allegories.

Works like the *House of Fame* which feature allegorical tableaux are dependent for coherence and narrative interest on actions extrinsic to the tableaux, generally involving the education of the narrator. On the other hand works in which personifications interact to make a developed story—which I refer to conveniently as narrative allegories—have their own continuity and do not require a linking action to make them cohere. Thus the personifications are intrinsic to the narrative; and because the processes depicted are given dynamic rather than static depiction, the possibilities of profound insight are increased appreciably. Such insight is produced by both *Everyman* and the first dream of *Piers Plowman,* two very successful narrative allegories which contrast markedly. The narrative of *Everyman* is quite simple and its action, the process of dying, integrally concerns but a single individual; the story of the first dream of *Piers Plowman,* on the other hand, is very complex, and many individuals are implicated in the action, which concerns the establishment of right reason in government.

Everyman, a morality play of the fifteenth century, is Dutch in origin, but because an English translator early gave it a distinguished rendering it has been a living part of English literature right up to the present. Its subject has the widest interest of all subjects: Death. Tableau allegories of Death have often been presented by artists. In these Death, a skeleton clothed in black robe and hood, brandishing his dart, or leading a procession in a ghastly dance over the countryside, has an awesome, perhaps frightening, presence. From the picture one can infer Death's fatal power, its suddenness, its relevance to mortals who are all engaged in the dance; little depth of insight into its operation, however, is produced. *Everyman,* on the other hand, provides each of its spectators with a lively and profound view of the phenomenon which each of them will experience one time only.

The play is, of course, Christian—Catholic—as is all medieval

English literature. A Catholic God sends Death to Everyman at the beginning of the play, and an angel appears to receive Everyman's soul at the end. Most things in the play, however, are quite understandable to the modern non-Catholic audience, except perhaps for the role of confession. One should understand that confession of one's sins and genuine repentance at the time of death, whether to a priest or privately to God if a priest is not available, can help even the most depraved soul to Heaven.

The perceptive viewer can gloss for himself the beautifully simple allegory of *Everyman*, but for the very reason that it is transparent it provides an excellent example demonstrating how personification allegory of its type operates. To begin with we might consider the overall action of the play, its beginning, middle, and end. The beginning is Death's summons to Everyman; this summons signifies a man's realization that his death is imminent. The middle concerns the successive desertions of Everyman by his earthly companions and possessions and his bodily faculties, and his recovery of his spiritual assets, his good works. At the end he enters the grave to be received by the angel into Heaven. The action, then, is simple and complete, and it is inspirited by masterly dramatization.

When Death delivers his summons to Everyman, our hero begs for more time, since he is not ready to die—unpreparedness being the common situation of men. Death is of course inexorable; he does, however, allow Everyman time to find companions for his journey from which there will be no return. Death's indulgence signifies the common belief that each person has some chance, though perhaps a very brief one, at the time of death to prepare himself. The hour of the play represents the process of a few seconds for some people, a few days for others. In search of companionship Everyman goes first to those people and objects that have been dearest to his heart: Fellowship, Kindred, and Goods. All three at first avow their faithfulness; Fellowship proclaims, in a speech involving considerable dramatic irony,

> Sir, I must needs know your heaviness;
> I have pity to see you in any distress.

If any have you wronged, ye shall revenged be;
Though I on the ground be slain for thee,
Though that I know before that I should die.
                              216–220

Such protests turn out to be so much wind and sound. Everyman soon finds himself deserted except for a weak, almost lifeless companion, Good Deeds, who cannot rise from the ground. However, when the hero turns his attention to Good Deeds, the turning point of the action is reached. For Good Deeds directs him to Knowledge and Knowledge to confession. The allegory gives the viewer to understand that though Everyman's good actions are miniscule in size and number, and are almost canceled out by his sins, they are sufficient to merit for Everyman the wisdom to repent. He is also granted time to receive Holy Communion and Extreme Unction, but it is to be noted that these latter are not represented as essential, since Good Deeds is able to arise when Everyman completes his penance before receiving these sacraments. This is the crucial moment in the story, since it is necessary for Everyman's salvation that Good Deeds be able to accompany him.

After Knowledge leads him to confession and the scourging of his body, then, Good Deeds is freed from the chains of Everyman's misdoings and is able to get up. Though a happy outcome has now become relatively certain (since Everyman is in the state of grace), the process still has dramatic interest, for death even for the repentant man is a formidable and frightening experience. The successive departures at the graveside, of Beauty, Strength, Discretion, Five Wits, and even faithful Knowledge, especially provide a moving correlative to the last gasps of a dying man. In this realm of abstraction the suffocation of the grave becomes strangely real. But Good Deeds remains with Everyman to avert ultimate tragedy and sum up the action:

All earthly things is but vanity:
Beauty, Strength, and Discretion do man forsake,
Foolish friends and kinsmen, that fair spake,
All fleeth save good Deeds, and that am I.
                              870–873

The angel receives his soul with the words of the Song of Songs, "Come, excellent elect spouse to Jesu"; then a cleric appears to remind the audience that if Good Deeds is not sufficient at the last hour, God may say, "Depart, ye accursed into the eternal fire."

An ordinary death, then, is represented in this play. Nothing is done to individualize the death; as a matter of fact, everything is done to universalize it, even to the final speech of the cleric which reminds us of the alternate possible outcome of the story: if Good Deeds is not freed by repentance, the successive desertions will still occur, and Everyman will find himself completely alone at the end, Hell-bound. Conducing to the generalization of the narrative, no cause of death—disease, violence, old age—is specified; no bodily sufferings are depicted; no widowing or orphaning is brought into question; no particular aborted hopes are discussed. As a realistic story, it has virtually no interest. Dramatized in a personification allegory, in which the abstract universal features of the experience are represented by actions of happily selected personifications, the story is rich and powerful.

While the 920 short lines of *Everyman* present a mostly lucid allegory, clarity is not always characteristic of works of this type. Indeed, the greatest masterpiece of personification allegory, *Piers Plowman,* is one of the most challenging to the interpreter. Oddly, the general reader may have more patience with *Piers* than the professional critic, for while the poem finds interested readers among all classes of students, Middle English scholars have been diffident about offering full-dress interpretations. Many perhaps agree with one of our country's most distinguished medievalists, who breaks off his analysis of the poem in the middle because, "The constant digressions, parenthetical discussions, and breaks in continuity show that the author was powerless to resist the impulse to pursue any idea suggested by another idea or even by a word that he happened to use." This scholar finds the work the despair of those who look for "completely orderly plan or logical development from episode to episode" (A. C. Baugh, *Literary History of England*). The student perhaps approaches *Piers* with fewer preconceptions than does the more advanced scholar; he at least senses that the "digressions" have a function in the poem, and that the work has its own kind of continuity and development, even if not "completely orderly."

The problems presented by *Piers Plowman* are compounded by the three parallel but distinct versions in which it exists, called A, B, and C. All three evidently were composed, in the span of the very decades in which Chaucer was writing, by a poet of western England named William Langland. We will deal only with the well-known B-text in this volume. The B-version has 7,241 long alliterative lines, and is formally divided into a Prologue and twenty books or *passus*. Larger sections are formed by the more significant divisions between the several dreams and the major break between the so-called Vision *(Visio)* and Life *(Vita)*. There are eight dreams (not counting the two dreams within dreams), the first two composing the Vision and the final six the Life. Morton Bloomfield says that in the Vision the dreamer is "given a picture of life in the work-a-day world," and then in the Life "he is led into a timeless world of Christian truth." This indicates generally the subject matter of the two parts, though it should not mislead one into believing that the two parts present tangential or parallel narratives. They rather form one consecutive experience. Perhaps it is helpful to think of the Vision as giving a general view of society and its progress toward perfection, and the Life as the individual's experience which must subsequently be depicted because social progress ultimately becomes dependent on (at least in terms of the poem) individual progress.

The dreams which make up the poem have in turn a sequential relationship. Thus, the second dream of the Vision is necessitated by the outcome of the first. The allegory in the first dream is concerned with government and its morality; in the second dream the preoccupation is with the morality of the people—the governed—as an entity. Both of these dreams display admirably Langland's virtuosity and range as an allegorist. We will inspect the first one at some length as our third major exemplar of the workings of personification allegory. The first two examples were chosen as clear and readily glossed representatives of two contrasting types, tableau and narrative allegory. The allegory in this first dream of *Piers Plowman*, however, while essentially narrative allegory, makes use of tableaux, realistic scenes, and extensive moral lectures, and its elucidation is quite complex. It demonstrates the range and potentialities of personification allegory.

The dream is divided into a prologue and four passus, 1217 lines. As in the *House of Fame,* the narrator in this dream is a witness to the allegory, and his education is an important aspect of the action. Like *Everyman,* the narrative in which the personifications participate is a developed and continuous story; it begins with the establishment of government and ends with the king's adoption of conscience and reason as the controlling political forces. The descriptive passages and moral lectures which are interspersed in the narrative grow out of the story, but since they do not contribute directly to it I will disregard them in this summary. Some of them associate *Piers Plowman* with mirror literature and provide material for a later section of this book.

The narrator, who is named Will and represents the willing faculty throughout the poem, goes to sleep while wandering among the Malvern Hills, and in his dream he sees the famous tableau of the poem representing the world between Heaven and Hell:

> As I bihelde into the est an hiegh to the sonne,
> I seigh a toure on a toft trielich ymaked;
> A depe dale binethe, a dongeon thereinne,
> With depe dyches and derke and dredful of sight.
> A faire felde ful of folke fonde I there bytwene,
> Of alle maner of men, the mene and the riche,
> Worchyng and wandryng as the worlde asketh.
>
> B, Prologue, 13–19

> [As I looked into the east toward the sun, I saw a well-constructed tower on a hill; a deep valley below with a dungeon and deep dark ditches dreadful to see. Between these I saw a fair field full of folk, of all sorts of men, poor and rich, who were working and going about as the world requires.]

This tableau has, of course, value as moral allegory in itself. The people, high and low, are seen preoccupied with the concerns of this world, entirely unconscious of the pit and the tower, objectifications of Heaven and Hell, which are such impres-

sive parts of the scene to the onlooker. The tableau also serves
to introduce a hundred-line description of the world at work,
but it most importantly acts as an anchor to the narrative of
the whole poem.

This narrative gets underway when onto the scene comes
Knighthood leading a king, whom the commons then set up as
ruler. Natural Knowledge (Kynde Witte) helps the king and
Knighthood to create Learning (Clergye), who in turn helps the
people divide themselves into craftsmen and laboring men.
The establishment of government is thus depicted in eleven
lines (B, Prologue, 112–122). Almost immediately the question
arises about the lack of any check on the king's power, the
commons complaining that "The precepts of the king are the
chains of law to us." In a dreamlike manner the commons of
the story suddenly become a crowd of rats and the king a cat.
In order to control the cat's arbitrary rule over them, the rats
decide to put a collar with a bell on the cat; but then no rat
can be found to bell the cat. All eventually decide that the
results would not be desirable anyway, for the rats could not
govern themselves. As a mouse reminds them, they would live
lawlessly,

> Nere that cat of that courte that can yow overlepe;
> For had ye rattes yowre wille ye couthe nought reule yowreselve.
> > B, Prologue, 199–200
> [If it were not for the cat that can control you; for if
> you rats had your way you could not rule yourselves.]

At the end of the Prologue the king is left with unchecked powers, since no logical check can be provided by the Commons.

The scene now shifts, but Langland does not simply drop the
subject he has broached; rather he develops the framing-story
of the narrator's education, and at the same time weaves another narrative strand which will allow him to analyze more
comprehensively the problems of governmental power when the
king reappears. At the beginning of the next section of this
dream (Passus I), Lady Holy Church appears to the dreamer to
explain the tower and the pit, and to counsel him to seek
Truth, who is to be identified with the tower. When the dreamer asks how he will know Truth, Lady Holy Church replies

that Natural Knowledge will teach him, and she discourses on the nature of Truth at length. The dreamer, still mystified, takes a different approach. How can I know Falsehood, he asks. To answer this question, Lady Holy Church shows him another scene.

Will sees Falsehood and Favel (Flattery) as they are arranging a wedding for Mede the Maid, who represents the power of money—both reward and bribery. She is to marry Faithlessness. Lady Holy Church, having started the allegorical action again, commends Will to Christ and disappears from the narrative. The allegory comes to the forefront. It will eventually show the establishment of right reason in government; at the moment, however, the situation does not seem propitious for the commonwealth. If the wedding of the power of money to Faithlessness takes place, the basis for honest government will be hopelessly undermined. At the last minute Theology appears to object to the wedding. She demands that the case be taken to Westminster and placed before the king, to which all assent. The objection by Theology represents metaphorically the contention of moral philosophers that the power of money is not bad in itself, and therefore that the permanent alliance of Mede to Faithlessness is unnatural—unsound theology.

The parade of rogues to court at Westminster vividly depicts the power of dishonesty when supported by money. Mede is mounted on a sheriff, Falsehood on a prior, and Favel on a sycophant; and Liar is hitched to a great cart to haul a load of friars and imposters:

> And thus Fals and Favel fareth forth togideres,
> And Mede in the myddes, and alle thise men after.
> I have no tome to telle the taille that hem folweth,
> Of many maner man that on this molde libbeth;
> Ac Gyle was forgoer and gyed hem alle.
> B, II, 183–187
> [Thus Falsehood and Favel went forth together with Mede
> in the middle and all these men following. I have not
> time to describe the rag-tag that followed, of all kinds
> of people that live in the world; but Guile was the
> leader who guided them all.]

Truthfulness, however, forewarns the king of this procession, and he orders the whole group arrested. Allegorically we may understand that Falsehood cannot operate openly where Truthfulness is heeded. The rogues flee and hide out with friars, merchants, pardoners, and doctors; Mede is left alone to be taken before the king.

Despite the disgrace of her arrest, Mede proves attractive to the whole court. The king decides to question her himself, and others crowd around anxious to please her:

Curteysliche the clerke thanne, as the kyng hight,
Toke Mede bi the middel and broughte hir into chaumbre,
And there was myrthe and mynstralcye Mede to plese.
They that wonyeth in Westmynstre worschiped hir alle;
Gentelliche with ioye the iustices somme
Busked hem to the boure there the birde dwelled,
To conforte hire kyndely by clergise leve,
And seiden, "Mourne nought, Mede, ne make thow no sorwe,
For we will wisse the kynge and thi wey shape,
To be wedded at thi wille, and where the leve liketh."

B, III, 9–18

[As the king ordered, the clerk courteously took Mede by
the waist and escorted her into the chamber. There was
laughter and minstrelsy to please Mede, since they who live
in Westminster all loved her. With joy the judges with the permission
of the clergy politely hastened to the booth where she sat to comfort
her. "Don't be sad, Mede," they said, "for we will talk
to the king and make it so that you can marry whom you wish."]

In this manner the universal appeal of money is represented. Mede is the *femme fatale* whom everyone deprecates until brought in contact with her. A friar hears her confession and absolves her, and the king offers her a pardon if she will marry Conscience. The reader infers that this proposal is only a shade better than the scheme to marry her to Faithlessness. If the conscience of the realm were to be tied to the power of money, then the rich would have absolute sway and the poor would be powerless. So it is that though Mede is quite willing, Conscience will have none of the match.

Happily, the king does not force the marriage; rather he summons Reason to court and Mede is branded as a whore (signifying the truism that money will take up with anyone).

Everything thus seems propitious for the smooth and just operation of government, with Mede discredited, Falsehood not allowed at court, and the king following Reason. But Conscience destroys the sense of euphoria by reminding the king that the support of the common people will be necessary to make morality in government effective. This provides the subject of the second dream: the reform of the commons and their search for Truth.

This summary inevitably has passed over many interesting details and ramifications which flavor the narrative of *Piers Plowman*. While Langland wastes little time on transitions, shifting abruptly from one scene to another, he misses few chances to add to the vividness of his portrayal or to draw a moral. It is interesting to note too how many apparently realistic people—friars, mayors, and judges—interact with the personifications in this dream. Most of these, however, are not individualized and may be seen simply as typifications of different classes of men. In any event they impart no awkwardness to the story. The incidents of the narrative, despite occasional relevance to particular historical situations, also are admirably adapted to an allegory which has general application. The fable of the rats, for instance, probably has special reference to the conflict between Parliament and Richard II in Langland's time, but this is only secondary to its broad reference to the relationships between all rulers and their subjects.

Langland is the greatest virtuoso among writers of personification allegory. In addition to his ability to draw vivid scenes and write racy narrative, characteristics of the good storyteller, he has an impressive capacity for analyzing the moral, psychological, and social aspects of human activity. In each dream of *Piers Plowman* human action of general importance is analyzed; in each Langland continually improvises, introducing new characters and new situations. The second dream begins with a sermon by Reason to the people, proceeds through the confession of the Seven Deadly Sins, which represents a general confession and repentance, and introduces the mystical figure of Piers the Plowman to lead the repentant pilgrims to Truth. At the close of the dream they get a general pardon, but the substance of the pardon is quite unsatisfactory to both Piers and the dreamer; and the whole Life *(Vita)*, over twice as long as the Vision, grows out of their dissatisfaction. In Chapter IV we will return to *Piers Plowman* to discuss the first two dreams of the Life, in which a rather different setting—the mind of the dreamer—is used, and a completely new cast of personifications is introduced. In dreams subsequent to these, allegorical portrayal of the life of Christ and the establishment of the Church again requires radical narrative changes.

The diverse individual visions of the work are held together by the logical sequence of their actions, each dream embodying a step toward the salvation of the world. They are also held together by the frame story, whose subject is the dreamer's education in his search for Truth, which sometimes merges with the main action. The work in detail and in total is most complicated; but Langland is always sure in his guidance of the narrative, and it would be a mistake to imagine him lost in his own mazes. If the reader will devote himself to Langland's allegory he will usually find it well constructed, and he may very well be led to profound insights.

Profound insights through an author's sound and often original analysis is what the best of personification allegory offers. The process of dying, of losing friend, kindred, goods, beauty, strength, and sense, is thus effectively presented in *Everyman.* The establishment of government under right reason, despite the king's unchecked authority, the schemes of Falsehood, and the corrupting power of money, is portrayed in an exciting series of narrative scenes which make up the first dream of *Piers Plowman.* Such allegories are quite different from the rather static representations of allegorical tableaux, like those that make up the *House of Fame,* which nevertheless can have their own effectiveness and charm.

The strong sense of literary tradition characteristic of medieval writers shows up particularly in these allegories. The writers freely make use of the materials of previous writers, so that many of the personifications and narrative motifs reappear from one work to another over a period of centuries. For instance, the brief allegory in *Blow, Northren Wind* discussed at the beginning of this chapter is in the tradition of the court-of-love poems; both the personifications and the narrative of the short passage involved have dozens of analogues. Likewise in the other works that we have discussed few of the characters are wholly new; Fame, Death, and Reason, for example, were commonplace literary personages before their appearances in the *House of Fame, Everyman,* and *Piers Plowman.* Each of the next three chapters takes up a traditional kind of allegory: Chapter III concerns love allegory, which found its most influential and original expression in the *Romance of the Rose,* and Chapters IV and V concern psychological allegory and the related "allegory of revelation," which grew in large part out of the *Consolation of Philosophy* of Boethius.

NOTE TO CHAPTER II

Editions and Translations

Romance of the Rose and *House of Fame.* The standard version of Chaucer's works, which includes the Chaucerian translation of the *Romance of the Rose,* quoted in Chapter II, is edited by F. N. Robinson, *The Works of Geoffrey Chaucer* (2nd ed., 1957). Still essential to the scholar is the seven-volume edition by Walter W. Skeat, *The Complete Works* (1894-1897), which has extensive notes and a volume of Chaucer apocrypha. Useful especially to the student are the collections edited by Albert C. Baugh, *Chaucer's Major Poetry* (1963), and E. T. Donaldson, *Chaucer's Poetry* (1959); and the briefer anthology of Robert A. Pratt, *Selections from the Tales of Canterbury and Short Poems* (1966).

Blow, Northren Wynd. Carleton Brown and Rossell Hope Robbins have edited the bulk of Middle English lyrics in several complementary collections. *Blow, Northren Wynd* is found in Brown's *English Lyrics of the XIIIth Century* (1932) and in many anthologies which include Middle English lyrics.

Everyman appears in most collections of early English dramas and in the standard anthologies of English literature. The text generally cited by scholars is that of the first edition reproduced by W. W. Greg (1904).

Piers Plowman. The three versions of the peom are edited in parallel texts by Walter W. Skeat, *Langland's Piers the Plowman,* two volumes (1886). This is being superseded by an edition of the texts separately under the general editorship of George Kane, of which only the A-version has appeared, *Will's Visions of Piers Plowman and Do-Well* (1960). J. F. Goodridge has made a sound and readable prose translation, *Piers the Plowman* (rev. ed., 1966), which contains very useful introductory material and summaries at the head of each passus. A substantial and well-glossed selection from the poem in Middle English, designed for the student, has been edited by Elizabeth Salter and Derek Pearsall, *Piers Plowman* (1967).

Personification and Personfication Allegory

Discussion and copious illustrations of medieval personifications in the visual arts are found in Émile Mâle, *Religious Art in France in the Thirteenth Century,* translated by Dora Nussey (1913; reprinted recently as *The Gothic Image*), pp. 1-130. Erwin Panofsky deals with iconographical significances in *Meaning in the Visual Arts* (1955). Jean Seznec relates numerous traditional medieval personifications to classical gods and heroes in *The Survival of the Pagan Gods* (1953), pp. 84-121. The standard study of medieval Fortune is Howard R. Patch, *The Goddess Fortuna in Medieval Literature* (1927).

Helpful insights into personfication allegory are provided by I. A. Richards, *Practical Criticism* (1929), pp. 198–203, and Angus Fletcher, *Allegory* (1964), pp. 25–35. The chapter entitled "Allegory" in C. S. Lewis, *Allegory of Love* (1936), pp. 44–111, can substantially assist an understanding of medieval personification allegory and its backgrounds, but I do not find his distinction between symbolism and allegory (pp. 44–48) accurate or helpful, nor is it true that "the *bellum intestinum* is the root of all allegory" (p. 68). Bertrand Bronson's useful article, which discusses eighteenth-century allegory in particular, is referred to in the Note to Chapter I. The theoretical discussion by Edwin Bloom, "The Allegorical Principle," *ELH,* 18 (1951), 163–190, which also focuses on post-medieval allegory, suggestively explores the qualities of successful allegory. Robert W. Frank's well-known treatment of the subject, "The Art of Reading Medieval Personification-Allegory," *ELH,* 20 (1953), 237–250, is helpful, though not definitive.

Criticism of Specific Works

Criticism of the *Romance of the Rose* is taken up in the Note to Chapter III. A convenient short discussion of the *House of Fame* is Paul Ruggiers, "The Unity of Chaucer's *House of Fame,*" *SP,* 50 (1953), 16–29. An important book-length study, which explores the poem's deeper significations, is B. G. Koonce, *Chaucer and the Tradition of Fame* (1966). A rather complete study of the court-of-love poems, to which the allegory in *Blow, Northren Wynd* is allied, has been made by William A. Neilson, *The Origins and Sources of the Court of Love* (1899). Two suggestive discussions of the structure of *Everyman* are Lawrence V. Ryan, "Doctrine and Dramatic Structure in *Everyman,*" *Speculum,* 32 (1957), 722–735, and Thomas F. Van Laan, "Everyman: A Structural Analysis," *PMLA,* 78 (1963), 465–475.

Morton W. Bloomfield, "The Present State of *Piers Plowman* Studies," *Speculum,* 14 (1939), 215–232, provides a good summary of scholarship on *Piers Plowman* up to 1939 and indicates the various aspects of the work which may be profitably explored. Useful interpretations of the first dream are contained in Thomas P. Dunning, *Piers Plowman: An Interpretation of the A-Text* (1937), and A. G. Mitchell, *Lady Meed and the Art of Piers Plowman* (1956). There are several important book-length studies of broader scope. Robert W. Frank, Jr., *Piers Plowman and the Scheme of Salvation* (1957) provides a usually clear summary of the narrative, though his restricted concept of its allegorical possibilities is a subject of debate (See review by D. W. Robertson, Jr., *Speculum,* 33 [1958], 395–397). Morton W. Bloomfield, *Piers Plowman as* a *Fourteenth-Century Apocalypse* (1962), is important for its bringing out of literary, social, and religious associations of the work. The study by D. W. Robertson, Jr., and Bernard F. Huppé, *Piers Plowman and the Scriptural Tradition* (1951), elucidates important implications of the poem's Scriptural associations. E. Talbot Donaldson, *Piers Plowman, the C-Text and its Poet* (1949), explores particularly the relationships between the three texts and discusses what the poet reveals of himself.

Chapter III

The Dance of Love

Important Works: *Romance of the Rose, Book of the Duchess, Troilus and Criseyde,* Merchant's Tale.

After the narrator of the *Romance of the Rose,* the Lover, has inspected the personifications of Old Age, Hate, Envy, and the like which are displayed on the exterior wall of the Garden of Mirth, he is admitted to the garden by Idleness. She leads him to a carole, a dance, in which the participants are personifications of the qualities of good lovers. Many of these represent qualities directly opposed to those depicted outside the garden. As the Lover approaches the carolers, he sees Mirth dancing with Gladness, Love leading Sweet Looking, Beauty with Wealth, and Largess, Candor, and Youth each with a chosen partner. When at the invitation of Courtesy the Lover joins the dance, he symbolically allies himself with these figures and begins his career of amour. The dance, a Dance of Love, provides a particularly apt metaphor for the conventionalized and patterned practices of love depicted in medieval courtly literature.

The poets were fond of the image of the dance for talking about love practices. Guillaume de Lorris and Chaucer, among others, attributed experience in the "old dance" to various of their characters. Guillaume's old duenna, Vekke, learned the *daunce* through youthful experiences in love play; as a result,

> She knew ech wrench and every gise
> Of love, and every wile.
>
> 4292–4293

Chaucer similarly imputes skill in the dance to the Wife of Bath, to governesses, and to Pandarus. Such savants in the art are able to teach those without experience the proper steps. So Vekke instructs Fair Welcome and Pandarus guides Troilus. The Lover in the *Rose,* however, has more than one teacher. He learns initially from his observations inside and outside the garden what is appropriate and inappropriate to love. Subsequently, lectures by the God of Love and Friend further prepare him for the allegorical affair in which he eventually becomes enmeshed.

The carole which the Lover joins in the *Romance of the Rose* is a Dance of Love, depicted here. The dancers with crowns are Beauty and the God of Love. Pierpont Morgan Library Ms. 324, f.6v. By permission.

The practices of love appropriate to people attached to medieval courts, as these practices are represented in narratives such as the *Romance of the Rose,* have been popularly classed under the collective label *courtly love.* Unfortunately courtly love has been understood to involve an invariable code and pattern of behavior. And equally unfortunately Andreas Capellanus' witty treatise, translated under the title *The Art of Courtly Love* (originally *De Arte Honeste Amandi* or simply *De Amore*), has been considered the Bible of medieval lovers. Such misapprehensions have resulted in many distorted notions about medieval love as manifested in literature. For example, analysts note Andreas' rule that no love can exist between people married to each other; they cite the adulterous affairs of famous couples like Lancelot and Guinevere and Tristan and Isolde; and they conclude that the only genuinely courtly love which married people in medieval fiction could enjoy would be an adulterous love. Yet there seems no sound reason for excluding from the classification *courtly-love* stories that use the conventions wherein the lovers are married or decide to marry.

The first lines of Chaucer's Franklin's Tale, for instance, tell of an exemplary knight who strives as best he can to serve his noble lady, and who accomplishes many an exploit in her honor:

> For she was oon the faireste under sonne,
> And eek therto comen of so heigh kynrede
> That wel unnethes dorste this knyght, for drede,
> Telle hire his wo, his peyne, and his distresse.
> But atte laste she, for his worthynesse,
> And namely for his meke obeysaunce,
> Hath swich a pitee caught of his penaunce
> That pryvely she fil of his accord
> To take hym for hir housbonde and hir lord.
>
> F, 734–742

Here are noble lovers who act strictly according to the conventions. He performs acts of heroism for her and is for a long time afraid to confess his love to her despite great sufferings. When at last he reveals his devotion, she is hesitant, but finally she secretly accords with his wish—to get married! It is courtly; it is love according to the conventions; but the end is marriage. Nor is Chaucer simply a late medieval innovator in love poetry. A notable example of the alliance of courtly love with marriage is provided in the great romance of *Parzival* by Wolfram von Eschenbach, written a full century and a half before Chaucer's major work. Repeatedly in Wolfram's masterpiece are found the requisite perfect knights and perfect ladies, the long service, the love longing, and eventual consummation of the love in bed; but consistently the delights of the bed are accompanied by marriage.

Courtly love, then, if this modern term is to be retained as a convenient label, is best conceived of as a set of conventions which may be mixed in various ways. The end of a courtly-love affair may be premarital love, adulterous love, platonic love, or love in marriage, depending on the desires and disposition of the participants. In the process of arriving at whatever conclusion may be envisaged or destined, the narrative will make use of conventionalized movements by standardized characters. Though the movements are stereotyped, their arrangement may be varied somewhat so that very different stories may be told. To put it in metaphoric terms, there are numerous steps which make up the dance, and these steps may be combined by the dancers in a variety of sequences.

The nearest approach to a standard pattern of love allegory applicable to Middle English literature is presented in the *Romance of the Rose*. Just as *Everyman* and *Piers Plowman* involve important actions common to most men (the experience of death and the search for salvation), so the *Romance of the Rose* concerns a crucial experience of youth: the first love affair of a young man and woman. The poem presents this experience so effectively that it became the central medieval love story, and it exerted a major influence on love poetry for more than two centuries.

The *Rose* is the work of two poets. Guillaume de Lorris wrote the first 4058 lines around 1235, and Jean de Meun forty years later stretched out the poem to more than five times that length. Guillaume's part, apparently unfinished, contains the major part of the love narrative. Jean uses the elements of Guillaume's story to construct a discursive and often satiric tract on the subject of love taken in its broader sense. Though Jean ostensibly continues and concludes Guillaume's allegory, he effects rather fundamental changes. Guillaume is interested in love as practiced by courtiers, while Jean's subject is universal love, especially the urge to procreate as ordained by nature;

the graceful dance of Guillaume ultimately becomes a fertility rite in Jean's part (though not, I may hasten to add, a pagan rite). Since Guillaume's story exerted the greater effect on Middle English love narrative, we are concerned here primarily with his part of the poem.

Guillaume's poem synthesizes a great number of the conventions of love poetry which it inherited. The Arts of Love of Ovid and Andreas Capellanus, the love stories of chivalric romance, the traditions embodied in contemporary lyric poetry, overtones of Platonic and Neoplatonic love, and Christian writings on the subject all are evident in the work. In turn the *Rose* was the primary purveyor of conventions of love to succeeding generations of poets, though to be sure there were other important influences on later love poetry. The love story of Chaucer's *Troilus and Criseyde* reflects not only Guillaume's *Rose*, but also the modified patterns of amorous behavior found in the poetry of Chaucer's French contemporaries, especially Machaut; essential features also were derived from the Italian poets, particularly Dante and Boccaccio.

Nevertheless, the influence of the allegorical *Rose* even on a realistic story like *Troilus and Criseyde* can hardly be overrated. One might even state that the story of the *Rose* developed into stories like *Troilus,* since almost every step in the narrative of Guillaume de Lorris may be found in transmuted- form in the story of *Troilus.* The medium changes from personification allegory to natural representation, but the conventions remain. An intermediate stage on the road from the allegorical to the realistic is found in the stories of Guillaume de Machaut and in Chaucer's *Book of the Duchess,* which was profoundly influenced by Machaut's work. The love story in the *Duchess,* while not allegorical like the *Rose,* possesses less of the flesh of realism, and more of the language of allegory, than *Troilus.* The *Rose,* the *Duchess,* and *Troilus,* then, provide a contrast in narrative media—the first allegorical, the second nonallegorical but hardly realistic, and the third overtly realistic. The directions which the stories take also contrast. The young Lover of Guillaume de Lorris is desirous of a nonmarital, and clearly physical, alliance with the virgin Rose; in the *Book of the Duchess* the Black Knight tells of a courtship which ostensibly had an impeccable, idealistic aim; in *Troilus* the inexperienced lover achieves a liaison with the widow Criseyde.

The love conventions provide the common element which relates these three stories to each other. An inspection of several of the more interesting conventions common to them should illuminate the kinship among them, and at the same time help to identify some qualities of that protean entity, courtly love, which has been the subject of much imprecise thought and comment.

To begin with, the settings of the poems and the participants in the stories have marked similarities. The story of the *Romance of the Rose* takes place in a dream, a vision which presages the truth with complete accuracy (28–30). The narrator awakens to a bright May day:

> That it was May me thoughte tho—
> It is fyve yer or more ago—
> That is was May, thus dremed me,
> In tyme of love and jolite.
>
> 49–52

The birds in this month are almost delirious in their happiness:

> Than doth the nyghtyngale hir myght
> To make noyse and syngen blythe.
> Than is blisful many sithe
> The chelaundre and papyngay.
>
> 78–81

Birds, lovely flowers, beautiful meadows, majestic trees, and gentle animals are the subject in many subsequent lines of description, and these lend a strongly pastoral flavor to the story, particularly suitable to the subject:

> Hard is the hert that loveth nought
> In May, whan al this mirth is wrought.
>
> 85–86

The lovers have the gentle breeding and fresh youth which accords with the setting: the Rose is a perfect bud, the Lover is "swoote and debonair,/ Of age yong, lusty, and fair" (3737–3738).

These elements recur in the *Book of the Duchess*. The narrator has a dream that is "inly swete," which is to say that it presents a true story. In the dream it is May; birds sing everywhere:

> Was never herd so swete a steven,
> But it had be a thyng of heven.
>
> 307–308

The narrator goes from his room and eventually walks down a flowery path into a grove of beautiful, green trees whose branches grow together overhead. The small animals again are present:

> And many an hert and many an hynde
> Was both before me and behynde.
> Of founes, sowres, bukkes, does
> Was ful the woode, and many roes,
> And many sqwirelles, that sete
> Ful high upon the trees and ete.
>
> 427–432

These lines, indeed, along with numerous others describing the setting in the *Duchess,* are based directly on description found in the *Rose.*

The lovers in this poem of Chaucer's are also nobly born and attractive. The man whom the narrator sees in the garden is

> A wonder wel-farynge knyght—
> By the maner me thoghte so—
> Of good mochel, and ryght yong therto.
>
> 452–454

The lady whom the knight describes is perfect both physically and morally. When he first saw her in a crowd of beautiful women, she outshone the rest as the sun does the stars (820–829).

In *Troilus and Criseyde* the lovers similarly are outstanding examples of youthful nobility. In the capsule portraits that Chaucer includes in Book V, Troilus is described as

> Yong, fressh, strong, and hardy as lyoun;
> Trewe as stiel in ech condicioun;
> Oon of the beste entecched creature
> That is, or shal, whil that the world may dure.
>
> V, 830–833

In the previous stanza summing up Criseyde's character, one

hardly notes that *sliding courage* is actually a fault, her other qualities are so exemplary:

> She sobre was, ek symple, and wys withal,
> The best ynorisshed ek that myghte be,
> And goodly of hire speche in general,
> Charitable, estatlich, lusty, and fre;
> Ne nevere mo ne lakked hire pite;
> Tendre-herted, slydynge of corage;
> But trewely, I kan nat telle hire age.
>
> V, 820–826

While the setting of *Troilus and Criseyde* is the whole city of Troy, as contrasted with the garden settings of the *Rose* and the *Duchess,* both springtime and the garden play important roles in *Troilus*. It is April when Troilus first sees and falls in love with Criseyde,

> whan clothed is the mede
> With newe grene, of lusty Veer the pryme,
> And swote smellen floures white and rede.
>
> I, 156–158

And when the lovers finally find themselves in bed together, it is May of another year. Criseyde's garden, furthermore, is crucial in her deliberations about whether to love or not to love Troilus. In this garden her niece Antigone sings her a song of love and speaks of its power:

> "For alle the folk that han or ben on lyve
> Ne konne wel the blisse of love discryve."
>
> II, 888–889

This song inclines her heart toward Troilus, and when she goes to bed a bird perched on a bough outside her window contributes to her inclination with a lay of love:

> A nyghtyngale, upon a cedir grene,
> Under the chambre wal ther as she ley,
> Ful loude song ayein the moone shene,
> Peraunter, in his briddes wise, a lay
> Of love, that made hire herte fressh and gay.
>
> II, 918–922

At this point the prophetic dream—which controls the *Rose* and the *Duchess*—figures importantly in this narrative, for Criseyde, under the influence of the songs of Antigone and the nightingale, dreams that an eagle claws out her heart and gives her his own in return. Troilus, we may deduce, allegorically the eagle, is now destined to claim her heart.

Thus the conventions of setting and participants are passed along from Guillaume to Chaucer's two poems, though some of them are preserved in somewhat transmuted form in *Troilus*. Similar resemblances may be found in every step of the narratives, from the first sight to the eventual outcomes. We will consider several of the more notable instances.

Andreas Capellanus records a rule that blindness incapacitates a person for love. Though we may recognize some irony in this dictum, it still suggests the importance of the physical sight of the beloved, especially the first sight. It is the first sight that inflicts on the lover a wound which never heals. In the *Romance of the Rose,* the impact of this look is forcefully shown in a complex series of allegorical metaphors. When the lover leaves the carole, he walks around until he comes upon a pool, which an inscription proclaims to be the Pool of Narcissus. Undaunted by the legend of Narcissus, he looks in the pool and sees two beautiful crystals that reflect the whole garden of love. We infer that he had discovered in the depths of his own eyes (the crystals) the broad range of attractive experiences available to him in this garden. The reflection of a beautiful rose arbor particularly takes his attention. When he is drawn to approach it, the perfume of the flowers and the beauty of one perfect *knoppe* (bud) strikes him "right to the herte rote" (1662). The sight of the lady has captured him. His efforts to get at the bud, however, are interrupted by the God of Love's arrows; these provide a further more explicit metaphor representing love on sight.

Love has been following the Lover accompanied by his bow-and-arrow carrier, Sweet Looking—the sight of the lady—who now provides the god with the arrow Beauty. He shoots it through the Lover's eye right to his heart:

> He streight up to his ere drough
> The stronge bowe, that was so tough,

> And shet att me so wondir smerte
> That thorough myn ye unto myn herte
> The takel smot, and depe it wente.
>
> 1725–1729

Though sorely wounded, the Lover succeeds in drawing out the arrow; the barbed head, however, remains permanently in his heart. The succeeding arrows with which he is wounded—Simplicity, Courtesy, Company, and Fair Semblance—symbolize the succeeding stages of his first experience with the lady.

The God of Love shoots an arrow into the Lover's eye, an allegorical representation of the effect of the first sight of the beloved. Pierpont Morgan Library Ms. 324, f.13. By permission.

The initial view of the beloved in the *Rose* is thus represented in three metaphorical stages: the pool with the crystals, the rosebushes, and the arrows of Love. In comparable fashion the Black Knight in the *Book of the Duchess* points up the importance of his first sight of Fair White by means of a full-dress eulogy on her beauty. He narrates first how he spent his youth in the service of Love, and how his heart was fastened on no particular object until one day he came into a company of beautiful ladies in which White stood out like the sun among the stars. By her look he was at once caught up in love:

> She ful sone, in my thoght,
> As help me God, so was ykaught
> So sodenly, that I ne tok
> Ne maner counseyl but at hir lok
> And at myn herte.

837–841

The Knight explains the impact of the sight of her in his ensuing 250-line description of the lady's beauty of person and character. She had perfect features, the goodness of Esther, and was absolutely unique, like the phoenix. Among ten thousand she would have been the "chief mirror of the feast." As a result of seeing her he immediately devoted himself wholly to her service.

Troilus is comparably thunderstruck the first time he sees Criseyde. The fact that he sees her in church reminds one of the Italian backgrounds of Chaucer's work: Petrarch and Dante both described seeing their ladies in church. Indeed, the whole sequence of Troilus' first sight of his beloved as described by Chaucer, like much of the poem, is based on Boccaccio's *Filostrato*. But Chaucer slows down the pace and adds much detail not found in the *Filostrato* so that his story hearkens back to the older French tradition. The God of Love is felt much more as an actual power than in Boccaccio's version, and the devastating effect of Criseyde's appearance on Troilus is dramatized with more force.

When Chaucer's Troilus in blasphemous fashion makes fun of the young men who serve Love, and looks up impertinently in smug self-satisfaction, the God of Love angrily observes him and plots revenge:

> At which the God of Love gan loken rowe
> Right for despit, and shop for to ben wroken.

I, 206–207

The god will soon manifest his power, but Troilus, like the Lover in the Garden of Mirth, walks around the temple quite unconscious of the god's presence until suddenly the arrow of Sweet Looking strikes him:

> And upon cas bifel that thorugh a route
> His eye percede, and so depe it wente,
> Til on Criseyde it smot, and ther it stente.
>
> I, 271-273

The verbs—"percede," "smot," "stente"—all suggest the speed and power of Love's arrows, which have fixed her image in his heart:

> And of hire look in him ther gan to quyken
> So gret desir and such affeccioun,
> That in his hertes botme gan to stiken
> Of hir his fixe and depe impressioun.
>
> I, 295-298

Though "astoned," Troilus is yet "nat fullich al awhaped" (I, 316). He manages to get home to his room, where he can mull over the image impressed in his heart:

> Thus gan he make a mirour of his mynde,
> In which he saugh al holly hire figure;
> And that he wel koude in his herte fynde,
> It was to hym a right good aventure
> To love swich oon.
>
> I, 365-369

As a result of one look, Troilus gives himself over completely to love.

Criseyde has a very similar experience when, after Pandarus has told her of Troilus' love, she sees him riding back from battle. His helmet is hewn, his shield shattered, and as the people salute him as a hero, he blushes from modesty. Criseyde, realizing that she is the conqueror of this conqueror, is deeply impressed:

> Criseyda gan al his chere aspien,
> And leet it so softe in hire herte synke,
> That to hireself she seyde, "Who yaf me drynke?"
>
> II, 649-651

His appearance has the force of a powerful potion; she too has been struck by Sweet Looking.

The look is the initial, and one of the most predictable, steps in the Dance. It has a permanent effect on the true lover; as a consequence of it, he forever after longs for the presence and love of the lady. When he is deprived of these, which happens very often, he complains. The God of Love in the *Rose* specifically warns the Lover that he will often think of the lady, and wherever he is he will have to go off alone to complain:

> Fro folk thou must departe in hie,
> That noon perceyve thi maladie.
> But hyde thyne harm thou must alone,
> And go forth sool, and make thy mone.
>   2393–2396

The god even puts an imagined complaint in the mouth of the Lover; he says that the Lover will dream of having his love naked in his arms, and will awaken to find it is not so. The Lover then will sigh because the dream has ended; he will pray that it might come true; then he will worry that he has asked entirely too much, for from a much lesser thing than the dream envisages he would have "full gret likyng,/ And full gret joye." She is so worthy, he will think, that simply a look of hers would satisfy him. But then, the god warns, he will worry that he has set his heart on too high an object even for the solace of a look, and he will toss and turn in his bed and long for the dawn, reproaching the sun for its slowness. Only with dawn will his complaint find an end.

Love's prediction of the Lover's complaint comes true after Jealousy has cast him out of the garden and built a great tower to guard Fair Welcome from him. In the resulting lament the Lover finds his pain inexpressibly severe, and feels quite seriously that it will prove his death:

> For I endure more hard penaunce,
> Then ony can seyn or thynke,
> That for the sorwe almost I synke.
> Whanne I remembre me of my woo,
> Full nygh out of my witt I goo.

>Inward myn herte I feele blede,
>For comfortles the deth I drede.
>
>4406-4412

In the love stories which followed the *Romance of the Rose,* the lover's complaint became an even more important part of the narratives. It was oftentimes set off by distinctive versification, and sometimes provided the mainspring of the narrative. The lengthy complaint in Chaucer's fragmentary *Anelida and Arcite* exemplifies these developments; Anelida's lament has both a distinctive form and a position of dominant importance in the poem. The Black Knight's complaints in the *Book of the Duchess* have analogous qualities. When the dreamer comes up behind the Knight, he hears him recite a formal complaint, an eleven-line set piece, evidently composed by himself, with a distinguishing rhyme scheme. Later the Knight adds another 150 lines of more spontaneous lament about the loss of his beloved (560-709). As is frequently the case with such laments, he makes great use of rhetorical devices prescribed in medieval textbooks like the *Poetria Nova* of Geoffrey of Vinsauf. Apostrophe, oxymoron, and repetition of initial words (anaphora) are particularly popular in lovers' complaints, and are well illustrated in the Knight's moaning.

A favorite target of the lover's lament is Fortune, the arbitrary power who upon whim unites and separates the servants of Love. The Knight is particularly bitter about Fortune's actions, and he excoriates her angrily:

>She is the monstres hed ywrien;
>As fylthe over-ystrawed with floures.
>Hir moste worshippe and hir flour ys
>To lyen, for that ys hyr nature;
>Withoute feyth, lawe, or mesure,
>She ys fals.
>
>628-633

Another traditional enemy of the lover is Death, who is said either to threaten the lover, or—as in the *Duchess*—to flee from him when he longs to die.

The Black Knight's complaints, standing at the head of his story, have a pivotal position in the *Book of the Duchess.* Troilus' complaints have an equally crucial place in *Troilus and Criseyde:* in Book I they precede the story of his conquest of Criseyde; in Book IV they adumbrate his loss of her. The laments in Book I are quite standard. After being struck by Criseyde's arrows, Troilus, like the Black Knight, turns poet; he composes a "Canticus Troili," in which the paradoxes of Love are soberly set forth:

> "If love be good, from whennes cometh my woo?
> If it be wikke, a wonder thynketh me,
> When every torment and adversite
> That cometh of hym may to me savory thinke,
> For ay thurst I, the more that ich it drinke."
>
>   I, 402–406

Just before Pandarus appears to offer help, Troilus is longing for the "port of deth." And after Pandarus arrives, he expresses his conviction that no help is possible for him, since cruel Fortune is his enemy:

> Ful hard were it to helpen in this cas,
> For wel fynde I that Fortune is my fo;
> Ne al the men that riden konne or go
> May of hire cruel whiel the harm withstonde;
> For, as hire list, she pleyeth with free and bonde.
>
>   I, 836–840

Troilus, the lover sepaiated from his lady, is expressing himself in conventional ways; his subjects are the paradoxes of love, the instability of Fortune, and the enmity of Death. His lamentations are in earnest, but the reader does not feel at this time that his case will really be fatal, however much he thinks so.

In Book IV, however, after the love of Troilus and Criseyde has been consummated and they have lived long in bliss, Troilus' desperation in the face of potential separation has more serious implications. When he hears that Criseyde is to be traded to the Greeks for Antenor, he immediately goes to his room, and after weeping, launches into a magnificent series of apostrophes, to Fortune, to the God of Love, to his soul—

> "O wery goost, that errest to and fro,
> Why nyltow fleen out of the wofulleste
> Body that ever myghte on grounde go?"
>
>   IV, 302–304

—to his weeping eyes, to Criseyde, to more fortunate lovers, and finally to Criseyde's father, Calkas, who has arranged the trade—"O oold, unholsum, and myslyved man" (IV, 330). His later apostrophe to Crisyede's empty house is yet more pitiful:

> "O paleis, whilom crowne of houses alle,
> Enlumyned with sonne of alle blisse!
> O ryng, fro which the ruby is out falle,
> O cause of wo, that cause hast ben of lisse!"
>
> V, 547–550

Not only does he feel that Fortune is against him, but also that Divine Providence has foreordained his loss:

> "For certeynly, this wot I wel," he seyde,
> "That forsight of divine purveyaunce
> Hath seyn alwey me to forgon Criseyde,
> Syn God seeth every thyng, out of doutance,
> And hem disponyth, thorugh his ordinaunce."
>
> IV, 960–964

This pessimistic analysis of Providence does not result from mere casual petulance on the part of Troilus; he spends the next sixteen stanzas proving logically man's lack of free will, to his own satisfaction at least. His desire for death, often expressed in the last two books, has an earnestness that demands fulfillment. Achilles, who eventually kills him, is simply an instrument of Troilus' death wish.

The situation of the typical lover in medieval stories, however, is not generally so desperate as that of Troilus becomes. To keep the Lover from despair, the God of Love in the *Romance of the Rose* promises to send four of his lieutenants: Hope, Sweet Thought, Sweet Looking (supplied by the sight of her), and Sweet Speech (words of praise of the lady by another). Sweet Speech, says the god, can be supplied by a carefully selected friend. One must be absolutely secretive about his love except to this friend, who can solace the Lover with praise of the lady and with advice. Preferably, states the god, the friend will himself be a lover, whose similar experience will enable him to understand his comrade's problems and even to further his cause with the lady herself. He can also offer consolation:

For it is noble thing, in fay,
To have a man thou darst say
Thy pryve counsell every deell;
For that wole comforte thee right well.
2887-2890

In accord with the God of Love's promise, the friend appears in different forms in numerous medieval love stories, including the *Rose, Troilus,* and the *Duchess.* When the Lover in the *Rose* is first dismissed by Danger from the bower of the bud, he is visited by Reason, who advises a rational—and therefore to the Lover an unsatisfactory—approach. After the Lover rejects Reason, he is reminded of Love's suggestion that in desperate times he call on a confidant; so he summons Friend, a comrade "Trewe and siker, curteys and hend" (3345). Friend's words are sweet indeed, since he assures the Lover that Danger is easily controlled. Though Danger is fierce at first, says Friend, he will later prove pliant; the Lover has only to be meek and humble, and above all to use flattery. This practical counsel proves efficacious, as does the more lengthy advice which Friend offers later in Jean de Meun's part, though the lady ultimately is won only through the direct intervention of the God of Love and Venus.

The friend, then, who appears in numerous guises in subsequent poetry, is a wholly trustworthy practical assistant to the lover. A character named Hope provides the advice and encouragement of the friend in Guillaume de Machaut's *Remedy of Fortune;* in Machaut's *Fountain of Love* the poet himself functions as the trusted comrade. In the *Book of the Duchess,* indebted to both of these works of Machaut, the dreamer-poet has a great desire to play the friend's part. He asks the Black Knight to tell him all of his troubles so that he can do his best to help him:

> But certes, sire, yif that yee
> Wolde ought discure me youre woo,
> I wolde, as wys God helpe me soo,
> Amende hyt, yif I kan or may.
> Ye mowe preve hyt by assay;
> For, by my trouthe, to make yow hool,
> I wol do al my power hool.
> 548-554

It turns out that the Black Knight's lady is dead, so the dreamer's powers to help are restricted. He perhaps assists a healthful catharsis by encouraging the Knight to tell his story, but his comment at the disclosure of White's death is simply a helpless, "Be God, hyt ys routhe!" (1310).

The narrator of the *Duchess* also plays the part of Reason, the rational counselor of the *Romance of the Rose;* and just as the Lover of Guillaume de Lorris rejects the sound advice of Reason, so the dreamer's admonitions to the Black Knight prove fruitless. Ignore the whims of Fortune, the dreamer advises, drawing on one of Reason's examples in the earlier poem:

> "Remembre yow of Socrates,
> For he ne counted nat three strees
> Of noght that Fortune koude doo."
>   717–719

To this rational counsel, the Knight answers abruptly, "I kan not soo."

Pandarus in *Troilus and Criseyde* likewise combines recognizably the roles of Friend and Reason. He moreover is like Jean de Meun's duenna, Vekke, in his setting Criseyde on the way of love. Both Pandarus and Vekke, we remember, are said to be experienced in the "olde daunce," which in theory should enable them to guard their protégées from lecherous men, but in practice assists their endeavors to bring lovers together. Consideration of Pandarus in his functions as duenna or Reason, however, would take us afield from the present subject, which concerns the conventional figure of the friend. In any event it is the role of friend that Pandarus most truly fills. As I will discuss in the next chapter, Pandarus as Reason is simply a caricature; and, despite the word his name has given to the language, he is no pander in the conventional sense like Jean de Meun's duenna. At the same time, he is all the God of Love posits in a friend, and more.

When Pandarus wrings from Troilus his lady's identity, he immediately offers Sweet Speech, pleasant words about her:

> "Ne I nevere saugh a more bountevous
> Of hire estat, n'a gladder, ne of speche
> A frendlyer, n'a more gracious
> For to do wel, ne lasse hadde nede to seche

What for to don; and al this bet to eche,
In honour, to as fer as she may strecche,
A kynges herte semth by hyrs a wrecche."

I, 883–889

Like the Friend in the Rose, Pandarus is himself a lover, albeit an unsuccessful one. As a result of his experience, he knows better how to help Troilus:

> "I, that have in love so ofte assayed
> Grevances, oughte konne, and wel the more,
> Counseillen the of that thow art amayed."

I, 646–648

The God of Love has suggested that the friend will further the lover's cause by praising him to the lady. When Pandarus accordingly sees Criseyde, he prepares the way for Troilus with a fulsome eulogy on his bravery and his character. Though Criseyde asks about Hector, Pandarus immediately shifts the subject to Hector's brother Troilus, "The wise, worthi Ector the secounde" (II, 158). Pandarus also like Friend in the Rose gives his comrade much sound, practical advice. But he goes quite beyond simple words of advice and praise; he woos and wins Criseyde for Troilus, and even pushes him into bed with her. In the prosecution of the affair he virtually becomes the lover himself; and he bears for Troilus the brunt of Criseyde's danger, the aspect of the lady which so terrifies the Lover of Guillaume de Lorris.

Among the conventional personifications of the Romance of the Rose, Danger is one of the most important and fascinating. The word danger in medieval English and French signifies something rather different from the Modern English word, describing a quality of personality rather than a matter of circumstance. It implies both the standoffishness of the lady and her direct refusal. Perhaps Danger is most easily specified as the opposite of Fair Welcome, who personifies an aspect of personality that presents no semantic problem. In the Rose, after the Lover has pledged his service to Love, Danger and Fair Welcome alternate in dominating the allegory. When one is at hand the other leaves; it is impossible for both to be present at the same time.

When the Lover approaches the rose arbor after the God of

Love's lecture, Fair Welcome, a handsome young man, greets him; allegorically, the pretty young thing's smile and friendliness to a new acquaintance are represented. Fair Welcome takes the Lover right up to the rose and allows him to draw near to the bud, and to touch the bush which holds it. Fair Welcome even pulls a leaf (a love token) for the Lover, who is thereby captivated and almost emboldened to make a request. But then he hesitates, for as he says he would rather be carved in pieces than to earn Fair Welcome's displeasure. Fair Welcome, nevertheless, leads him on:

> "Sey boldely thi will," quod he,
> "I nyl be wroth, if that I may,
> For nought that thou shalt to me say."
> 3098–3100

So the Lover asks for the Rosebud. Fair Welcome, despite his previous assurances, is shocked right off the scene, protesting as he leaves that the bud is too young:

> "Ye are not curteys to aske it.
> Late it still on the roser sitt,
> And growe til it amended be,
> And parfitly come to beaute."
> 3123–3126

The Lover has not been conscious of the "cherl" Danger, who has been lurking behind the rosebush and now appears with his club like an uncouth ruffian:

> Ful gret he was and blak of hewe,
> Sturdy and hidous, whoso hym knewe;
> Like sharp urchouns his her was growe;
> His eyes reed sparclyng as the fyr glowe;
> His nose frounced, full kirked stood.
> 3133–3137

He chases the Lover from the rose-bower with great threats: "Fle hennes, felowe! I rede thee goo!" Only with the help of Candor and Pity does the Lover later see Fair Welcome again.

In *Troilus and Criseyde,* as I have said, Pandarus takes the brunt of Criseyde's initial rebuffs. Her Danger and Fair Welcome alternate as with the lady of the *Rose,* and with similar motivation. When Pandarus attempts to win Criseyde for his friend, he praises him effusively and tells her of his love and suffering. She, inquisitive and friendly, but inwardly wary, leads Pandarus on—just as Fair Welcome led on the Lover—to imprudence. Saying to herself, "I will find out what he really wants," Criseyde asks her uncle ingenuously what he would suggest (II, 388–389). "Well said," he answers, falling into her trap. He then advises that she gather rosebuds while she may:

> "Thenk ek how elde wasteth every houre
> In ech of yow a partie of beautee;
> And therefore, er that age the devoure,
> Go love; for old ther wol no wight of the."
>
> II, 393–396

The Fair Welcome of Criseyde now flees, and in comes Danger. She laments bitterly that Pandarus, the uncle who should pro- tect her, rather pushes her into the lion's jaws. "What!" she wails,

> "Is this al the joye and al the feste?
> Is this youre reed? Is this my blisful cas?
> Is this the verray mede of your byheeste?
> Is al this paynted proces seyd, allas!
> Right for this fyn? O lady myn, Pallas!
> Thow in this dredful cas for me purveye,
> For so astoned am I that I deye."
>
> II, 421–427

Pandarus of course is less easily put off than the inexperienced Lover, and with his counter-emotionalism succeeds in daunting Danger.

In any event Fair Welcome is more congenial than Danger to Criseyde's friendly temperament and "sliding courage." In her dealings directly with Troilus, she is dangerous only insofar as she demands her rights as his lord, king's son or not. When at last they find themselves in bed together, Danger is very far away. Troilus says jubilantly, "Now be ye kaught," and she answers complacently that she was caught long ago; if she had not been, she would not be in bed with him. Then she cuts short his verbal effusions with a simple statement that further talk is unnecessary:

> "But lat us falle awey fro this matere,
> For it suffiseth, this that seyd is heere,
> And at o word, withouten repentaunce,
> Welcome, my knyght, me pees, my suffisaunce!"
>
> III, 1306–1309

Troilus could not ask for a fairer welcome.

As in *Troilus and Criseyde,* so in the *Book of the Duchess,* personifications of Danger and Fair Welcome do not figure in the action or diction; nevertheless, the successive appearances of these qualities are quite obvious. When the Black Knight with trepidation and hesitation requests her mercy, the lady's danger immediately comes forward. As the Knight recalls,

> "And whan I had my tale y-doo,
> God wot, she acounted nat a stree
> Of al my tale, so thoghte me.
> To telle shortly ryght as hyt ys,
> Trewly hir answere hyt was this;
> I kan not now wel counterfete
> Hir wordes, but this was the grete
> Of hir answere: she sayde 'nay'
> Al outerly."

1236–1244

Despite the apparent finality of this rebuff, the Knight succeeds in dispelling White's danger by dint of faithful service over a long period of time. When finally she becomes sure that he only works for her benefit and to further her good name, she changes her attitude and accepts his service:

> "My lady yaf me al hooly
> The noble yifte of hir mercy."

1269–1270

The reaction of the courtly lady to the lover's first request is generally *dangerous;* nevertheless, her beauty provides a visible guarantee that she possesses pity and generosity which will eventually bring out Fair Welcome.

The garden setting, the noble participants, the stunning first sight of the beloved, the rebuff, the despairing complaint, and many other aspects of the love affair in medieval narrative are matters of convention. Yet not all conventional aspects are always present. Indeed, in a single story never are all of them present; nor are they always arranged in the same way, though something like an ideal order exists. Furthermore, the poets oftentimes vary subtly the nature of these apparent constants, and in so doing alter the indicated course of the story; for instance, Criseyde's sliding courage, a minor flaw in the otherwise ideal lady, changes the model love story into a tragedy. Thus the Middle English Dance of Love is not an endlessly repeated minuet of automatons; it is rather a set of decorous components and graceful movements which each writer can make use of in moving his characters in subtly varied patterns toward divergent outcomes.

Differing patterns appear in the three stories which I have dealt with, and the results contrast sharply. At the end of Guillaume de Lorris' section of the *Rose* the Lover seems hopelessly separated from his beloved by Wicked-Tongue (Slander) and Jealousy (the parents). The successful courtship of Chaucer's Black Knight is terminated by the death of his beloved. And Troilus in the last book of the story, betrayed by his lady love, gazes with futile longing at the Greek camp.

Love conventions such as I have discussed are found in many other works of Chaucer and his imitators, and in Middle English romances. Each of these stories has its individuality, though each might be described as a courtly love narrative. The essentials of this kind of story are young, good-looking participants who comport themselves in ways appropriate to the courts of medieval romance. If these essential elements are varied—if in a love story the lovers are old or ugly or act in uncourtly ways—the result is usually humorous. Such variation for humorous purposes indeed is a favorite device of Chaucer's; he depicted for comic effect unsuitable lovers and inappropriate behavior in at least six of the *Canterbury Tales:* the Miller's Tale, Reeve's Tale, Wife of Bath's Tale, Shipman's Tale, Merchant's Tale, and Nun's Priest's Tale.

A relatively minor use of this device is found in the depiction of Pandarus as lover in *Troilus and Criseyde.* Pandarus, who has a fine sense of irony, recognizes his own unsuitability for the part of lover, and he occasionally uses his lack of success in love as a subject for banter. "How ferforth be ye put in loves daunce?" asks Criseyde:

> "By God," quod he, "I hoppe alwey byhynde!"
> And she to laughe, it thoughte hire herte brest.
>   II, 1106–1108

Too old and too much of a clown to be the courtly lover, the able counselor of Troilus cuts a humorous figure when cast in that role.

The Merchant's Tale supplies a larger and particularly fascinating study of Chaucer's courtly-love comedy. The love story in this tale involves a triangle: January, the sexagenarian knight who suddenly decides to marry; May, his new wife, as fair and fresh as her name, of "age tendre"; and Damian, January's squire, of whom January himself says,

> "He is as wys, discreet, and as secree
> As any man I woot of his degree
> And therto manly, and eek servysable,
> And for to been a thrifty man right able."
> E, 1909–1912

January thinks so much of Damian that when he discovers the squire is sick, he sends May to him, with instructions to help him: "Dooth hym disport—he is a gentil man" (E, 1924).

January is too lost in his own conceit to realize that Damian is his rival and no gentleman. As a matter of fact much of the humor in the story arises from the misapprehensions of January. Not the least of these is his conceit of himself as lover. In bed with May, he fancies himself Venus' knight; his ludicrous appearance is far from his thought (though not from May's):

> He was al coltissh, ful of ragerye,
> And ful of jargon as a flekked pye.
> The slakke skyn aboute his nekke shaketh,
> Whil that he sang, so chaunteth he and craketh.
> But God woot what that May thoughte in hir herte,
> Whan she hym saugh up sittynge in his sherte,
> In hys nyght-cappe, and with his nekke lene.
> E, 1847–1853

The implicit contrast of this crack-voiced old lecher with someone genuinely equipped for the lover's part, such as the Squire of the pilgrimage, points up his ludicrousness. The Squire is wholly attractive and pleasantly musical:

> Embrouded was he, as it were a meede
> Al ful of fresshe floures, whyte and reede.
> Syngynge he was, or floytynge, al the day;

> He was as fressh as is the month of May.
>
> A, 89–92

January thinks of himself as such a man. He obviously has no insight into himself, May, or Damian; he certainly has not the least notion that in the story being enacted he is not the lover, but is rather the *jaloux* (the jealous husband).

The actual love story, that of May and Damian, is a travesty on the conventional narrative typified in the *Romance of the Rose*. In the *Rose* Venus, the sexual instinct, exerts her power to overcome the lady's inhibitions. But Venus applies her torch to the body only after the arrows of her son, the God of Love, have had a chance to work; the source of love is rather psychological than physical, found in the action of the visual images on the psyche. With Damian, however, there is no generalized astonishment at the first sight of May; he does not wonder, like Palamon in the Knight's Tale, whether she is woman or goddess. Instead the brand of Venus strikes him at once with overwhelming sexual desire:

> He was so ravysshed on his lady May
> That for the verray peyne he was ny wood.
> Almoost he swelte and swowned ther he stood,
> So soore hath Venus hurt hym with hire brond,
> As that she bar it daunsynge in hire hond.
>
> E, 1774–1778

It is this desire that sends him forthwith to bed, where he writes a letter to May in the form of a "complaint or lay." He is like Troilus and the Black Knight in being sick for love, in his lament, and in his composition of poetry; but his motivation, unlike theirs, is wholly animal:

> This sike Damyan in Venus fyr
> So brenneth that he dyeth for desyr.
>
> E, 1875–1876

Damian as a squire has a proper position in life for a noble lover, and he presents a properly courteous front; but he clearly has not innate *gentilesse,* the quality which distinguishes genuine nobility and the proper lover.

The level on which May acts and reacts is the same as Damian's. Chaucer's descriptions of another pseudo-courtly lady, Alisoun of the Miller's Tale, filled as they are with barnyard simile, would be most appropriate to her. May and Damian are two attractive animals parodying the behavior of polite lovers. Damian declares his love and cries "Mercy!" in courtly form, and May's response ostensibly is conditioned by appropriate womanly feelings. Chaucer even applies to her Dante's famous line describing the love of Francesca for Paolo: "Lo, pitee renneth soone in gentil herte!" (E, 1986). But May's procedure makes quite clear that she too has no *gentilesse*, and that calling her reaction *pity* is sharply ironic. Whereas Damian's proposal should certainly have brought forth her womanly *danger*, upon small reflection May accepts his blunt overtures and her dominant interest at once becomes the satisfaction of their lust:

> She moot outher dyen sodeynly,
> Or elles she moot han hym as hir leste.
>
> E, 2094–2095

The place and position in which the two eventually consummate their desires aptly expresses the vulgarity of their inclinations. Their adultery is both awkward and beastly; no illusion of amorous idealism is possible.

At no time in his stories does Chaucer impute "gentilesse" to adulterers. The French writers of romance had on occasion idealized the affairs of adulterers like Lancelot and Guinevere. At the same time, however, many of the polite lovers in Old French literature are unmarried, and the aims of many of these are not sinful by strict Christian interpretation. When Chaucer depicts adultery, the participants are always beastlike; he uses the typical triangle of *jaloux*, wife, and lover only for low comedy. Troilus and Criseyde, who generally strive to be *gentils* in practice as well as in name, are sinful, but they are not adulterous; and the Epilogue explicitly imposes a Christian ethic on their tragedy. Chaucer in other works allies the conventions with marriage. The destiny of the courtly lovers in the Knight's Tale and the *Parliament of Fowls* (ultimately) is marriage; and success in courtly love is identified with marriage in the Franklin's Tale and the Wife of Bath's Tale.

Not only in Chaucer, but also in all of Middle English literature, one is hard put to find explicit or implicit approval of adultery. Though in Malory the adulterous Lancelot and

Guinevere are sympathetically presented, it is their sin which prevents Lancelot from gaining the Grail, and which contributes heavily to the downfall of Arthur's kingdom. Thus, while Andreas Capellanus enunciates the rule that "Marriage is no excuse for not loving," writers of medieval England manifest no approval of this rule in their imaginative creations.

In this chapter I have discussed a few examples from the set of conventions which constitutes courtly love. The persistence with which these conventions appear in literature has no doubt fostered the illusion that the medieval aristocracy had a consistent and continuing philosophy of love. If the same conventions appear in fourteenth-century narrative as in twelfth-century, then it has been assumed that the same ethic informs the actions and works of both times. Yet consideration of the writings themselves indicates that the conventions are literary counters which the artist could manipulate to suit numerous attitudes toward love between the sexes. In Middle English literature one finds that while the implicit attitudes varied somewhat, they were seldom—probably never—non-Christian. The viewpoint of earlier French works seems at times less conformable to Christian doctrine, but it would surely be a mistake to find in the treatise of Andreas Capellanus a forthright declaration of practices and beliefs directly applicable to any group of works.

The examples which I have used show that a patterning of conventional counters into what might be termed a dance persisted not only through time but also through changes in narrative media, from the personification allegory of the *Romance of the Rose* to the skeletal realism of the *Book of the Duchess* to the developed natural representation in *Troilus and Criseyde* and the Merchant's Tale. Inherent in all of these works are love allegories in which Lover, Friend, and Fair Welcome participate. The same persistent recurrence of generalized abstract actions from allegory to apparently realistic stories is found in the psychological allegories which are dealt with in the next chapter.

NOTE TO CHAPTER III

(The main bibliographical listing for Chaucer's works is found in the Note to Chapter II.)

Editions and Translations

Romance of the Rose. I quote from the Chaucerian translation, the *Romaunt of the Rose,* in Robinson's edition of Chaucer's works. This translation, of which only a part could be Chaucer's, contains all of Guillaume de Lorris' part, but only a fraction of Jean de Meun's. The standard edition of the original French is Ernest Langlois, ed., *Le Roman de la Rose,* five volumes, SATF (1914-1924). Parallel texts with the French original facing the Middle English translation have been edited by Ronald Sutherland, *The Romaunt of the Rose and Le Roman de la Rose* (1967). A pleasant and useful translation by Harry Robbins of the complete *Roman de la Rose* in Modern English blank verse is available in illustrated paperback (1962).

Troilus and Criseyde has been edited separately by Robert K. Root, *The Book of Troilus and Criseyde* (1926); his notes on the specific congruencies of Chaucer's work with Boccaccio's *Filostrato* are particularly helpful. The *Filostrato* itself is edited with parallel English translation by Nathaniel E. Griffin and Arthur B. Myrick. *The Filostrato of Giovanni Boccaccio* (1929).

Love Allegory and Courtly Love

Maurice Valency, *In Praise of Love* (1958), a study of the love lyric from the Provencal troubadours to Dante, provides a good introduction to medieval love poetry in general. For the development of love allegory before the *Romance of the Rose,* see Charles Muscatine, "The Emergence of Psychological Allegory in Old French Romance," *PMLA,* 69 (1953), 1160-1182; for the subsequent history of love allegory up to Chaucer's time, see James I. Wimsatt, *Chaucer and the French Love Poets* (1968).

The standard translation of Andreas Capellanus' *De Amore* is John J. Parry, *The Art of Courtly Love* (1941); his introduction presents a good deal of valuable information about medieval love literature along with a conventional interpretation of its development. A background in the real world for courtly love is constructed by Amy Kelly, "Eleanor of Aquitaine and Her Courts of Love," *Speculum,* 12 (1937), 3-19. Her assumptions are disputed by John F. Benton, "The Court of Champagne as a Literary Center," *Speculum,* 36 (1961), 551-591; see especially his remarks on Andreas Capellanus, pp. 578-582. Standard, though opposed, viewpoints on medieval love are presented by C. S. Lewis, *Allegory of Love,* pp. 1-43, and Alexander J. Denomy, *The Heresy of Courtly Love* (1947). Sharp issue with the critical commonplaces about medieval love, particularly as regards Andreas' *De Amore,* is taken by D. W. Robertson, Jr., *A Preface to Chaucer* (1963), especially pp. 391–463. (For a balanced evaluation of Robertson's *Preface,* see the review article by Robert E. Kaske, "Chaucer and Medieval Allegory," *ELH,* 30 [1963], 175–192). A moderate corrective to critical preconceptions on the subject is provided in W. T. H. Jackson, "The *De Amore* of Andreas Capellanus and the Practice of Love at Court," *Romanic Review,* 49 (1958), 243–251.

Criticism of Specific Works

The basic study of the backgrounds of the *Romance of the Rose* is Ernest Langlois, *Origines et sources du Roman de la Rose* (1891). Chaucer's specific uses of the *Rose* are detailed in Dean S. Fansler, *Chaucer and the Roman de la Rose* (1914). C. S. Lewis provides a lucid interpretation of the allegory of Guillaume de Lorris and an unsympathetic view of Jean's accomplishment in *Allegory of Love,* pp. 112–156. Students of medieval and Renaissance critical traditions have lately called into question much of Lewis' interpretation which has been for many standard (and of which I make some use); his judgment of Jean de Meun's section is rather clearly misguided. See Rosamond Tuve, *Allegorical Imagery* (1966), pp. 233–284; D. W. Robertson's *Preface, passim;* and John V. Fleming, "The Moral Reputation of the *Roman de la Rose* Before 1400," *Romance Philology,* 18 (1965), 430–436, and Professor Fleming's forthcoming book on the *Rose.* The most complete study to date of both parts of the poem is Alan M. F. Gunn, *The Mirror of Love* (1952), reviewed by C. S. Lewis, *Medium Aevum,* 22 (1953), 27–31. Charles Muscatine, *Chaucer and the French Tradition* (1957), contrasts the styles of the two poets of the *Rose* and the respective literary traditions in which he finds they worked. He relates these to Chaucer's development; see especially pp. 1–97.

Though the *Book of the Duchess* was in low repute among critics until the past twenty years, it is now generally admired; two essays which well represent the modern view are Bertrand H. Bronson, "The *Book of the Duchess* Reopened," *PMLA,* 67 (1952), 863–881; and John Lawyor, "The Pattern of Consolation in *The Book of the Duchess,*" *Speculum,* 31 (1956), 626–648. James I. Wimsatt, *Chaucer and the French Love Poets,* explores the relationships of the poem to its French ancestry and provides summaries of the poems of Machaut and other French works which influenced the *Duchess.*

Criticism of *Troilus and Criseyde* is especially voluminous. Two important book-length studies are Thomas A. Kirby, *Chaucer's Troilus: A Study in Courtly Love* (1940); and Sanford B. Meech, *Design in Chaucer's Troilus* (1959). The former provides a convenient summary of the development of medieval love poetry (Provençal, French, Italian); the latter features close explication in the light of the sources. Extensive discussions of *Troilus* are also found in three books referred to above in this Note: Robertson, pp. 472–502; Muscatine, pp. 124–165; and Lewis, pp. 176–197. Among the numerous valuable articles on *Troilus,* I will mention only two of particular relevance to this chapter: Roger Sharrock, "Second Thoughts: C. S. Lewis on Chaucer's *Troilus,*" *Essays in Criticism,* 88 (1955), 123–137, which calls attention to the attitude toward love expressed in the Epilogue; and Sister Mary Charlotte Borthwick, F.C.S.P., "Antigone's Song as 'Mirour' in Chaucer's *Troilus and Criseyde,*" *MLQ,* 22 (1961), 227–235, in which attitudes toward love in *Troilus* are analyzed in connection with the elucidation of Antigone's song.

Two articles which are particularly concerned with the subject of love in the Merchant's Tale are D. W. Robertson, Jr., "The Doctrine of Charity in Medieval Literary Gardens," *Speculum,* 26 (1951), 24–49; and C. Hugh Holman, "Courtly Love in the Merchant's and the Franklin's Tales," *ELH,* 18 (1951), 241–252.

Chapter IV

The Allegory of Reason

Important Works: *Consolation of Philosophy, Romance of the Rose, House of Fame* (Book II), *Troilus and Criseyde, Anticlaudian, Tale of Melibee, Piers Plowman* (Passus VIII–XV).

A. M. Severinus Boethius (480–524) was an important Roman statesman and philosopher who rose to power and fell in the reign of Theodoric the Ostrogoth. On the early death of his father, Boethius was adopted by Symmachus, a man of eminence who exemplified the traditional Roman virtues, and he eventually married his stepfather's admirable daughter, who provided him with an ideal domestic situation. Continuing his family's tradition of distinction in public service, Boethius became a Roman consul, and he had the pleasure of seeing both of his sons assume the same high office at early ages. At the same time that he distinguished himself in public affairs and enjoyed a private life of prosperity and love, Boethius also wrote tracts on the liberal arts, and religious treatises which aimed at reconciling the philosophy of the ancient pagans with Christian doctrine. These writings, which have earned him a reputation as the last of the Roman philosophers and the first of the Scholastics, were studied and followed throughout the Middle Ages.

When this dedicated philosopher-statesman was at the zenith of his career, however, he incurred the enmity of Theodoric. He was summarily condemned by the Senate in 523, and sent to prison in Pavia where he was eventually executed. In prison, stunned by the turn of events, he found a practical use for the philosophical wisdom which his studies had acquired for him; and he portrayed the process by which he reconciled himself to his misfortunes in the *Consolation of Philosophy*, the best-known of his writings and among books second only to the Bible in influence in the Middle Ages.

The *Consolation* is written in the alternate passages of prose and poetry which are characteristic of so-called Menippean satire; intrinsically, it strongly resembles the Platonic dialogue, with Lady Philosophy playing the role of Socratic teacher and Boethius as the respectful student. At the beginning of the work Boethius is seen attempting to achieve consolation in exile by writing poetic laments. Suddenly above him appears a lady of ageless beauty. Her eyes burn with wisdom; her height seems to change, varying from the size of men to great altitude; the garment she wears, which she has woven herself, is symbolically decorated; and she holds books in her right hand and a scepter in her left. This is Lady Philosophy, who reproaches Boethius for his pointless complaining, reminding him that her wisdom has nourished him from childhood. Boethius tries to justify his behavior by citing his previous upright life and selfless public service which have brought only misfortune to him.

Lady Philosophy thereupon states that Boethius is in much worse condition than she had first thought, for he has even forgotten his native country. She resolves to cure his malady and recall him to his true home; her efforts to do this provide the subject for the remainder of the treatise. The first remedy which Philosophy applies is designed mainly to prepare Boethius for stronger treatment—it is, so to speak, a soothing salve to alleviate his pain. She demonstrates that none of the goods of the Goddess Fortune rightly belong to anyone; people come into the world naked and Fortune arbitrarily bestows or witholds her benefits. She further points out that, since Boethius' wife and family are still safe and in good health, Fortune has left him with his most valuable possessions, even though she has taken away others. (The description and discussion of Fortune at this point in the *Consolation* provide a basis for most medieval references to the fickle goddess.) Her pupil having been fortified by these arguments, Philosophy administers stronger treatment. Not only are Fortune's goods impermanent, she shows, but also none of them—pleasure, wealth, honor, power, or even fame—is worthy of pursuit, all being but partial aspects of good. True good, and thus true happiness, is to be found only in our native country, with God.

Boethius in following Philosophy's argument becomes disturbed by two problems about the nature of God: he wonders how evil exists if God is all good and the source of being, and how man can have free will if God is omniscient and sees his actions before they are performed. In answer to the first question Philosophy demonstrates that evil, rather than being a positive force, is negative, an absence of good; thus, evil men may be said to lack their very existence. Also, God's providence uses apparent evil to bring about good ends. The question of free will and God's foreknowledge is complex, a chief argument being that God's having foreseen an action is no more a cause of the action than one person's observation of another's movement is a cause of the movement. In the final analysis, of course, man's understanding is imperfect, incapable of fathoming the mysterious ways and powers of God.

The exegesis of providence, fate, foreknowledge, and free will concludes the *Consolation*. The whole work is in effect a theodicy, a justification of the ways of God to man (a variety of exposition that has appealed greatly to Christian writers). The work was translated many time into several languages, commented upon frequently and at great length, and was used extensively in original literature by most prominent medieval writers, most notably by Jean de Meun, Chaucer, and Dante. Jean de Meun and Chaucer also translated the *Consolation*, Chaucer's *Boece* including interpolations provided by the commentary of Nicholas Trivet, an early fourteenth-century English friar. A previous English translation of Boethius, made by King Alfred in the tenth century, had made use of two continental commentaries. Queen Elizabeth's version was only one of several Renaissance English translations, and the popularity of the treatise through the eighteenth century is evidenced by further translations and frequent references. Even late in the century, when a lady of letters asked Dr. Johnson to recommend to her a literary project, his quite earnest suggestion was that she translate Boethius.

The *Consolation's* manifold influence on medieval literature may be analyzed under three headings. There is first the repetition in later works of philosophical ideas found in the treatise; again, there is imitation of the personifications and allegory that readers saw in it; and finally, there is realistic use of the dramatic situation and events of the work. In practice, one kind of use is rarely found exclusive of the others. In *Troilus,* for instance, the dramatic situation when Pandarus suddenly appears to console Troilus is clearly Boethian; at the same time, the content of Troilus' complaints against Fortune is also drawn from the *Consolation.* I will talk about all three kinds of use in this chapter, though the ultimate focus will be on personification allegories which are significantly related to Boethius.

In philosophical content the *Consolation* is in the best sense a popularization; as such, it is a thesaurus of classical and early Christian thought. Its ideas are drawn from such diverse sources as Plato, the Stoics, and St. Augustine; they include also commonplaces which Boethius no doubt encountered more than once in his wide reading, on subjects such as friendship, the Golden Age, and the value of noble birth. Boethius passed along these ideas in clear and convenient form to his medieval successors. In Jean de Meun's *Romance of the Rose* many of them are repeated by Reason, Nature, and Genius. Dante, too, frequently employs and transforms the thoughts of Lady Philosophy, notably those about fortune, fate, free will, and gentility. Chaucer's characters again and again express Boethian ideas about Fortune; in the Knight's Tale concepts of Providence and Destiny drawn from the *Consolation* explicitly impel the narrative to its happy conclusion; and Troilus in Book IV of his story flounders in Boethian speculation about free will. Much of the thought content of several of Chaucer's lyrics also is drawn from this source, particularly "The Former Age," "Fortune," "Truth," and "Gentilesse." Indeed, few of Chaucer's works are without echoes of the philosophy of Boethius; and all important medieval poets show the influence of his thought.

The female personification Philosophy is ubiquitous; she appears under her proper name or some kind of equivalent in many works of imaginative literature. Thus Reason in the *Romance of the Rose* is clearly one embodiment of Lady Philosophy, and Reason offers for present purposes a particularly apt example because she has most of the characteristics by which Lady Philosophy under any name may be discerned. The manner of Reason's appearance in the *Rose* is, in the first place, recognizably Boethian; as Philosophy appears suddenly from above to Boethius, so all at once Reason descends from her tower to accost the Lover. Reason's physical attributes also are analogous to those of Philosophy, for she too has burning eyes, and uncertain age and height:

> But she was neither yong ne hoor,
> Ne high ne lowe, ne fat ne lene,
> But best, as it were in a mene.
> Her eyen twoo were cleer and light
> As ony candell that brenneth bright.
>
> 3196–3200

The attitude of these mentors to their pupils are likewise comparable. Philosophy patronizes and scolds Boethius; Reason in the *Romance of the Rose,* while somewhat more patient with the Lover, inclines to corrective sarcasm. Finally, the kinship is signaled by the fact that numerous passages in the lectures of Reason are derived from the *Consolation,* particularly from Philosophy's lengthy speeches on the nature of Fortune.

The name *Reason* itself is one of the most likely for a surrogate of Philosophy. While the literary representative of Boethius' mentor appears as Philosophy in a love poem of Froissart, as Esperance (Hope) in one of Machaut's works, as Minerva in the Chaucerian *Kingis Quair,* and as Love in Thomas Usk's *Testament of Love,* more commonly she is designated by the name of a mental faculty or quality; Wisdom, Reason, Knowledge, Wit, and Prudence are some of the possibilities. Translation of Philosophy's name led to some of these designations. The Greek *philo* means *love,* and this, one may assume, resulted in Usk's Lady Love. *Sophia,* the second element, signifying *wisdom,* produced personified ladies named Wisdom, Reason, or Minerva. The personality of Beothius' counselor also made the

Reason instructs the Lover (as Philosophy instructed Boethius) about the capricious behavior of Fortune. Photo Bibl. Nat. Paris, Ms. Fr. 14968, f.43.

names appropriate; to the distraught man she embodies Hope, Love, and Wisdom.

If the character and name of Philosophy helped to make her a personification of considerable adaptability, so also the elaborate description of her in the *Consolation* conduced to interpretation of the whole treatise as basically a personification allegory. No stretch of the imagination was needed to find in that description an allegorical tableau, since the details have evident metaphorical significances. For instance, Philosophy's varying height represents the diverse subject matter that she deals with. Boethius mentions three heights which she assumes, and each has an obvious meaning. When she is of normal height, we understand that her attention is focused on worldly phenomena such as the natural sciences deal with; when her head touches the heavens her concern is astronomy and probably music; when her head reaches through the heavens, her subject is theology, above the normal ken of man. The description of her garment too has an almost transparent significance: low on her dress is a *pi*, which designates *p*ractical knowledge; high up is a *theta*, signifying *th*eoretical knowledge; between these letters are stairs (often represented as a ladder) which lead from the *pi* to the *theta*, thus indicating that one arrives at the theoretical by way of the practical. Her garment is torn, having been rent by thinkers who find all of philosophy in mere fragments of wisdom. Other details in her description complete a rather full representation of the abstract entity *philosophy*.

The commentators on the *Consolation*, alerted by this allegorical tableau, postulated that the whole frame of the work is allegorical. Under cover of the abstraction Philosophy's conversation with the troubled man, they inferred, is a psychological action. The real story, says Nicholas Trivet, is not of "Boethius complaining and Philosophy consoling. These figures are none other than the Soul complaining because of wounded sensibility and Reason consoling from the vigor of wisdom." To Nicholas and apparently to most medieval thinkers Boethius is the troubled soul and Philosophy is the rational power. The action of the narrative is the process by which the soul or will, which has been injured by events out of its control, corrects and comforts itself through the resources of the mind. This is an apt subject for allegory; like the process of dying, or the course of a love affair, or the attainment of salvation, the story involves a situation and process which is common to most men. Indeed, it seems that man's condition is chronically that of the wounded soul striving through reason to find consolation.

The two appearances of Lady Reason in the *Romance of the Rose* result allegorically in aborted versions of the *Consolation's* narrative. Reason enters first in Guillaume de Lorris' part when the despondent Lover has been expelled from the rose arbor by Danger. She pleads with the Lover to give up his allegiance to Amor, but he dismisses her summarily for her trouble. This dismissal, of course, has psychological truth, for lovers as a rule are anything but rational; it is also humorous in its stubborn wrongheadedness, especially when compared to Boethius' docile acquiescence to his master. Jean de Meun underlines this humor when Reason appears in his continuation of the *Rose*. After Jealousy has built a castle in which he imprisons Fair Welcome, and the Lover is left once again outside the rose garden, the Lover complains in Boethian terms against Fortune. This complaint sets the stage for Reason's return when she harangues the Lover for three thousand lines, many of which stem from the *Consolation;* she lectures him on the benefits of adverse Fortune, on Fortune's overthrow of great men, and on the complete insufficiency to man of earthly wealth. She is again wasting her breath on the Lover, however, for he once more rejects her and goes to Friend for additional pragmatic advice.

The parallels between the main characters and action of the *Consolation* and those of later narratives are not always as simple as with the *Romance of the Rose*. In works such as *Piers Plowman* descendants of Lady Philosophy multiply and become involved in more complex psychological allegories. In other places the Boethian comforter and the pattern of consolation appear in more realistic narratives, as in several stories of Chaucer. We will look at two examples of parallels in realistic stories before taking up the more complex allegories.

The eagle who in Book II of the *House of Fame* carries Geffrey in his claws up to the castle of Fame is a semirealistic deputy of Lady Philosophy. When the dreamer at the end of Book I has inspected the mural depictions of the Troy story in Venus'

temple, he leaves the temple to find himself alone in a vast des-
sert; immediately, he becomes the desperate complainer. "O
Crist!" he prays,

> "that art in blysse,
> From fantome and illusion
> Me save!"
>
> 492–494

Then he catches sight of the eagle in the sky, who swooping
down from above grabs him in her claws and carries him
speechless into the air. Like Lady Philosophy who reproaches
Boethius for his silence, the eagle commands his victim,
"Awak!/ And be not agast so, for shame!" (556–557). When the
eagle takes him above the clouds, Geffrey is reminded
specifically of Boethius' situation:

> And thoo thoughte y upon Boece,
> That write, "A thought may flee so hye,
> Wyth fetheres of Philosophye,
> To passen everych element."
>
> 972–975

The earth from above appears to him as a "prikke" (907), even
as Philosophy in Chaucer's translation of *Boece* has described
the world as a "prikke" in relation to the size of the heavens.

Like Lady Philosophy the eagle lectures Geffrey at length on
various matters—sometimes in her very words—playing the role
of schoolmaster even though Geffrey is reluctant to be taught:

> "Wilt thou lere of sterres aught?"
> "Nay, certeynly," quod y, "ryght naught."
> "And why?" "For y am now to old."
>
> 993–995

The dialogue in this portion of the *House of Fame* has a humorous relationship to the dialogue of the *Consolation*, which itself,
partly by virtue of its relationship to the Platonic dialogues, has
the touch of humor implicit in a pupil's monosyllabic ignorance
and a master's wordy wisdom. The garrulous eagle, with the
pedant's confidence in the efficacy of his advice, is a delightful
caricature of Lady Philosophy, who provided Boethius with a
vision of the heavens on the wings of "swifte thought." The

figure of Geffrey also reflects in a humorous way the person of Philosophy's more willing pupil.

The story of the *House of Fame,* however, is quite different from that of the *Consolation.* Chaucer's work aims at instructing the narrator about the workings of Fame: in Book I through the exemplum of Dido; in Book II through the instruction of the eagle; and in Book III through the allegorical exposition which was discussed in Chapter II. In Boethius' work, on the other hand, the main character is led through a series of logical demonstrations to a belief in and understanding of God's providence. The narrative and philosophical concerns of *Troilus and Criseyde* have much more in common with those of the *Consolation.* In this work of Chaucer's Pandarus and Troilus act as teacher and pupil; from his mentor Troilus first finds, then later fails to find, answers to problems of life which are much the same as problems of Boethius. His complaints against Fortune are answered in Book I, but no answer is forthcoming in Book IV to his questioning of God's providence.

In the last chapter we saw Pandarus as primarily a counterpart to Friend of the *Romance of the Rose.* Though this is no doubt his true role, he often parades as Reason or Lady Philosophy. He adopts this persona most obviously in his first appearance when Troilus is complaining mournfully in bed against Fortune, whose wheel no man may ride unharmed. As he complains Pandarus comes up behind him and in Lady Philosophy's very words demands to share—"parten"—his pain. Pandarus subsequently imitates a famous simile of Philosophy in which she asks Boethius sarcastically if her words are to him like the music of the harp to the ass, who listens without appreciation; and as Troilus sinks into numb despondency, Pandarus exhorts him (so the eagle exhorted Geffrey) to "Awake!" (I, 729–735). Pandarus reassures Troilus that his case is not desperate and proceeds to counsel him with sentiments drawn from the *Consolation* (though using none of the "sharper remedies" which Philosophy applies). He reminds Troilus of the true nature of Fortune, whose only constancy is in mutability, and he comforts him with the thought that since her wheel is never still then a change from the present situation may be in the offing. Subsequently, by action rather than words, he succeeds

in helping Troilus; unfortunately, his help is not of the permanent kind which Philosophy gives.

The wheel does turn in Troilus' favor: he is picked up from
the mud and raised to the heights of amorous joy; but the
wheel turns again to throw him down. When Criseyde is traded
to the Greeks for Antenor, Troilus is more despondent than
before:

> "Allas, Fortune! if that my lif in joie
> Displesed hadde unto thi foule envye,
> Why ne haddestow my fader, kyng of Troye,
> Byraft the lif, or don my bretheren dye,
> Or slayn myself?"
>
> IV, 274–278

Pandarus still knows some of the answers of Lady Philosophy
concerning Fortune: no man may trust in her; her gifts are
made to all alike (IV, 386–392). But these words are not
helpful, nor does he have any that are, for only the sharper
remedies can help here. Troilus now recalls, but to no advantage, Pandarus' Boethian warning that one of the greatest sor-
rows of the man who is cast down from good fortune is to remember his past happiness (IV, 482–483), and he longs for
death in the language of Boethius. Pandarus' advice, that he
should simply seize Criseyde, is impossible to Troilus, who now
comes to feel victimized by powers over which he has, and has
had, no control. This leads to his long statement, drawn almost
word-for-word from the *Consolation*, about the certainty of God's
foreknowledge and man's consequent lack of free will (IV, 958–
1078). When Boethius was in a similar quandary in the *Consolation* Philosophy offered ready answers; but in *Troilus and
Criseyde* Pandarus, who parades as a stand-in for Philosophy,
offers only silence.

It is humorous at the beginning of the story to see the pragmatic procurer Pandarus appear in the very robes of divine
Philosophy to advise and assist Troilus to the achievement of
his worldly ends by worldly means. But in the end disastrous
consequences result from Pandarus' perversion of true wisdom.
A true Friend, but false Reason, he can then help with none of
the genuine remedies; and Troilus is fated because all along he

has lacked a real Lady Philosophy. What in Book I is comedy, then, becomes tragedy in Book IV. The parallel in situation and action to the *Consolation* first sharpens the humor and afterwards points up the tragedy, which in a larger sense is Troilus' failure to find the proper answers.

Other narratives of Chaucer present stand-ins for Lady Philosophy: the dreamer in the *Book of the Duchess,* Theseus in the Knight's Tale, and even the old hag in the Wife of Bath's Tale. With varying degrees of success they use the words of Boethius to bring comfort to the grieving. Their voices, along with the voices of Pandarus and the eagle, speak the wisdom of Reason; the psychological allegory of the *Consolation* thus becomes imbedded in stories with realistic participants and actions. In the alternative development in literature of the Allegory of Reason, the narrative remains a personification allegory of the psyche, but it is often elaborated through the introduction of multiple personified faculties of the intellect. Though aspects of this latter variety of allegory are found in numerous Middle English stories and dramas, the Dowel section of *Piers Plowman* represents the central development of it. I will deal here only with *Piers* and with two preceding Latin allegories which provide some introduction to the analysis of Dowel: the *Anticlaudian* of Alan of Lille and the *Book of Consolation and Counsel* of Albertan of Brescia, which was translated by Chaucer as the *Tale of Melibee.*

Alan of Lille (Alanus de Insulis), called the Universal Doctor, was one of the leading philosophers and Latin poets of medieval France. His poetry is informed by his philosophy, which was particularly influenced by the Platonism associated with the twelfth-century cathedral school of Chartres. His masterworks, the *Complaint of Nature* and the *Anticlaudian,* written in hexameters in a very florid style, were held in high esteem as epics for at least two centuries; Chaucer and Jean de Meun seem to have known them well. The *Anticlaudian,* with which we are here concerned, makes use of personified faculties of the intellect which are manifestly related to Lady Philosphy. Alan's division of the rational faculty into two parts makes the poem particularly valuable for demonstrating the analytical development of the Allegory of Reason.

The *Anticlaudian* presents an allegory of the creation of a new man. The story is quite simple. Nature, disillusioned with her previous works, vows to endow one man with all the virtues which have previously been scattered among many. At a council called by Nature for the purpose of effecting her plan, the virtues accord with her and dispatch Prudence (who acts by present-day concepts more as a faculty than a virtue) to Heaven to bring back a soul for the new man. Prudence ascends, accompanied first by Reason, then by Theology, and in the final stages by Faith. God complies with Prudence's request and sends her back to Earth with a suitable soul. Nature places the soul in the body which she has carefully fashioned; after a battle between the vices and virtues, the new man establishes a golden age on Earth.

The most interesting part of the *Anticlaudian*—the section most laden with philosophical and psychological implications—is the ascent of Prudence and Reason to Heaven. Since these two personifications represent faculties that may be attached to individual intellects, it is appropriate that Alan endows both of them with features originally used by Boethius to describe Lady Philosophy. Like Philosophy Prudence has varying height, and her garment woven of fine thread has been torn in various places. Reason in turn looks exactly like Prudence, except that she is older. Whereas Lady Philosophy embodies for the commentators the intellectual faculty as a whole in the *Consolation*, two personifications who resemble the mentor of Boethius represent the intellect in the later work.

The identification of Lady Philosophy with these two mental faculties is simply one of the numerous divisions of the psyche which were to be made in medieval allegory. One would seek in vain to regularize the terminology and analysis of the mind employed in the various narratives of this type. Nevertheless, if one keeps in mind the individuality of each story, a comparison of the various allegories may be useful, particularly in untangling the complexities of works like *Piers Plowman*. For instance, it is enlightening to note that Alan's twins who resemble Lady Philosophy, Reason and Prudence, were in a sense anticipated by Alfred the Great (among others) in his Old English translation of the *Consolation*, in which he designates Lady Philosophy alternately—and sometimes simultaneously—as Wisdom and Reason. Alan's and Alfred's designations are comparably binary: Reason and Prudence on the one hand, and Reason and Wisdom on the other. Both use the name Reason, and if one thinks of Wisdom in its earthly aspect as the ability "to deal sagaciously with facts" (a dictionary definition), then Alan's Prudence provides a reasonable equivalent for it, for Prudence in medieval terms is a lady with three eyes (or three faces or three heads), these representing her functions of knowing, remembering, and foreseeing. The function of Reason, by contrast, at least in terms of the *Anticlaudian,* is to observe through the senses, to abstract useful truths from the observations, and thence to inform Prudence, who will make use of the truths.

Alan portrays the functions of these faculties allegorically by showing Reason as the driver of the five horses which pull the chariot of Prudence. The horses are the five senses, Reason's means of observing. It is thus logical that when the chariot of Prudence reaches Heaven, Reason's power fails, since the senses no longer can make observations which avail Prudence.

The chariot which carries Prudence also fails. It has been built by the Seven Arts, daughters of Prudence and subdivisions of the human knowledge which Prudence uses. (A common depiction of medieval iconography shows Lady Philosophy, in her character as Wisdom [or Prudence], presiding over seven figures who personify the Arts; compare Figure 8.) Since in Heaven human knowledge is of no relevance, at the borders Prudence leaves the chariot of the Arts, the horses of the senses, and Reason, and proceeds under the direction of a new guide, Theology. We thereby see that Prudence can operate with whatever materials she is given, whether derived from the senses by Reason or obtained from supersensory sources by Theology. Prudence's ensuing journey will be discussed in the next chapter when we take up allegories of Revelation.

Another allegory of the intellect appears in the *Book of Consolation* of Albertan of Brescia, translated by Chaucer from a French version as the *Tale of Melibee.* Like the *Anticlaudian,* the narrative is simple though the work is long. Melibee is a prosperous landowner whose daughter is attacked by three enemies through the windows of his house; she is severely wounded in five places. Distraught, Melibee vows vengeance; his wife

Prudence, however, counsels forbearance, and the remainder of the work is taken up with her many arguments which suggest the wisdom of forgiveness. The simple allegory of the story is interpreted by Prudence in the course of her lecture to Melibee: "You have sinned against our Lord, for you have allowed the three enemies of man, who are the world, the flesh, and the devil, to enter freely into your heart by the windows of the body without defending yourself sufficiently against their assaults and temptations, so that they have injured your soul with five wounds, that is to say, with all the mortal sins, which enter into the heart by the five senses of the body." Thus in Prudence's gloss the daughter who is wounded through the five senses is the soul; Chaucer in his translation names her *Sophie* (Greek for *wisdom;* the second element of Philo*sophy*). Since access to Sophie is achieved by way of the five senses, it is clear that she, like Reason in the *Anticlaudian,* is nearly allied with the faculties of perception. Prudence in her extensive display of knowledge and her plentiful advice corresponds well to Alan's personification of the same name. Melibee himself is a complainer in the Boethian tradition, who in the allegorical division of functions may be seen as the will.

Semantics in medieval allegories of the psyche, it may be seen, present a substantial problem. *Reason* in Alfred and Alan has a counterpart in Sophie (or Soul) in Albertan; Alfred's *Wisdom,* on the other hand, correlates with Prudence in the other two works. The semantic problem looms even larger in the Dowel section of *Piers Plowman,* where several intellectual faculties participate in the allegory: Thought, Wit, and Imaginatif are faculties of observation and assimilation which correspond approximately to Alan's Reason. To complicate matters Langland also employs a personified Reason in several places. (But not as a faculty of the individual psyche; obviously, poets used the personifications of other writers in quite different ways.) Further confusing the correspondences, no Prudence or Wisdom participates in Langland's narrative; however, his Clergy—Knowledge—is closely related to Alan's Prudence, though Clergy is a more limited character. The functions of the various participants can perhaps best be explained through an analysis of the section known as Dowel.

Dowel is made up of the third and fourth dreams (not count-ing dreams within dreams) of *Piers Plowman*. In Chapter II we analyzed the first dream of the work, which depicts the process by which truth or right reason is adopted as the standard of government. At the end of this dream it becomes apparent that the adoption of truth by the king is not enough, that the mo-rality of the nation depends on the morality of the people; the second dream, therefore, shows the people as a whole con-fessing their sins and setting out on a pilgrimage to Truth. Toward the end of this dream the people receive a disappoint-ing "pardon," which merely states that those who do well go to Heaven and those who don't to Hell. This points up the in-dividual's responsibility for his salvation; since there is no blan-ket pardon, each person must find out for himself what it is to *do well*. The first two dreams of *Piers,* known as the Vision, thus have presented an allegory of public progress, and they have shown that the progress possible on this level, while no doubt important, is ultimately limited. Eventually, each person must set out on his own quest for Dowel (Do Well). In the next six dreams, called the Life, the dreamer describes his personal search for Dowel, which quickly expands into a triple quest—for Dowel, Dobet (Do Better), and Dobest. Most of the allegory in the poem in which faculties of the psyche operate to instruct the bewildered dreamer is contained in the two dreams of Do-wel, which open the Life.

It is particularly appropriate to the psychological allegory that William Langland identifies his narrative persona by a diminutive of his name, Will. The mental faculties which instruct the narrator thus are seen accurately as counselors of the faculty which chooses: the will. The first instructor whom Will encounters in Dowel is Thought, a tall man who looks very much like the dreamer. Thought represents cogitation uninstructed by learning—the thinking that one engages in be-fore more seriously applying himself to the question at hand. Thought offers a ready definition of Dowel, Dobet, and Dobest, which does not quite satisfy Will; so Thought agreeably and appropriately introduces Will to the basic faculty of perception, Wit. Wit, like Alan's Reason who drives the steeds of the senses, is associated with sensory perception. He immediately identifies

the home of Dowel as the castle of the body in which nature
has enclosed Anima, the soul, and over which Inwit and the
five senses are set as guards (We are of course reminded of Melibee's house):

> "Ac the constable of that castel that kepeth al the wacche,
> Is a wys knighte withal, sire Inwitte he hatte,
> And hath fyve feyre sones bi his first wyf;
> Sire Sewel and Saywel and Herewel the hende,
> Sire Worche-wel-wyth-thine-hande, a wighte man of strengthe,
> And sire Godfrey Gowel, gret lordes for sothe.
> Thise fyve ben sette to save this lady *Anima,*
> Tyl Kynde come or sende to save hir for evere."
>
> B, IX, 17–24
>
> ["But the constable of that castle that keeps the watch
> is a wise knight called Sir Inwit, who has five fine sons
> by his first wife, Sir See-Well and Say-Well and Hearwell
> the gentle, Sir Work-well-with-your-hands, a strong man,
> and Sir Godfrey Go-Well, great lords indeed. These five
> are posted to preserve this lady *Anima,* until Nature comes
> or sends a deputy to save her forever."]

Inwit and the five senses taken together (the "Outwit") are
the two aspects of Wit; the outward senses feed perceptions to
the inward sense, which organizes that which is perceived. As
the subsequent narrative shows, Wit has an inflated opinion of
his own powers. He claims:

> "Ac Inwitte is in the hed and to the herte he loketh,
> What *Anima* is lief or loth he lat hir at his wille;
> For after the grace of God the grettest is Inwitte."
>
> B, IX, 56–58
>
> ["Inwit is in the head and looks to the heart; what *Anima*
> is pleased or not pleased to do he allows according to his
> will. For Inwit is second only to the grace of God."]

Wit thus promises great things, as one's rational faculty forever
promises, and Wit reels off several answers to the problems of
Dowel, Dobet, and Dobest, all of which seem possible, but none
wholly satisfactory. Thus one may find in his personal experience solutions to philosophical and ethical questions.

There comes a point, however, at which the lessons of sense
and experience are exhausted and in order to go further one

Natural Understanding and Reason flank the pilgrim in Guillaume
Deguilleville's *Pilgrimage of the Life of Man*. Natural Understanding,
because inherently uneducated, cannot help Pilgrim's reading and draws
back. Pierpont Morgan Library Ms. 772, f. 39. By permission.

must seek the assistance of the various branches of learning in
which man has organized the percepts of his wit; which is to
say in medieval terms that he must study the Seven Arts which
comprise systematic knowledge. The representation which follows therefore shows that, since common sense is helpful only to
a certain point, one must eventually turn to laborious study of
books. Langland well depicts the grim moment when the
student discovers this truth. Wit's wife, a crabbed-face woman
named Study, suddenly interrupts her husband and scolds him
for wasting his instruction on a loafer. She tells him not to
throw pearls before hogs who are interested only in temporal
well-being:

"Wisdom and witte now is nought worth a carse,
But if it be carded with coveytise as clotheres kemben
    here wolle."

B, X, 17–18

[Wisdom and Wit today are not worth a cress, unless they
are carded with covetousness as clothiers comb their wool."]

Will indeed has been consulting Thought and Wit in a rather
passive manner, but now he shows himself as more than a des-
ultory seeker after Dowel. Bowing meekly before hostile Study,
he promises to be her man all of his life if she will show him the
way to Dowel. As books quickly become less formidable when
they are given close attention, so Dame Study is immediately
placated. She promises to help Will by introducing him to her
cousin, Clergy (Learning or Knowledge), who has recently married Scripture. The road to Clergy which she offers Will is no
easy one; he must go through Suffer-well-and-woe, avoid riches
and the pleasant land of Lechery, and continue on to a court
where he will meet Sobriety and Simplicity of Speech. Will,
undaunted, follows her directions and at length meets Clergy.

Clergy, as I have said, is a partial counterpart to Prudence of
the *Anticlaudian*. For one thing, both are parents of systematic
knowledge: Prudence in Alan's work rides on a chariot made by
the Seven Arts, who are her daughters; Clergy identifies himself
as the father of the Arts, who serve in the castle of the body
(the same castle where Inwit and his sons are the guards):

"I have sevene sones," he seyde, "serven in a castel,
There the lorde of Lyf wonyeth, to leren hym what is Dowel."

B, XIII, 119–120

["I have seven sons," he said, "who serve in a castle
where the lord of life dwells in order to teach him what
Dowel is."]

It is Clergy's business to codify the lessons of Wit and serve as
the mentor of the soul. He thus can provide Will with further,
even likelier, answers to the question of Dowel, Dobet, and
Dobest.

Will, however, soon comes to feel that Clergy's answers are
not only limited but also obscure, and he rejects them. In justi-
fying his anti-intellectual stance, Will points out the failure in
their personal lives of the most eminent scholars, Solomon and
Aristotle (Aristotle's life was the subject of slanderous medieval

legends). Citing Augustine's authority, he claims that none are sooner saved than plowmen and shepherds, and none taken from true faith more quickly than cunning clerks;

> "I se ensaumples myself and so may many an other,
> That servauntes that serven lordes selden falle in arrerage,
> But tho that kepen the lordes catel, clerkes and reves.
> Right so lewed men, and of litel knowynge,
> Selden falle thei so foule and so fer in synne
> As clerkes of holikirke that kepen Crystes tresore,
> The which is mannes soule to save as god seith in the gospel:
> 'Ite vos in vineam meam.'"

B, X 468–475

["I myself see the examples, and so may many others, of servants of lords who seldom fall into arrears, unlike those who are entrusted with the lords' property, clerks and reves. In the same way unlearned, ignorant men seldom fall so foully and far into sin as clerks of the Church that keep Christ's treasure—man's soul which they should save according to God's instruction in the Gospel: 'Go ye into my vineyards.' "]

The progress of Will toward Dowel thus becomes mired in his doubts about the usefulness of Learning—Clergy—in the quest of salvation. Alan's allegory had answered this question affirmatively, representing worldly learning as an important step in the ascent to God. Though in the *Anticlaudian* Reason, the steeds of the senses and the chariot of the arts could not penetrate the empyrean, they performed a vital function in carrying Prudence to the limits of Heaven. In *Piers* the importance of learning is comparably justified by Imaginatif.

Preoccupied with his repudiation of learning, Will falls into a deeper sleep and has a dream within his dream in which his anti-intellectual arguments are expanded and Reason (a supernatural power, not a faculty) reproaches him for presumptuous complaining. Waking from this deeper dream, Will sees before him a new counselor, Imaginatif. Imaginatif is a superior faculty of perception, a higher form of Wit. Boethius in the final book of the *Consolation* says that *sense* (Langland's Wit) looks on form "as it is constituted in matter," while *imagination* discerns it "without matter." By virtue of his abstracting power

Boethius with Lady Philosophy and the Seven Arts (from left): Grammar, Rhetoric, Logic, Music, Geometry, Astronomy, and Arithmetic. Pierpont Morgan Library Ms. 222, f.39. By permission.

Imaginatif is able to answer questions which were too abstruse for Will's previous psychic instructors, and to defend Wit and Clergy. He chides Will for his thoughtless talking and explains that Wit and Clergy arise respectively from sight and from teaching (B, XII, 66–69). Though they cannot teach anything about God's grace, they are still to be commended, especially Clergy which was founded by Christ's love. Since Moses testifies that God wrote out the Ten Commandments (writing being a chief manifestation of learning), and in the New Testament Christ saved the woman taken in adultery by writing on the ground, learning is a godly skill which must be revered:

> "Forthi I conseille the for Cristes sake Clergye that thow lovye,
> For Kynde Witte is of his kyn and neighe cosynes bothe
> To owre lorde, leve me; forthi love hem, I rede;
> For bothe ben as miroures to amenden owre defautes,
> And lederes for lewed men and for lettred bothe."

> B, XII, 94–98

["Therefore I counsel you for Christ's sake to love Clergy,
for Natural Wit is his kin and both are near cousins to

our Lord, believe me; therefore, love them, I advise; for
both are as mirrors to amend our faults and are guides
for both lettered and unlettered men."]

Imaginatif expatiates on the great importance of Clergy in
Christian life; despite the admitted limitations of learning,
without it priests could not administer the sacraments and men
would live in general ignorance. At the end of the defense Imaginatif vanishes and the dreamer awakens, quite frantic with
bewilderment, only to go back to sleep rather soon.

The second dream of Dowel is a sermon to Will in dramatic
form. As had been the case in most of the Vision, Will here is
mainly a spectator; he observes Conscience and Patience as
they lead Hawkyn, a representative of the active life, to confession of his sins and belief in a life of patient poverty. When
Will awakens again, he wanders around, still trying to understand about Dowel. Sleep rescues him once more, and the final
episode of the psychological allegory takes place with the appearance of Anima.

The teaching of Anima provides the Prologue to Dobet; it
leads to a higher level of doctrine, a level which is beyond the
power of human faculties, as Anima makes clear. Anima himself, as has been stated, is the fully integrated psyche; he is described, curiously but appropriately, as a creature without
tongue or teeth. As if by magic he appears and makes everything clear which Will has sought: "He told me whither I
should go, whereof I came, and of what sort I am." In answer to
Will's questioning, Anima explains first who he is. Anima is
Soul, Life, Mind, Memory, Reason, and several other entities
including Wit and Wisdom:

"And whan I fele that folke telleth my firste name is *Sensus,*
And that is wytte and wisdome, the welle of alle craftes;
And whan I chalange or chalange noughte, chepe or refuse,
Thanne am I Conscience ycalde, goddis clerke and his notarie;
And whan I love lelly owre lorde and alle other,
Thanne is lele Love my name, and in Latyn *Amor:*
And whan I flye fro the flesshe and forsake the caroigne,
Thanne am I spirit specheles, and *Spiritus* thanne ich hatte."
                                              B, XV, 29–36
["And when I hear what people say, my first name is *Sensus,*

which is wit and wisdom, the origin of all skills; and when
I claim something or do not claim it, buy or refuse to
buy, then I am called Conscience, God's clerk and notary;
and when I love loyally our Lord and all men, then is
loyal Love my name, in Latin *Amor;* and when I leave the
flesh and forsake the body, then I am a mute spirit, and
am then named *Spiritus.*"]

The sermon of Anima is prefatory to Will's vision of the theological virtues of Faith, Hope, and Charity. Anima explains
that Charity is above the ken of the senses and of learning:

"Therefore by coloure ne by clergye knowe shaltow hym nevere,
Noyther thorw wordes ne werkes but thorw wille one."

B, XV, 203–204

["Therefore neither by senses nor by knowledge will you
ever know him (i.e., charity), nor through words or works,
but by way of the will alone."]

It is only through direct revelation that one comes to know
charity. When Will subsequently has a vision of the Tree of
Charity, the reader understands that the Allegory of Reason is
finished, and that Will's experiences are now provided by supernatural powers rather than his own reasoning processes. The
remaining dreams of *Piers Plowman* are related to the Allegory of Revelation which provides the subject for our next
chapter.

We have seen in this chapter that the *Consolation of Philosophy*
is an ancestor of many stories in which the reasoning power is
personified or in which realistic figures play the part of Reason.
Events and characters in the *Romance of the Rose,* the *House of
Fame, Troilus and Criseyde,* the *Anticlaudian,* the *Tale of Melibee,*
and *Piers Plowman* exemplify a set of Boethian narrative motifs
which are found commonly in medieval literature. The reasonable counselors in these works have many different forms and
names: Reason, the eagle, Pandarus, Prudence, Wit, Clergy,
Imagination, Mind, Understanding, Memory, even Hope and
Love. The various figures reveal their ultimate relationship to
the *Consolation* by their narrative functions, by what they say,
and by the pattern of the actions in which they are involved. In
the Middle Ages the wisdom of Boethius was on every man's
tongue, and the allegory of the *Consolation* on every writer's pen.

NOTE TO CHAPTER IV

(The main bibliographical listings for the *Romance of the Rose* and *Troilus and Criseyde* are found in the Note to Chapter III; for the *House of Fame* and *Piers Plowman* in the Note to Chapter II.)

Editions and Translations

   Consolation of Philosophy. The Loeb Library *Boethius,* ed. H. F. Stewart and E. K. Rand (1918) provides a Latin text of the *Consolation* along with a fine seventeenth-century English translation by I. T. which employs alternate prose and verse comparable to the original. Chaucer's prose *Boece* is contained in the editions of his complete works. The translation into Modern English prose by Richard H. Green, *The Consolation of Philosophy* (1962), is precise and readable; his introduction contains the basic information about the author and the work. King Alfred's translation has been edited and translated into Modern English by Walter J. Sedgefield (1899 and 1900).

   Anticlaudian. The standard edition is Robert Bossuat, *Alain de Lille: Anticlaudianus* (1955). William H. Cornog has made a complete English translation, *The Anticlaudian of Alain de Lille* (1935).

   The Book of Consolation and Counsel of Albertan of Brescia. The Latin original is edited for the Chaucer Society by Thor Sundby, *Liber Consolationis et Consilii* (1873). The French version, which Chaucer translated as the *Tale of Melibee,* has been edited by J. Burke Severs in *Sources and Analogues of Chaucer's Canterbury Tales,* ed. W. F. Bryan and Germaine Dempster (1941), pp. 560–614.

   Related English Works. I have mentioned Thomas Usk's *Testament of Love,* which is edited by Walter W. Skeat in his volume of Chaucerian pieces, *The Complete Works of Geoffrey Chaucer,* VII (1897); and the *Kingis Quair,* ed. W. M. McKenzie (1939). Three personification allegories of particular relevance might also be noted: the fifteenth-century *Court of Sapience,* ed. Robert Spindler (1927); and the morality plays *Wisdom* (also called *Mind, Will, and Understanding*), ed. F. J. Furnivall and A. W. Pollard in *The Macro Plays,* EETS (1904), and *Wyt and Science,* ed. Joseph Q. Adams in *Chief Pre-Shakespearean Dramas* (1924).

Psychological Allegory

   Though medieval theory of human mental processes exercised no strict control on writers of allegory, it is clearly relevant to our discussion. Richard H. Green, "Alan of Lille's *Anticlaudianus:* Ascensus Mentis in Deum," *Annuale Medievale,* VIII (1967), 3–16, brings in important collateral writings in explaining Alan's analysis of the psyche. Though my interpretation of Prudence differs somewhat from his, I find his discussion and references very valuable. A detailed exposition of St. Thomas Aquinas' theories of human perception and cogitation is contained in George P. Klubertanz, S. J., *The Philosophy of Human Nature* (1953), which also has a useful bibliography. One introduction to the general subject, relevant to this chapter and the next, is Étienne H. Gilson, *Reason and Revelation in the Middle Ages* (1938).

Charles Muscatine's article on psychological allegory, referred to in the Note to Chapter III, deals with pertinent aspects of Old French romances. The metaphorical castle found in *Piers Plowman* is related to several other such edifices, particularly the one in *Sawles Warde;* see C. L. Powell, "The Castle of the Body," *SP,* 16 (1919), 197–205. A broader treatment of the subject is Roberta D. Cornelius, *The Figurative Castle* (1930). The connection of Lady Philosophy with the Seven Arts is set forth by Marie-Thérèse d'Alverny, "La Sagesse et ses sept filles," *Mélanges Félix Grat,* I (1946), 245–278; see also articles of Mlle. d'Alverny referred to in the Note to Chapter V.

Criticism of Specific Works

Most aspects of Boethius' influence on medieval literature are documented and discussed in Howard R. Patch, *The Tradition of Boethius* (1935), which includes an extensive bibliography. E. K. Rand, *Founders of the Middle Ages* (1928), pp. 134–180, presents a concise portrait of the man and his work. An important relationship of the *Consolation,* literary as well as philosophical, is identified in Edmund T. Silk, "Boethius' Consolatio Philosophiae as a Sequel to Augustine's Dialogues and Soliloquia," *Harvard Theological Review,* 32 (1939), 19–39. Chaucer's uses of the *Consolation* are set forth in Bernard L. Jefferson's *Chaucer and the Consolation of Philosophy of Boethius* (1917). For those interested in the commentaries on Boethius the basic work is Pierre Courcelle, "Étude critique sur les commentaires de la Consolation de Boèce," *Archives d'histoire doctrinale et littéraire du Moyen Age,* 14 (1939), 5–140. Also important is Courcelle's broader recent work (which, however, takes a narrow view of "literary tradition"), *La Consolation de Philosophie dans la tradition littéraire: Antécédents et postérité de Boèce.* (1967).

In addition to Green's article referred to above, brief, readily accessible discussions of the *Anticlaudian* may be found in Ernst R. Curtius, *European Literature and the Latin Middle Ages,* translated by Willard R. Trask (1953), pp. 117–122; and F. J. E. Raby, *A History of Christian Latin Poetry* (2nd ed. 1953), pp. 297–300. The comments of C. S. Lewis in *Allegory of Love,* pp. 98–106, ignore the positive values of Alan's work.

Among the numerous essays and books which take up the Boethian elements and concepts in *Troilus and Criseyde,* two of the more basic discussions are Theodore A. Stroud, "Boethius' Influence on Chaucer's *Troilus,*" *MP,* 49 (1951–1952), 1–9, and Howard R. Patch, "Troilus on Determinism," *Speculum,* 6 (1929), 225–243. Both are reprinted in *Chaucer Criticism,* II, ed. Richard J. Schoeck and Jerome Taylor (1961). Boethian implications of the dramatic situation in *Troilus* are taken up by Jefferson (cited above), pp. 121–130, and by Alan Gaylord, "Uncle Pandarus as Lady Philosophy," *Papers of the Michigan Academy of Science, Arts, and Letters,* 46 (1961), 571–595. Robert M. Lumiansky, *Of Sundry Folk* (1955), pp. 34–39, elucidates the narrative of the Knight's Tale in terms of Providence, Destiny, and Fortune, agents of the hierarchy set forth in the *Consolation.*

Chapter V

The Allegory of Revelation

Important Works: *Consolation of Philosophy, Anticlaudian, Divine Comedy, Pearl, Piers Plowman* (Passus XVI–XX).

Men try in similar ways to find solutions, justifications, and consolation for their troubles through reasoning; the process by which they do became, as we saw in the last chapter, a common subject of allegorical representation in the Middle Ages. Some problems, however, transcend the solutions of reason, and direct divine revelation is needed. Alan of Lille's Reason is unable to take Prudence into the Empyrean; Virgil cannot show Heaven to Dante; nor can the rational faculty assuage the narrator's grief in the Middle English *Pearl* or reveal Charity to Will in *Piers Plowman.* The processes entailed in each of these cases, which are represented by Allegories of Revelation, provide a supplement to the Allegories of Reason. These too have roots in Boethius' *Consolation of Philosophy.*

In terms of the contents of the *Consolation* the attitude of Boethius toward divine revelation is problematical. And as a matter of fact the question of his religious beliefs has always been a problem to scholars. Tradition formerly established him as a Christian saint, Saint Severinus, martyred by Theodoric for activities on behalf of his faith. Nineteenth-century scholars, on the other hand, denying his authorship of the theological tracts ascribed to him, saw him as a pagan or an apostate. Neither theory about Boethius has stood scrutiny. It is now accepted that he was an orthodox Christian throughout his life, but that he did not die for his religion; his own testimony in the *Consola-*

tion rather presents him as a political martyr, betrayed by his colleagues in the Senate.

The primary evidence formerly adduced to prove the paganism of Boethius is the complete lack of Christian reference in the *Consolation:* Christ is not named or alluded to, Biblical references are not used, and pagan philosophers are relied upon. However compelling such evidence might be superficially, the fact remains that paganism was not tolerated by Theodoric, who was himself a Christian. Furthermore, Boethius as a Christian had very good reason for suppressing Christian material: he wanted to show the rationality and inevitability of much of Christian theology. As E. K. Rand says,

> The thinker [in the *Consolation*] reasons solely with his own powers, without any revelation, save that of Philosophy, who is naught but the idealization of his own intellect. But the results fit in neatly with the revealed truth of Christian theology. The latter is in the background of the thinker's consciousness. He is proving as much of *fides* as *ratio* will allow him. That explains why there is not a trace of anything Christian or Biblical in the entire work; the assumption of any portion of faith in an endeavor of the unaided reason would defeat its very purpose.

Lady Philosophy embodies the powers of human reason; for this reason she appears frequently in various transmuted forms in medieval literature, particularly as Reason, Prudence, or Knowledge. Yet she also has divine possibilities. Even though in the *Consolation* she does not use wisdom beyond the capacity of man, there are indications that she could pursue superhuman topics. In the description of her Boethius says that her head sometimes pierces the clouds so that she cannot be seen. Allegorically one understands that at such times she is concerned with matters of a supernatural order. Later in the *Consolation* Philosophy herself claims to have "swift wings which will ascend the heights of Heaven." These passages permitted the association of Philosophy with Wisdom of the Bible, a power which subsumes both natural and supernatural knowledge. The Seven Pillars of Wisdom spoken of in Proverbs (ix, 1) were interpreted as the Seven Arts, and iconographic depictions of Wisdom frequently show him (or her) holding the book and scepter of Lady Philosophy and presiding over seven figures who represent the Arts (compare Figure 8.)

The fourteenth-century *Revelation of St. Bridget,* like *Pearl* and Dante's *Paradise,* describes a vision of Heaven. Bridget, while assisting at Mass, sees Christ and Mary in an aureole surrounded by cherubim, angels, saints, and patriarchs. Pierpont Morgan Library Ms. 498, f.4v. By permission.

As a consequence of Lady Philosophy's association with Divine Wisdom, literary personifications of powers superior to the rational faculty are often related to her. Such figures may be identified as Revelation, who makes available to man's intellect information beyond his power of reason, as Theology, celestial philosophy, or as Wisdom. A figure of this sort appears in the *Anticlaudian*. We have seen that both Prudence and Reason in that work are identified descriptively with Lady Philosophy, each possessing certain of her traditional properties; but they lack others, notably the books and the scepter of authority which Boethius describes Philosophy as holding, and the crown with which iconography subsequently endowed her. When Prudence in Alan's work reaches the borders of Heaven, her guide Reason and her chariot made by the Arts fail her; a new guide appears who bears the attributes of Lady Philosophy which Reason lacks: scepter, crown, and one book (apparently the Bible). This is the *Regina Poli,* the Queen of the Heavens, an embodiment of Revelation or Theology. Prudence follows the Regina Poli into the Empyrean on the single horse of the senses left to her, Hearing (of the five corporal senses, we are thus given to understand, Revelation speaks only to the hearing), and contemplates her surroundings. While Prudence on her ascent from Earth, in the company of Reason and the sensory faculties, contemplated natural phenomena such as clouds and lightning, with her new guide she observes the supernatural— the orders of the angels, the communion of saints, and the glory of the Virgin. When Prudence arrives at the Divine Palace a third guide, Intuition or Faith, conducts her up to the throne of God. This last guide is a sister to the Regina Poli; thus she too is of the family of Lady Philosophy.

Though nothing proves conclusively that Dante read the *Anticlaudian*, the tropological (or moral) allegory of the *Divine Comedy* bears a close resemblance to Alan's story. As in Alan's work, in Dante's ascent to the divinity there are three major instructor-guides: Virgil, who embodies Reason; Beatrice, who embodies Revelation; and Saint Bernard, who embodies mystical Intuition. Virgil first meets Dante in the initial canto of the *Comedy* as he is being pursued through a dark wood (the Wood of Error). With the aid of Virgil (Reason) Dante explores the very depths of sin in the *Inferno.* In the *Purgatory,* having recognized the ugliness of sin and still under the conduct of Reason, he corrects his inclination toward sin. He is thus prepared for the coming of supernatural revelation, to be represented by Beatrice.

On the top of the Mount of Purgatory Dante and Virgil enter the Earthly Paradise. They pass through a "divine forest," where birds sing melodiously in the treetops; thence they proceed to a plain fragrant with flowers, in the midst of which is a dark river flowing with pure water. On the other side of the river appears Matilda, a maiden who will take Dante to Beatrice. She explains the garden as the original abode of Adam, then she on one side and Dante and Virgil on the other proceed upstream to where they encounter the procession in which Beatrice manifests herself. At the approach of the procession Virgil is puzzled, and when Beatrice appears he vanishes: Reason is of no assistance in explaining the supernatural. From this point in the *Purgatory* till Beatrice leaves Dante's side to join the celestial rose in the thirty-first canto of *Paradise,* Revelation is his guide.

The reunion of the poet with Beatrice is the climax of the *Divine Comedy.* Beatrice was in real life the beloved of Dante, whom he was content to worship with an unspoken love. He first saw her when she was nine years old, and he was devoted to her until she died sixteen years later. Dante recounts in his *Convivio (Banquet)* how after Beatrice's death he abandoned her memory in favor of another woman, who turns out to be Lady Philosophy. In other words, in his bereavement he had resort to philosophy and the philosophers—he singles out Boethius particularly—to supply Beatrice's place in his thoughts. But his desertion of her was not permanent. He left the *Convivio* unfinished to write the *Comedy,* wherein the figure of the courtly mistress and Lady Philosophy merge in an apotheosized Beatrice.

In the *Purgatory* Beatrice appears more beautiful than ever as a transcendent Lady Philosophy, an embodiment of Divine Wisdom, to reassert her mastery over Dante. The similarity of the dramatic situation established here to that of the *Consolation of Philosophy* is manifest. Charles Grandgent states, "Just as Lady Philosophy greets with stern rebuke the captive Boethius

. . . so the divine Beatrice chides Dante for his recreancy after the death of her mortal part. Without entering upon specific charges, she accuses him of having forsaken the true way and 'given himself to others,' following 'images of good.' " (Dante's *images of good* echoes Boethius' *imagines veri boni.*) Beatrice's disdainful attitude toward Dante signals her role as Boethian adviser. We have seen the patronizing, scolding attitude parodied by Chaucer's eagle and Pandarus; here in the *Divine Comedy* the analogue which Beatrice presents to the mentor of Boethius has more serious implications.

Beatrice appropriately appears to Dante in a pageant which represents the books of the Bible. Twenty-four elders, who stand for the divisions of the Old Testament, precede the chariot bearing Beatrice; four "living creatures" who signify the evangelists surround her; and suitable figures representing the Acts of the Apostles, the Epistles, and the Apocalypse (Revelations) follow the chariot. Among other things, the procession indicates the grounding of revelation on Scripture. The direct dependence of Dante's *Paradise* on the Bible, however, is not great. The discussions in the canticle are mostly based on the speculations of scholastic philosophy, and the visions depend in great part on literary and philosophic traditions modified by personal inspiration. In this regard the Middle English *Pearl,* which may be seen as a kind of *Paradiso,* differs markedly from Dante's work, for both discussion and vision in the English poem are based closely on Biblical texts.

In other ways *Pearl* and the *Divine Comedy* are remarkably similar, so similar that it would indeed be wonderful if the Pearl Poet had not been familiar with Dante's work. A contemporary of Chaucer's, the poet was in a good position to know the *Comedy*; moreover, the complex artistry of his poems indicates a man not only of genius but also of broad culture and experience.

Pearl has been transmitted to us in a single small manuscript along with three other poems written in the same Northwest Midlands dialect: *Sir Gawain and the Green Knight, Purity,* and *Patience.* All four works are assumed with good reason to be the work of the same writer. *Pearl* is probably the most artful long poem in English, the poet's mastery of complex form being comparable to Dante's control of the demanding *terza rima* rather than like the skill of French contemporaries whose technical tours de force have limited aesthetic worth. The Pearl Poet's virtuosity in versifying substantially enhances the semantic richness and sensuous vitality of his work. He uses alliteration heavily throughout to bind the verses together; the verses are arranged in twelve-line stanzas with a complex rhyme scheme (which has significant similarities to *terza rima*); and the stanzas and groups of stanzas are related and connected by refrains and refrain words. In order to find the lexicon needed to maintain this form the poet strains the resources of his own and of neighboring dialects to the utmost, but almost always to good effect. With the formal elements working together, the luminous imagery has a magical, hypnotic effect in creating a picture of the celestial world.

The vision which the dreamer is granted in *Pearl* is in many ways comparable to the last cantos of *Purgatory* and to the *Paradise* of Dante. When the narrator of the English poem goes to sleep he is taken to an earthly Paradise where he looks over a stream into the heavenly Paradise; as he stands dazzled, he sees across the stream a very young maiden, even as Dante in a comparable landscape observes Matilda and later Beatrice across the stream of Lethe. The disdain which Beatrice at first manifests to Dante is recalled by the hauteur with which the maiden in *Pearl* receives the dreamer's remarks. Furthermore, just as Beatrice discusses with Dante the nature of Heaven and afterwards leads him to a vision of it consummated by the sight of God himself, so the maiden talks at length with the dreamer about Heaven, then conducts him to the Heavenly City where he observes the procession of the Lamb. When the maiden has led the dreamer to his final vision, she leaves him and joins the procession; similarly, Beatrice departs from Dante to take her place in the Celestial Rose. Thus the narrative of *Pearl* is analogous with the story of the *Comedy* from the time of Beatrice's appearance until the end of Dante's poem.

The comparison of *Pearl* to the *Divine Comedy* is relevant and productive in understanding the nature of the English poem. Particularly enlightening is the parallel which the Pearl Maiden presents to Beatrice. The Maiden is evidently a loved one whom the dreamer lost through death and bitterly mourned, even as Dante lost and mourned for Beatrice. Though she was not, like Beatrice, the poet's courtly beloved, her clothing and deportment are those of the courtly gentle lady. More important, the allegorical significance of the two female guides is similar, each of them being an embodiment of Revelation; through their offices the poet-narrators are enabled to understand and actually see Heaven.

The existential status of the Pearl Maiden, a matter of much controversy, is made clear by Dante's work. She, like Beatrice, is to be seen as a real person who was very important to the poet before she died and who returns to the poet in a vision as an embodiment of supernatural Revelation. Though a number of critics have seen the girl as purely symbolic, several passages of the poem point to her actuality, at least in terms of the fictional narrative; these strongly suggest that she is a daughter of the dreamer who died before her second birthday. She is thus significant not only as a symbol but also for her literal self.

Besides Beatrice another literary analogue to the Pearl Maiden is the *Marguerite* that was celebrated in French and English literature of the late fourteenth century. In addition to being a popular lady's name, Marguerite in French signifies both *daisy* and *pearl*. Several French poems utilize the meanings of the name in praising the Marguerite flower as a symbol of a real woman and at the same time of a transcendent ideal whose nature we may infer from a poem of Chaucer. In his Prologue to the *Legend of Good Women*, the daisy which the narrator worships symbolizes explicitly *womanly virtue* (F, 298). The daisy even has a female counterpart in this work who embodies this virtue. She is Alceste, the companion of the God of Love, who is dressed in the foliage and petals of the daisy. The crown of Alceste, furthermore, is cut from a single great pearl. This pearl broadens the Marguerite associations and shows a connection of the whole group of works with *Pearl* (where the pearl is on occasion called a *margery*).

Womanly virtue in medieval terms can have a range of mystical associations that would tie in with the Pearl Maiden's symbolization of revelation. In his prose *Testament of Love*, another imitation of Boethius, Thomas Usk is quite explicit about the meaning of his exemplary "Margery-pearl": "Marguerite, *a woman*, betokeneth grace, lerning, or the wisdom of God, or els holy church" (Book III, Chapter ix). In this statement ascribing several significances to a woman symbolized by a pearl, it should be noted that before all else the Marguerite is said to be an actual woman. The same may be said of the Pearl Maiden, who is first introduced in the metaphoric guise of a jewel. Of the other significations attributed by Usk to his Marguerite in this statement, two belong traditionally to Lady Philosophy— *lerning* (Langland's Clergy) and the *Wisdom of God*, which comprehends Revelation.

The Wisdom of God and Revelation are near cousins, and Beatrice, Marguerite, and the Pearl Maiden are closely related literary ladies. They provide an excellent lesson in the range and capacity of medieval allegory and symbolism. The medieval mind felt no limits to the analogies which manifestations of the physical, moral, and spiritual world offer to each other. A beautiful lady of virtue in particular seems to suggest a great variety of analogues. Beatrice, a woman, signifies Revelation, Sanctifying Grace, and by analogy the Host and Christ himself. Marguerite, a woman represented by both the daisy and the pearl, can fill the whole series of symbolic functions named by Usk. The Pearl Maiden, too, is a real woman, and she stands for Revelation, a product of the Wisdom of God. She seems to represent other things in addition, including the very Kingdom of God which she shows the dreamer, for like Usk's Marguerite she is associated with the Pearl of Great Price which Christ compared to the Kingdom of Heaven (Matthew, xiii, 45–46). Usk states that after first seeing his lady he has thought constantly of that Biblical pearl: "Ever sithen I have me bethought on the man that sought the precious Margarytes; and whan he had founded oon to his lyking, he solde his good to bye that jewel" (I, iii, 83–85). Comparably the Pearl Maiden says that the pearl which she wears at her neck is the "perle of prys" of the Scriptures.

It is quite possible—though such an assumption is not necessary—that the Pearl Maiden in life was named Margery or Margaret, since pearls in the poem three times are called *margeries*. We should recognize, of course, that the girl in the poem may have had no living counterpart, that the poet perhaps invented a fictional situation to suit his artistic purpose. This would make the Maiden no less a real person in terms of the poem. This is to say that, regardless of her actual historicity, the literal action in which the Pearl Maiden and the narrator are involved, as well as the allegorical action in which she functions as a personification of Revelation, has important significance.

Like Lady Philosophy and Beatrice, the Pearl Maiden acts as corrector, comforter, and counselor to the narrator. But whereas Boethius is comforted by Lady Philosophy acting as human reason, the dreamer in *Pearl* receives consolation through revelation, which the Pearl Maiden embodies and purveys. In this respect *Pearl* is basically similar to the *Consolation of Theology,* a religious treatise by the great French scholar, Jean Gerson (1363–1429). Writing his *Consolation* in virtual exile, Gerson imitates Boethius' story in many ways, except that faith and revelation perform for his narrator what reason had accomplished for his predecessor. Since he was unable to rationalize the corrupt condition of his country, he had to call on a higher wisdom. In *Pearl,* rather than to political and religious abuses, the narrator must reconcile himself to the early death of a child. But his problem is essentially like Gerson's in that it involves a human tragedy which Reason is inadequate to cope with.

At the beginning of *Pearl,* as the narrator stands before the burial mound, care seizes him. Though he believes that he should be able to rationalize the death of the beloved child, he finds no peace:

> A devely dele in my hert denned,
> Thagh Resoun sette myselven saght.
> I playned my perle that ther wats spenned
> Wyth fyrce skylles that faste faght;
> Thagh Kynde of Kryst me comfort kenned,
> My wreched Wylle in wo ay wraghte.

51–56

[A dreary sorrow lurked in my heart, though Reason
offered me peace. With fierce thoughts that contended
sharply, I lamented my pearl that was imprisoned. Though

Nature from Christ counseled me to comfort, my wretched
Will ever wrought in woe.]

Reason attempted to appease his sorrow; Nature, a vicar of
Christ and assistant to Reason, in the process of time should
have brought him forgetfulness; but his contrary Will fights
against these common comforts to the bereaved, making him
inconsolable. Only the lessons and revelations of the Pearl Maid-
en can reconcile him to his loss.

Boethius found reason at least sufficient, if not all-powerful.
But it is obvious that reason is not adequate to all occasions, as
Montaigne was to point out effectively in the "Apology for
Raymond Sebond." Montaigne, it will be remembered, says
that Raymond Sebond in his treatise *Natural Theology* argues as
well as one might for the reasonableness of Christian doctrine;
nevertheless, human reason is a severely limited faculty, and
one must rely primarily on simple faith to justify his religion.
The attitude of the Pearl Poet and Gerson is comparable to
that of Montaigne. Indeed, situations like those which provide
the occasion for their writings, in which natural reason is found
insufficient to the problems at hand, are common. The processes by which revelation or theology comfort and correct the
misguided will are therefore well suited to allegorical representation.

Pearl thus lies in a second tradition of allegory which grew
out of the *Consolation of Philosophy;* it represents a kind of narrative that takes up where the Allegory of Reason leaves off, or
that is used in situations where reason is simply not effective.
Reason is not able to relieve the dreamer's grief, but Divine
Revelation can. Gerson likewise in reconciling himself to the
state of the world finds revelation rather than reason efficacious.
Both *Pearl* and the *Consolation of Theology* present parallels to
Boethius' narrative, and because they do the ineffectiveness of
reason in them becomes more pointed, since the whole of the
Consolation of Philosophy consists of the narrator's finding a solu-
tion to his spiritual dislocation through unaided reason. Dante
in the *Divine Comedy,* by contrast to the Pearl Poet and Gerson
on one hand and Boethius on the other, combines the forces of
reason and revelation in leading the poet to Heaven. Virgil, an

embodiment of human reason, takes the poet to the top of the Mountain of Purgatory where Beatrice, Revelation, becomes his guide for the journey to the outermost Heaven. In the conception of the *Comedy*, then, natural reason leads man to the threshold of Heaven. Even though it can go no further, the fact that reason can take the poet so far imparts to that human power great importance.

The *Divine Comedy* in the matter of combining reason and revelation is like the *Anticlaudian* and also has much in common with *Piers Plowman*. The Dowel section of *Piers*, which we considered as an Allegory of Reason in the last chapter, corresponds to the parts of the *Comedy* in which Virgil is the guide; the remainder of the Vita (Dobet and Dobest) corresponds to the parts in which Beatrice leads. When physically Dante enters Heaven under the guidance of Beatrice, in the allegory his mind achieves contemplation of the divine through the inspiration of revelation; his attention previously had been directed to matters which his own faculties could deal with. A similar change takes place on the allegorical level in the Dobet section in *Piers*. Of course the physical site of the literal action in Langland's work—unlike the *Comedy*—remains on Earth; the similarity to Dante's work comes in the psychological allegory.

In Dowel Will's insights become progressively more acute under the tutelage of progressively higher modes of reason—Thought, Wit and Clergy, Imagination, and finally the integrated soul, Anima. Anima tells Will almost everything he has sought to know, "Whither I should go, whereof I came, and of what sort I am" (B, XV, 13–14). Nevertheless, however broad the perceptions of Anima, they have definite limitations. His powers do not go beyond those of the faculties with which man is naturally endowed. Talk as he will about Charity (and he discusses it quite eloquently), Anima admits that he cannot show it to Will:

> "By Cryst, I wolde that I knewe hym," quod I, "no creature levere!"
> "Withouten helpe of Piers Plowman," quod he, "his persone seestow nevere."
>
> B, XV, 189–190

["By Christ, I wish I knew him" (i.e., Charity), I said,
"there is no one I'd rather know." "Without the help of
Piers Plowman," he said, "you will never see him."]

The mystical Piers the Plowman, then, can bring Charity, but
Anima cannot. Charity, being divine, cannot be described by
even the highest human power. So it is that after Anima's long
speech Will thanks him for his teaching, but adds, "Yet I am in
doubt about the meaning of charity" (B, XVI, 3).

Charity is the primary of the three theological virtues of
faith, hope, and charity. In Christian thought these virtues are
gifts from above, not to be attained or understood through the
efforts of man. When Beatrice (Revelation) descends to Dante
clothed in the red of charity, Virgil (Reason) is no longer present. Were he present he could not see Beatrice or her apparel,
since revelation on an intellectual level and charity on a moral
level are beyond the ken of natural reason. It is necessary that
Beatrice on her first appearance should bring charity, signified
by her red clothing, for charity is basic to all that is heavenly,
including revelation. So also is charity necessary to Will in *Piers
Plowman* to achieve a supernatural vision.

Anima as a human faculty shares most of Virgil's limitations.
He can describe the Tree of Charity to the dreamer, but he
cannot show it to him. In other words the intellect at its best
can express ideas about charity, but charity is essentially
ineffable, indescribable; one must experience it to know it, and
the experience is on a supernatural plane, God-given. For this
reason the dreamer's vision of the Tree of Charity, which is at-
tended by Piers the Plowman himself, is attained just after
Anima—like Virgil on the appearance of Beatrice—has disap-
peared (B, XVI, 20ff.).

Piers' presentation of the Tree of Charity to Will represents
allegorically the infusion of charity in Will and leads to the
subsequent vision. Comparably Beatrice brings the infusion of
charity requisite for Dante's vision of Paradise. What Will sees
is quite different in substance from the celestial vision enjoyed
by Dante and by the dreamer in *Pearl*, but like the other visions
his is on a supernatural level. Will's vision is of the spiritual history of the Church: successively he meets with Abraham in the

garb of Faith, Moses as Hope, and the Good Samaritan as Charity; then before his eyes come Christ's crucifixion, the harrowing of Hell, the establishment of the Church, and the advent of Anti-Christ. Though the events and people depicted are historical, they are clothed with spiritual significance, and they may properly be seen as the matter of a supernatural vision. Langland's verse in these sections becomes especially vivid and powerful, and he succeeds remarkably, as do Dante and the Pearl Poet, in poetically suggesting divine truth which is ultimately beyond human reach. The last five passus of *Piers Plowman*, then, form another version of the Allegory of Revelation.

In the course of this chapter we have had repeated occasion to refer to the *Divine Comedy*. This masterpiece of Dante is often spoken of as something of its own kind, not basically comparable to other medieval works. Yet it has its roots deep in the broad literary and philosophical tradition which Dante's time saw as stretching from the Athens of Socrates through Roman history directly to the fourteenth century. On every hand in the *Comedy* one encounters aspects of this tradition. For example, as we have seen, patterns in the narratives of the *Consolation of Philosophy* and the *Anticlaudian*, part of Dante's heritage, are comparable to patterns in the *Comedy*. These similarities do not in themselves constitute evidence that Dante used the works, but rather witness the breadth of the tradition and the centrality of the *Comedy* in the tradition. In turn works which succeeded Dante's reflect aspects of the *Comedy*—*Pearl* and *Piers Plowman*, for example. We cannot be positive that the Pearl Poet read the *Comedy*, and one inclines to think that Langland did not. Dante's poem nevertheless provides illuminating parallels to and commentary on both poems. Other Middle English works, Chaucer's particularly, are elucidated by reference to many aspects of Dante, and we shall have occasion to refer to his great poem again in subsequent chapters.

The subsequent chapters of this book deal primarily with the literary mirror, and not only the *Divine Comedy*, but also many works which we have treated as allegories may be related to the mirror tradition; like the literary mirrors which we will discuss, they present comprehensive and inclusive images of discrete segments of existence. *Pearl* is a good example.

As a mirror, the *Divine Comedy* provides a complete picture of the afterlife: Hell, Purgatory, and Heaven. *Pearl*, too, though only a fourth as long as Dante's *Paradise*, qualifies as a mirror of Heaven. Indeed, *Pearl* in its own way has as complete a picture of Heaven as does the *Paradise*, since the base on which its image is built is much narrower than Dante's. Dante makes use of much medieval speculation in the discussions of Heaven and the organization of the vision; he draws material from diverse vision literature; and he fills out the picture with his personal vision. The Bible figures in the *Paradise* mostly as a secondary source for this large body of materials. The Pearl Poet, on the other hand, uses almost nothing but the limited relevant sections of the Bible for his picture of Heaven. It seems that he intends to display only as much of Heaven as the Bible, the primary record of divine revelation, directly warrants.

The poetic situation in *Pearl* is particularly well suited to such an exposition of Heaven. The confrontation by the bereaved man of the sanctified child, who is symbolized by a pearl, makes appropriate to his conversations with her central texts of the New Testament on the nature of Heaven: the parable of the vineyard, the image of the pearl of great price, the marriage of the Lamb, and Christ's statement that the kingdom of Heaven is "arrayed" with little children. Furthermore, the process of correcting the dreamer's misplaced grief provides an ideal narrative frame for discussing celestial matters. The Maiden, like Lady Philosophy, first clears away some of the dreamer's misapprehensions; then, when he recognizes and acknowledges his errors, she invites his questions about Heaven and its inhabitants. After answering several of these, she reveals that she (like Beatrice) has been granted special permission to show him Heaven.

The vision of the heavenly city is described in ten enraptured stanzas, 973–1092, that are based on the Apocalypse. Despite its complete dependence on arcane apocalyptic images, the poetry approaches the magnificence of Dante's description in the last cantos of *Paradise:*

> On sunne ne mone had thay no nede;
> The self God wats her lombe-lyght,
> The Lombe her lantyrne, wythouten drede;

Thurgh hym blysned the borgh al bryght.
Thurgh woghe and won my lokynge yede,
For sotyle cler noght lette no lyght.
The hyghe trone there moght ye hede
Wyth alle the apparaylmente umbepyght,
As John the appostel in termes tyghte,
The hyghe Godes self hit set upone.
A rever of the trone ther ran outryghte
Wats bryghter then bothe the sunne and mone.

1045–1056

[They had no need of sun nor moon. God himself was their
lamp-light, the Lamb their lantern in truth; by Him the
city gleamed very brightly. My sight went right through
the walls and dwellings, for the transparent clarity did
not hinder the light. One might see the high throne set
about with its adornment, as John the Apostle describes it.
High God himself sat upon it. A river ran out from the
throne that was brighter than both the sun and moon.]

This description, developed from the only substantial description of Heaven in Scripture, is the culmination of the experience of the narrator and of the mirror of Heaven. When the
dreamer sees the Maiden in the celestial procession, he tries to
leap the stream to join her, and the dream ends.

Though his vision is truncated by his impetuosity, through
the Maiden's revelation the dreamer is brought to a thorough
reconciliation to the loss of the child:

Over this hyul this lote I laghte,
For pyty of my perle enclyin,
And sythen to God I hit bytaghte
In Krystes dere blessynge and myn.

1205–1208

[On this mound I had this experience, lying prostrate with
grief for my pearl. Afterwards I committed it to God,
with Christ's precious blessing and mine.]

Furthermore, despite the vision being represented as incomplete, it provides nearly as complete a mirror of Heaven as the
Bible directly warrants, with all the most familiar texts finding
a place in the poem. The narrator's unnatural grief has been
assuaged, and the central texts of the Bible about Heaven have

been presented to the reader in a coherent form. The work has reached its natural conclusion; allegory and mirror are complete.

The combination of the modes in works other than *Pearl* and the *Divine Comedy* will be discussed in the final chapter of this study. The intervening three chapters attempt to elucidate the origin, nature, and purpose of Middle English mirrors; they are as characteristically medieval as the allegories.

NOTE TO CHAPTER V

(The main bibliographical listings for the *Consolation of Philosophy* and the *Anticlaudian* are found in the Note to Chapter IV; for *Piers Plowman* in the Note to Chapter II.)

Editions and Translations

Divine Comedy. For the English-speaking student the edition of the original by Charles H. Grandgent, *La Divina Commedia de Dante Alighieri* (rev. ed., 1933), with commentary and notes in English, is most useful. A parallel-text edition has been made by John D. Sinclair, *The Divine Comedy of Dante Alighieri*, three volumes (1961), with prose translation printed on pages facing the Italian verse. Many translations have been made into English verse; I might mention two in *terza rima* of good quality. Dorothy Sayers' translation *(Paradise* completed by Barbara Reynolds) in three-volume paperback, *The Comedy of Dante Alighieri* (1949–1962), has particularly full and helpful introductions and notes. The Viking *Portable Dante* (1947) presents in one volume Lawrence Binyon's translation of the *Comedy* and makes use of Grandgent's commentary and notes; included in this volume is Rossetti's rendering of the *Vita Nuova.*

Pearl. The most complete edition, with full introduction, notes, and glossary, is that of Eric V. Gordon, *Pearl* (1953). *The Pearl: A New Translation and Interpretation*, edited and translated by Sister Mary Vincent Hillman (1961), is a useful edition, presenting text and prose translation on facing pages. The four poems of the Pearl Poet are translated by John Gardner, *The Complete Works of the Gawain Poet* (1965).

De Consolatione Theologiae. The current edition of Gerson's *Complete Works* (1960) will make his *Consolation* generally available. Older editions are quite rare. No English translation is available.

Revelation, Visions, and Mysticism

Revelation, Wisdom, and Theology are variously seen as the inspirers and guides of supernatural visions, and as such are nearly synonymous (Beatrice might be identified by any of the three names). A series of articles by Marie-Thérèse d'Alverny makes clear some interrelationships of traditional treatments of the three: "La Sagesse et le Crist de Saint Dunstan," *Bodleian Library Record*, 5 (1956), 232–244; "Alain de Lille et la *Theologia*," *Mélanges Henri de Lubac*, II (1964), 111–128; "Notes sur Dante et la Sagesse," *Revue des études italiennes*, 11 (1965), 5–28.

A survey of the many medieval descriptions of supernatural places, with full bibliography, is provided by Howard R. Patch, *The Other World According to Descriptions in Medieval Literature* (1950). Literary visits to Heaven and visions of the godhead, such as are found in Dante and

Pearl, always bring up the question of mysticism. A lucid introduction to the history of mysticism and to the prominent medieval English mystics is provided by David Knowles, *The English Mystical Tradition* (1961). A representative anthology in translation of the Latin and vernacular writings of English mystics, with informative introduction, has been compiled by Erec Colledge, *The Medieval Mystics of England* (1961). See also below on individual authors.

Criticism of Individual Works

A general introduction to Dante's work is provided by Thomas C. Bergin, *Dante* (1965). The commentary in Grandgent's edition of the *Comedy* (see above) supplies perhaps the easiest access to a basic understanding of this most complex work. Indispensable for an adequate comprehension of the allegory of the *Comedy* are the *Dante Studies* of Charles S. Singleton: *1, Commedia; Elements of Structure* (1954); and *2, Journey to Beatrice* (1958). The first nine chapters of *Journey to Beatrice* elucidate the transition from Virgil to Beatrice in the *Purgatory;* the action of *Piers Plowman*, I have suggested, provides an analogy to this transition. Much about the symbolism in the *Comedy* is contained in the encyclopedic study of Helen Flanders Dunbar, *Symbolism in Medieval Thought and Its Consummation in the Divine Comedy* (1929); the chapter on Dante's "Relation to Mysticism," pp. 331–395, presents several aspects of that problem. Two very readable books about the *Comedy*, learned but without footnotes, are Francis Fergusson, *Dante's Drama of the Mind: A Modern Reading of the Purgatorio* (1953), and Charles Williams, *The Figure of Beatrice* (1943). The former correlates with Singleton's studies to present an analysis in depth of the *Purgatory;* the latter works from the premise that Dante in his masterwork follows the mystical "Way of Affirmation."

The problem of *Pearl* which has most concerned the critics is whether the Maiden is a real person or is simply symbolic—of the dreamer's soul or something else. Gordon's introduction to his edition contends that she had a real existence, at least in the poet's mind, whereas Sister Hillman's introduction finds her simply a personification. A compelling and well-documented argument for the latter viewpoint is the article by Marie P. Hamilton, "The Meaning of the Middle English *Pearl,*" 70 (1965), 805–824. In what is still probably the best overall reading of the work, however, René Wellek argues for the girl's actuality: "The Pearl: An Interpretation of the Middle English Poem," first published in the Charles University (Prague) *Studies in English* (1933), now generally available in a collection of essays edited by Robert J. Blanch, *Sir Gawain and Pearl: Critical Essays* (1966). Stanton deV. Hoffman, "The Pearl: Notes for an Interpretation," *MP*, 58 (1960), 73–80, summarizes previous interpretations and discusses some major obstacles which readings such as Miss Hamilton's present. A provocative essay which points out important contrasts between the earthly and heavenly in *Pearl* is Wendell S. Johnson, "The Imagery and Diction of the *Pearl:* Toward an Interpretation," *ELH*, 20 (1953), 161–180.

The symbolism of the Marguerite in French and English literature, which is related to the pearl symbolism, is taken up in James I. Wimsatt, *The Marguerite Poetry of Guillaume de Machaut* (forthcoming); and S. K. Heninger, Jr., "The Marguerite-Pearl Allegory in Thomas Usk's *Testament of Love,*" *Speculum,* 32 (1957), 92–98.

One of the livelier topics in studies of *Piers Plowman,* as with studies of Dante, is the problem of mysticism in the poem. Edward Vasta summarizes previous discussions of Langland's possible mysticism and makes a beginning at a mystical reading of the whole poem in *The Spiritual Basis of Piers Plowman* (1965). Some relationships of *Piers* to mystical writings are particularly pointed up in Elizabeth Zeeman (Salter), *"Piers Plowman* and the Pilgrimage to Truth," *Essays and Studies,* N. S. 11 (1958), 1–16.

Chapter VI

Summas, Manuals, and Mirrors

Important Works: the Parson's Tale, *Ancrene Riwle,*
Piers Plowman, Handlying Synne, Confessio Amantis.

Surrounded by more complex scientific wonders, we today
scarcely pause to analyze the reflecting mirror. Indeed, the
discussions of mirrors and optical theory in the *Romance of the
Rose* (18013–18298) and the *Paradiso* (II, 73–105) seem to us the
very dullest parts of the poems. Mirrors nevertheless have found
a substantial place in modern literary imagery. The mirror of a
lake brings Heaven to Earth in a poem of Frost; distorting mirrors show inward truth in Hawthorne's fiction; and the Lady
of Shallott's mirror, through which she views the world, indicates her separation from reality. Medieval writers, as their interest in optical phenomena might forewarn us, found even
more plentiful uses for mirror images, though they generally
employed the images more predictably to refer to a *compendium,*
or an *exemplar,* or a combination of these. With such referents
the word commonly appears in the titles of both imaginative
and expository writings, as well as within the texts.

Medieval compendiums of all kinds have *mirror* as an element
in their titles. As the mirror of the Lady of Shallott sums up in
small compass the whole of the outside landscape—the winding
river, the city, the churls, and the girls—so a literary work may
offer a summary, brief but complete, of a substantial slice of

existence. *Pearl* and *Paradiso* are mirrors of Heaven, small in their extent with respect to Heaven itself but meant to reflect all of it. An early example of an imaginative work called a mirror is the twelfth-century Latin *Speculum Stultorum (Mirror of Fools)*, which relates the odyssey of Brunellus the Ass; Brunellus' meetings with a spectrum of knaves and fools provide occasion for an inclusive view of their kind. Among nonfictional *speculums* one perhaps thinks first of the thirteenth-century *Speculum Maius* of Vincent of Beauvais, which includes three great encyclopedias—of nature, history, and doctrine, each of which is itself known as a mirror: the *Speculum Naturale, Speculum Historiale,* and *Speculum Doctrinale* (the *Speculum Morale,* which completed Vincent's scheme, was added in the fourteenth century).

Gluttony, astride a pig, strikes with her dart the pilgrim of Deguilleville's *Pilgrimage of the Life of Man.* Pierpont Morgan Library MS. 772, f.75. By permission.

The use of *mirror* or its Latin equivalent *speculum* in a title generally implies an attempt at inclusiveness or completeness. Such a title further suggests that the work has exemplary features, that its content reflects ideals or archetypes. This latter signification of the mirror image in literature perhaps becomes most clear in some of its applications outside of titles to paragons. Blanche in the *Book of the Duchess* is "chief myrour of al the feste," in other words, the lady who of all present most nearly reflects perfection. In *Hamlet* Ophelia's lament for the Prince's decline—for one who, though now "quite down," was once the "glass of fashion and the mold of form"—supplies its own gloss for *mirror* or *glass*. *Mold* and *glass* in her statement are equivalent terms signifying *ideal pattern*. In Ophelia's mind, then, Hamlet had once been the model, the mold or mirror, of decorous appearance *(fashion)* and proper behavior *(form)*. A person might also be a mirror through inappropriate behavior, when by actions opposed to the ideal he becomes a negative exemplar. It is in this sense that in *Piers Plowman* Jesus tells Judas and the Jews that their behavior will be a mirror to men (B, XVI, 156).

Works called mirrors generally aim in some way both at inclusiveness and the presentation of ideals; they are either compendiums of exemplars or compendiums of more or less corrupted entities in which exemplars are implicit. A mirror of Heaven is certainly a mirror of the ideal, and it is therefore composed of a compendium of exemplars; the compendium in *Pearl,* for example, includes such ideal elements as the Maiden, the City, and the Lamb. In a *speculum* of fools or of wrong behavior, the ideal may be made implicit through the very opposition to propriety which is represented. The *Canterbury Tales,* as we will see in the next chapter, is a Mirror of Society; it is that with respect both to inclusiveness and the depiction of archetypes, for virtually ever sort and condition of man, in each of whom the archetype is present or implicit, is represented.

The great number of medieval works classifiable as mirrors is accounted for in large extent by the encyclopedic tendencies of the age. Such tendencies were nursed by a belief that the world is ordered rationally and logically in ways which man can often discover. Making plentiful use of Biblical and classical traditions, philosophers confidently located organizing principles for most worldly and otherworldly phenomena, and then used these principles as a basis for classification. The elements were four, the humors of the body four, the spheres of the heavens nine, the orders of angels nine, the ages of the world four, the ages of man seven, the virtues seven, the vices seven, and so on. In dealing with each aspect of existence a scholar could take such classifications as a basis for extended treatises and could subdivide and correlate as convenient and necessary. If the scholar aimed at complete treatment of one phase of thought or existence, then he would likely call his work a *summa* or a *mirror*. Thomas Aquinas' *Summa Theologica*, a monumental survey of all theology, is probably the best-known summa, but many of Thomas' thirteenth-century contemporaries were also writing similar treatises. Summas written for semischolarly or popular purposes might alternatively be called *manuals* or *handbooks*. All such designations imply summary inclusiveness.

In this chapter our attention is directed at treatments of the Seven Deadly Sins contained in the works known interchangeably as summas, manuals, or mirrors. The Sins were a very popular subject in works of this sort; through looking at several treatments of them in English we can see how the encyclopedic tendencies of medieval scholarship came to be manifested in literature of substantial aesthetic worth. Relatively mechanical catalogs in works like the Parson's Tale contrast with the more artful discussions and visualizations found in the *Ancrene Riwle* and *Piers Plowman*. The scheme of the Seven Sins also provided a framework for extensive collections of narrative exemplums like Robert Mannyng's *Handlyng Synne* and John Gower's *Confessio Amantis*. The *Canterbury Tales,* while not employing the framework of the Sins, nevertheless shows in its plan and its characterizations the influence of English treatments of them. This influence provides one very good reason for calling Chaucer's Canterbury period his "English Period."

The Seven Deadly Sins (also called the Seven Capital Sins), were usually dealt with in the order Pride, Envy, Wrath, Sloth (more properly Acedia), Avarice, Gluttony, and Lust. Theologically, this is merely one of several ways to classify vice, but only occasionally in literature, as in Dante's *Inferno,* does another system appear. Sometimes the scheme of the Seven Sins alone provides the organizing principle of an extensive work, for example, William Peraldus' *Summa de Vitiis (Summa of Vices,* 1236). More often it is used as one section in compilations of teachings of the Church, as in Friar Lorens' *Somme le Roy (Summa of the King,* 1279), known in other versions as the *Miroir du Monde (Mirror of the World);* or it is employed in confessional manuals, works such as the Anglo-Norman *Manuel des Péchés (Manual of Sins,* c. 1260), designed to assist the priest in hearing confessions.

Various forces in the thirteenth century contributed to a flood of religious treatises which included exhaustive exegeses of the Sins. In the first place the status of Penance (Confession) as a Sacrament had become generally recognized by 1200, and the Fourth Lateran Council of 1215 focused attention on Penance by making more strict the obligation of yearly confession. As a result priests anxious to improve their confessional practices created a demand for penitential handbooks, like the *Manuel des Péchés,* in which the Seven Sins were extensively treated. Furthermore, there was a general growth of interest in preaching in England. Of great import in this regard were the fraternal orders. The Dominican and Franciscan orders of friars had been founded early in the thirteenth century and were very soon established in England. Their particular interest was in ministering and preaching to the people. Sermon literature, which might include treatments of the Sins, was called for, as were collections of exemplums—illustrative stories appropriate for sermons—for which the scheme of the Seven Sins could provide a basis of organization.

Several episcopal decrees seconded the friars' efforts to take religion to the folk; these bolstered the standards of preaching by codifying for the parish priest his duty to inform his parishioners on basic matters. The first friar to become Archbishop of Canterbury, John Peckham, in 1281 made such a decree applicable to all of England. The Constitutions of Lambeth directed all parish priests to give instructions from the pulpit four times a year on Six Points: the Articles of the Creed, the Ten Commandments, the Works of Mercy, the Seven Deadly Sins, the Seven Virtues, and the Sacraments. This decree naturally created a demand for treatises which dealt with the Six Points. In these the Seven Deadly Sins usually came in for disproportionate attention.

In practice much of the literature which resulted, especially of the more popular sort, was useful both for guiding the clergy and as devotional reading for the layman. Chaucer's Parson's Tale is a good example of such a treatise being appropriate for more than one use. The Parson's presentation had its origins in summas like William Peraldus' *Summa de Vitiis,* a scholarly work in Latin that presents in detail a philosophy and psychology of sin. From such summas were derived the confessional manuals for the use of priests and ultimately the more popular books and sermons for the laity. The Parson's Tale might serve as a guidebook for a confessor, as a sermon, or as a treatise for the edification of the learned layman. In the *Canterbury Tales* it is a sermon; its subject is the Sacrament of Penance, and it provides the last word on the pilgrimage. Though it is not particularly valuable for its literary properties, Chaucer gave the humble Parson's performance the place of honor, thereby implying that in the end moral considerations transcend the aesthetic. At the conclusion of the earthly pilgrimage must come penance.

The Sacrament of Penance has three aspects: contrition, sorrow for one's sins; confession, verbal acknowledgement of them; and satisfaction, atonement for them. These three aspects provide the organization for the three parts of the Parson's Tale. Our interest is in the second part, which concerns confession, where the Parson makes an analysis of sin based on the Seven Deadly Sins; this occupies 60 per cent of the whole Tale. Like all of the Tale the discussion is workmanlike and relatively unimaginative. It is workmanlike in its aiming at comprehensive coverage and in its proceding toward that goal in an orderly fashion. The Seven Sins, says the Parson, are called the "chieftaynes of synnes" because from them spring all the other sins (I, 386). To illustrate how more specialized classifications are included under the major vices, he uses the conventional metaphor of the tree. "And everich of thise chief synnes hath his braunches and his twigges, as shal be declared in hire chapitres folwynge" (I, 388). The Parson subsequently enumerates the subdivisions in full and discusses them; and he analyzes the remedial virtues, the opposites of each of the Sins. In its inclusiveness the Tale may well be said to provide an expository *mirror of sin* within a larger work which might itself be called a *mirror of Penance.*

The Tale is unimaginative in that the discussions are often perfunctory and generally are restatements in flat prose of the commonplaces found in older treatises. At times the principles of analysis have a poor logical basis. The treatment of gluttony provides an example of the Parson's procedure; I will use other discussions of the same sin for illustration later in the chapter to facilitate comparison. The Parson defines gluttony as "unmesurable appetit and desordeynee coveitise to eten or to drynke" (I, 817), makes the conventional statement that "This synne corrumped al this world, as is wel shewed in the synne of Adam and of Eve" (I, 818), and then he cites Saint Paul who says of the enemies of Christ that their "wombe is hire god" (I, 819). In his further discussion of the sin the Parson uses two systems for subdividing it: the first is perhaps his own extempore system, the other is a conventional one. He begins the discussion by stating that the species of gluttony are many: one is drunkenness, the second is that the "spirit of a man" grows troubled from drunkenness, the third is the incontinent devouring of one's food, the fourth is that the humors of the body become distempered from gorging, and the fifth is that a man often forgets what he has done the morning after his drinking. This subdivision obviously sorts causes with effects and so provides no real analysis—nor is there colorful comment to make up for the lack of logic.

The second system for classifying gluttony has more logic, but is presented even more perfunctorily (I, 827–830). The basis for it is an analysis by Gregory the Great which was commonly used—in Peraldus' *Summa,* for instance, where Gregory's classification is filled out with copious citations of Biblical and patristic texts. The Parson by contrast merely notes briefly that Gregory distinguishes five sorts of gluttony: eating too soon, eating too delicate food, eating too much, worrying overly about the preparation of the food, and eating greedily. The Parson's remedy for gluttony is abstinence, which he also analyzes in a manner unsatisfactory both from a literary and logical standpoint. After citing one text from Augustine to the effect that abstinence is worth little unless reinforced by patience and charity, he says that the "felawes of abstinence" are temperance, sufficiency, measure, and sparing.

Not all of the Parson's performance, however, is as deficient in style as his treatment of gluttony. In accordance with the Host's view of the Parson as something of a prude, he waxes most eloquent about sins such as profanity, immodest dress, and fornication. In the discussion of pride, for instance, he laments the short mantles which men are accustomed to wearing over their tight-fitting, and therefore revealing, undergarments (which resemble the ballet dancer's tights). When these are half white and half red, says the Parson, it appears as if "half hir shameful privee membres weren flayne [flayed]" (I, 424). And if they are of other colors then it seems "by variaunce of colour, that half the partie of hire privee membres were corrupt by the fir of seint Antony [erysipelas], or by cancre, or by oother swich meschaunce" (I, 426). The view from the rear is even worse, for there "the buttokes of hem faren as it were the hyndre part of a she-ape in the fulle of the moone" (I, 423). Their buttocks, he goes on, are indeed "ful horrible for to see. For certes, in that partie of hir body ther as they purgen hir stynkynge ordure, that foule partie shewe they to the peple prowdly in despit of honestitee, which honestitee that Jesu Crist and his freendes observede to shewen in hir lyve" (I, 427–428). Unfortunately the heat of the Parson's indignation is not sustained, and the reader of his Tale in the end applauds his righteous perseverance considerably more than his eloquence.

Other works in the same tradition have more interest; for example, the treatise commonly called the *Ancrene Riwle (Rule for Anchoresses)*. This title seems to classify it with monastic documents like the *Benedictine Rule,* which prescribes the forms and observances proper to the life of the contemplative. But in content the *Riwle* actually reflects the thirteenth-century vogue of confessional literature. Whereas the emphasis in St. Benedict's book is on practical rules of conduct, only a small part of the *Ancrene Riwle* is taken up with such matters. Four-fifths of the English work has to do with the occasions of sin and the Sacrament of Penance: the guarding from sin of one's outward and inward senses, temptations to sin, confession, and the performance of penance. These materials ally the *Riwle* with penitential treatises like the Parson's Tale.

In literary value, however, the superb *Ancrene Riwle* is no fellow of the drab Parson's Tale. The writer of the *Riwle,* a priest assisting three young ladies in establishing themselves as hermitesses, has a gentle, paternal manner which sharply contrasts with the Parson's prosaic, impersonal approach. Instead of the mechanical organization of the Parson's Tale, the writer uses an informal, fluid form in dealing with traditional materials. And in place of the dry, flat style of the Parson, the *Riwle* provides perhaps the foremost example of Middle English prose which has come down to us. It is easy, varied, and versatile. A brief consideration of the treatment of the Seven Deadly Sins in the *Riwle* may suggest in some fashion the author's skill.

The work has eight sections. A substantial portion of the long fourth section, on temptation, is devoted to classification and subclassification of the vices, and to consideration of their consequences and remedies. While the author deals with these systematically, he avoids the impression of mechanical listing. One way in which he does this is through continuing metaphors and other imagery. The image of man as a pilgrim traveling through a wilderness to heavenly Jerusalem, who is like the Jews in Exodus traveling to earthly Jerusalem, introduces the discussion of temptation. In his journey through this wilderness, the writer says, man meets with many wild animals: the lion of pride, the serpent of envy, the unicorn of wrath, the bear of dull sloth, the fox of avarice, the sow of gluttony, and the scorpion of lust. As in the Parson's Tale where each limb of the tree of sin has its branches, so here each animal has its offspring. For example, the lion of pride has ten cubs, each of which the author identifies and briefly discusses. He spends little time on a sin like gluttony: since the anchoresses are not troubled with it, he merely enumerates the sow's little pigs, a list which roughly follows the Gregorian division:

> The suwe of yivernesse, thet is, glutunie, haveth pigges thus i-nemmed: to erliche hette thet on; thet other, to estliche; thet thridde, to urechliche; thet feorthe·hette to muchel; thet fifte, to ofte ine drunche more then i-mete.

[The sow of gluttony has pigs named thus: one is called Too Early, the second Too Daintily, the third Too Greedily, the fourth Too Much, the fifth Too Often in drinking, more than moderation.]

The priest is evidently more concerned about the possible attractions of lechery to these young ladies, for he describes the young of the scorpion of lust at length, and then deals with the scorpion itself:

> The scorpiun is one cunnes wurm that haveth neb ase me seith sumdel iliche ase wummon, ant is neddre bihinden. Maketh feir semblaunt ant fiketh mid te heaved, ant stingeth mid te teile. Thet is lecherie thet is thes deofles best thet he let to chepinge ant to everich gederinge ant cheapeth hit forto sullen ant biswiketh monie thuruh thet heo ne biholdeth nout bute thet feire heaved.
>
> [The scorpion is a kind of serpent that has a face, as they say, something like a woman, but is a reptile behind. It makes a fair face and flatters with its head while it stings with its tail. This is lechery, the devil's beast that he takes to the market and every gathering where he bargains to sell it, and he deceives many because they look at nothing but the fair head.]

Before purchasing the beast, suggests the author, go all around it, as you would before buying any animal. When you see its hind parts you will know to run from it.

The Seven Sins and their young include all vice, the author states: "I know no sin that may not be connected with one of the seven or their offspring." If in the wilderness through which the anchoresses are walking as pilgrims, they allow themselves to be subdued by these beasts, they will become dead to God and alive to the devil. The author then adopts another metaphoric framework to discuss the effects of the Sins when one succumbs to them. When a man has entered a sinful life, he says, he becomes a servant and companion to the devil: the proud are the devil's trumpeters, the covetous his ashmen, and so on. The glutton is the devil's steward, for he is always in the cellar or the kitchen:

> His heorte is ithe dissches, his thouht is al ithe neppe, his lif ithe tunne, his soule ithe crocke. Kumeth forth bivoren his loverde bismitted and bismeoruwed, a dischs ine his one hond, and a scoale in his other. Matheleth mid wordes ant wigeleth ase

vordrunken mon thet haveth imunt to vallen. Bihalt his greate wombe, ant te veond lauhweth thet he tobersteth.

[His heart is in the dishes, his thought in the cups, his life in the casks, his soul in the crocks. He comes forth before his lord besmutted and besmeared, a dish in one hand, a bowl in the other. He mouths words and totters like a man completely drunk about to fall. Look at his great belly! The devil laughs so that he bursts.]

God's judgement against such a man is "Give the drunkard boiling brass to drink!"

These images of what the soul becomes when it has succumbed to the various sins amount to personifications of the Seven Sins. The animals have previously provided emblems for each of the vices; now individuals are seen, as in Dante's *Inferno*, virtually becoming their sins. Personifications such as these in the *Ancrene Riwle* are grounded in the tradition which provided a basis for Langland's depictions of the Sins. And John Gower in the *Mirour de l'Omme* and Edmund Spenser made even more extensive use of imagery of the Sins such as is found in the *Riwle*. They combined the animal emblems with the personifications by the expedient of having the personified Sins ride in procession astride the emblematic beasts.

After a discussion of the comforts which one is given to counterbalance the pains of temptation, the writer of the *Riwle* comes back to the Sins. He tells how to overcome each of them, citing inspirational examples from Christ's life. Against late sleeping is the example provided by Christ's resurrection early Easter morning; against overeating is the "poure pitaunce" of food He had on the cross: "His pitaunce was but a sponge of gall." Subsequently the writer names the virtues opposed to five of the Seven Sins. That he does not oppose a virtue to each of them is hardly a defect; it simply demonstrates the flexibility with which he deals with all of the conventional materials he employs. He had inherited as models for his treatments of the Sins schemes of animals, of personifications, of inspirational examples from Christ's life, and of the remedial virtues. But he makes an entirely new entity from the old materials, a dissertation rich in aesthetic values which yet serves its didactic purpose at least as well as the wholly functional treatises do. The mirror of sin in the *Ancrene Riwle* is not merely a serviceable encyclopedia, which is about the best one can say for it in the Parson's Tale. In the *Riwle,* and in numerous subsequent works, the treatment of the vices is imbued with literary values.

In narrative works, of course, the tendency is generally toward even greater flexibility in the ordering of materials inherited from expository writings. Such a tendency is notable in Langland's *Piers Plowman.* Scattered throughout *Piers* are many of the materials which one finds in confessional manuals or in handbooks of Archbishop Peckham's six points. In every passus discussions of the sins, the virtues, the various sacraments, and of most aspects of Christian life may arise in connection with the allegory. Langland's coverage of these matters, however, is not systematic as it is in the summas and their direct progeny, nor is it complete. When he paraphrases the Ten Commandments and the Apostles' Creed in Passus V, for instance, some of the Commandments and Articles of the Creed are left out. In the same passus he presents his famous personifications of the sins. He includes all seven, but two—Pride and Lechery—are barely mentioned while the other five are described extensively. In the descriptions, moreoever, the poet does not offer so much an inclusive pictorial analysis as a dramatic representation of one or two characteristic aspects of the sins.

Thus his picture of gluttony primarily illustrates drunkenness; the various abuses in eating are barely hinted at. Shortly after Glutton is introduced, the "gret cherle" is intercepted on his way to Confession by Betty the Brewer. Soon he is at the tavern with Great Oaths and is joined by such regular customers as Wat the Warner, Tom the Tinker with two of his men, Clarice from the red-light district (Cock Lane), and the clerk of the church. After a game of New Fair, all treat Glutton to ale until he has drunk a gallon and a gill. His guts groan like two sows, then he urinates abundantly, makes a foul-smelling trumpet of his "rounde ruwet," and staggers to a door where he stumbles. When Clement the Cobbler tries to pick him up, he vomits in Clement's lap. At last, Glutton's wife and daughter get him home and put him to bed:

> And after al this excesse he had an accidie,
> That he slepe Saterday and Sonday til sonne yede to reste.

> Thanne waked he of his wynkyng and wiped his eyghen;
> The fyrste worde that he warpe was, "Where is the bolle?"
> > B, V, 366–369
> [And after all this excess he had an attack of sloth, so
> that he slept Saturday and Sunday till the sun went down.
> Then he woke from his sleep and wiped his eyes; the first
> word that he spoke was, "Where is the cup?"]

Finally Glutton gets to church, where his confession of eating too much, too early, and overdelicately covers three of Gregory's five points; but Langland is not at pains to include the other two.

The same sin had been a subject in Passus II where gluttony is said to be a part of the marriage portion of Lady Mede and Fraud. The description there has much in common with the later personification:

> Glotonye he gaf hem eke, and grete othes togydere,
> And alday to drynke at dyverse tavernes,
> And there to jangle and to jape and jugge here evene cristene,
> And in fastyng-dayes to frete ar ful tyme were.
> And thanne to sitten and soupen til slepe hem assaille,
> And breden as burgh swyn, and bedden hem esily,
> Til sleuth and slepe slyken his sides;
> And thanne wanhope to awake hym so with no wille to amende.
> > B, II, 92–99
> [He gave them gluttony also, together with great oaths;
> and leave to drink at various taverns all day, and to
> jangle and joke and judge their fellow-Christians there,
> and on fastdays to eat before time; and then to sit and
> sup until sleep overcomes them, and to breed like town
> pigs, and to loaf in bed until sloth and sleep fatten
> their loins; and then despair to awaken them with no
> will to amend.]

The path which leads from gluttony to sloth to despair is a well-worn one in descriptions of the Sins. Langland is as conscious of the traditional materials as are the writers of encyclopedic treatments, but he organizes them differently for a different purpose.

There are several other parts in which gluttony figures in *Piers Plowman.* For instance there is a passage suggesting a conventional remedy for gluttony, temperance (B, VI, 259–269). And Gluttony is again treated together with the other Sins in Passus XIII when Hawkyn the Active Man appears. Each of the Sins is discussed from time to time in the poem in much the same way as Gluttony, so that all in all the passages devoted to the vices in *Piers* are comparable in extent to the treatments in the *Ancrene Riwle,* and even to the Parson's Tale. Though these materials of themselves are fragmentary and are assembled in no consistent manner, they add up virtually to a mirror of vice.

It is not inevitable that treatments of the vices employing narrative will be diffuse or fragmentary. Systematic expositions consisting largely of exemplary stories, for instance, are quite feasible. An important Middle English example of such a work is Robert Mannyng of Brunne's *Handlyng Synne (Handbook of Sin,* 1303), a large portion of which (about 45 per cent) is composed of illustrative *exempla.* Robert's *Handbook* is a free adaptation of the *Manuel des Péchés* of William of Wadington, one of the many works written in French by Englishmen in the Middle English period. Both the *Handbook* and William's *Manuel* are written in short-line couplets, and both show significant affinities to confessional manuals, to the encyclopedias of religious instruction, and to collections of exempla. In design their closest affinity is to confessional manuals, guides to the Sacrament of Penance. They contain discussions, liberally supplemented by supporting stories, of the Ten Commandments, the Seven Deadly Sins, Sacrilege, the Seven Sacraments, and the Ten Points and Eight Graces of Shrift. Though the form of the English work and much of what it says derives from its Anglo-Norman model, Robert at the same time exercises considerable originality, and he forcefully impresses his personality and individuality on the *Handbook.*

In his moral judgements, his pictures of Hell, and particularly in a digression in which he attacks tournaments, minstrels, and miracle plays, Robert shows a puritanical streak comparable to the Parson's. But despite his rigorous standards of behavior, he also evidences in his stories a broad familiarity and sympathy with the people and their customs. In the course of *Handlyng Synne* he inserts sixty-three illustrative stories. None of these is over four-hundred lines in length, and they average less than ninety lines. As may be imagined from such brevity, the narratives are very simple and there is no real character development. Moreover, they are filled with events that seem wildly improbable. Yet in the meager descriptions of people and reports of their behavior the characters come alive. The century-old statement of Robert's editor, F. J. Furnivall, well describes the breadth of observation that is manifested in the work:

> An intimate knowledge of the life of his countrymen is his too: the earl and the knight at their robbery; the lord in his grasping, the rich man in his oaths, his adultery, his gluttony, sloth, and indulgence to his children in their insolent ways; the landowner in his covetousness; the priest with his 'mare' or concubine; the judge and the assizer in their harshness; the lawyer with his wicked counsels; the merchant in his usury; the trader at his tricks; the scold in her household; the flunkey of the time at his riotous supper; the poor in their sufferings; the bearded bucks; the beauties with their saffron wimples and whitened faces, all pass under his review, and none without those individualizing touches that show he had studied from the life. He must have seen the rich man's sluggardry, and heard his yawn, on Sunday mornings, as well as been witness of the shrew's airs and "veyes moy sy" ["look at me"], ere he could have put his sketches on paper. And one can fancy his monk's disgust at hearing men in church chattering, telling tales, asking where they can get the best ale—and thinking what much better fun it would be at the ale-house, or larking with the girls—as well as share his indignation at seeing poor men kept shivering all day in the cold, crying at rich men's gates for alms, or getting them only with beating and abuse.

Robert imparts to nearly all of his stories a characteristic touch. Favorite selections of anthologists are the story about a hermit who is bereft of his sociable and serviceable pet bear by envious monks; another concerning a witch who has a magic cow-milking bag which the bishop cannot make to work because he lacks faith in it; and a third about carolers who dance in the churchyard at Mass time, and end up dancing continuously for a year as punishment.

Though the stories are the more distinctive portion of *Handlyng Synne*, they arise incidentally from the discussions of the various topics. The tale of the hermit and his bear illustrates the sin of envy; the story about the witch arises in the discussion of the first commandment; and the story of the carolers is relevant to sacrilege. Easily the longest section of *Handlyng Synne,* forming almost half of the treatise and located at its very heart, is the discussion with illustrative examples of the Seven Sins. Robert takes them up in the standard order of Pride, Anger, Envy, Sloth, Covetousness, Gluttony, and Lust. He discourses at length on each of them, interspersing twenty-seven stories to illustrate the vices or their remedies. If the logic of his treatments is not always scrupulous, nevertheless what he says is always in some way pertinent to his subject. The discourse on gluttony illustrates his characteristic procedure.

He begins his exposition with a conventional but effective image; he plans to show the species of gluttony, he says, so that none will fall on its grease, for

> Ful many on stumble up and down
> On the greces of syre glotown.
> 6521–6522
> [A great many stumble on the greases of Sir Glutton.]

Before beginning an analysis of the sin, Robert advocates a traditional remedy for gluttony: moderation. He then advises that one shun the undesirable company of excommunicants when eating or drinking; and he warns against leading one's companions to drunkenness. Eventually he arrives at the Gregorian analysis of the sin. He deals with two of Gregory's species before being diverted: do not ask for your food "overtymely" (too early), he advises, and avoid having too many courses, eating "over delysyusly." The idea of such gourmandizing suggests to Robert the Biblical story of Dives and Lazarus, which he recounts colorfully. Then the greed of Dives prompts two stories of generosity, a subject which is somewhat tangential to the main topic of gluttony. The first is of St. John the Almoner who gave to a beggar three times in a day even though he knew the beggar was tricking him. The second is about one of St. John's avaricious subordinate bishops, Bishop Troilus.

Despite Troilus' exotic name, and the setting of the story in the Near East, the Bishop seems every bit the English miser, and his hoarding is appropriately calculated in English pounds. One day, the story goes, Troilus has the misfortune to be with

St. John when his superior has no money and is feeling particularly generous. When John finds out that the Bishop has thirty
pounds with him, he takes it and gives it all away to the poor.
This so offends the soul of Troilus that he takes to his bed,
gravely ill. John intuits the niggardly Bishop's problem, so lest
he die of grief John pays him back the thirty pounds with a
gently ironic nod to his generosity:

> "Thy golde that was to me so redy,
> To me thou lentyst hyt, graunte mercy;
> For y was yn wyl, for the feste,
> That every hadde a peny, who so hadde leste.
> But y myght nat so of myne,
> But y hadde borowed at the of thyne;
> Tho thrytty pounde, God hath me sente,
> And here they are now, thy presente."
>
> 6983–6990

["Your gold that was so available to me, much thanks that
you lent it to me. For I was in the mood for the feast
to wish everyone who desired it to have a penny. But I
couldn't give mine unless I borrowed yours from you.
God has sent me those thirty pounds, and here they are
now, your present."]

With the return of the money, Troilus immediately is cured.
But later he has a dream that makes him repent his stingy
ways. In the dream he sees a wonderful palace of flaming gold,
and over the palace is a sign designating it his. While enraptured he contemplates the beautiful dream palace, however,
his name is erased and John's is substituted, with the new inscription:

> "Rest, and hous, and wonyng,
> Graunteth, and gyveth, hevene kyng,
> To Jhon the patryark so fre,
> Withouten ende in joye to be,
> For thrytty pounde that he boghte,
> And to almes dede hem broghte."
>
> 7051–7056

["Rest, and house, and dwelling, Heaven's king grants and
gives to the very generous Patriarch John, to be in joy
without end. He bought it for thirty pounds, which he
gave as alms."]

Waking from the dream, Troilus recognizes his false values and thenceforward reforms. Nevertheless, says the poet, the Bishop had given up the first palace that God had designed for him (7056–7066). The moral that Robert draws is that "lordynges" should give willingly and without regret to the poor.

The two stories in which St. John the Almoner figures seem more apt to the treatment of avarice than of gluttony; but generosity is one of Robert's favorite themes, and he finds—no doubt rightly—that giving is a good antidote for the greed of gluttony. In any event he continues to talk about generosity subsequently by expatiating on St. Paul's text on charity in I Corinthians. At length he returns to the analysis of gluttony proper, and he deals with the three species defined by St. Gregory which he has not already covered. Do not eat too greedily, "over brennynglye and lustly" (7202–7203), he says; do not eat too often, more than two meals a day; and do not be overparticular about the preparation of the food. Chaucer's portrait of the Franklin is evoked by his description of the lords who are particularly fastidious about their food:

> Anouther vyce is yit to graunte,
> That ryche men mochel haunte,
> That many one are so daungerous,
> And oute of mesure esquaymous,
> That his koke may no day
> Graythe hym hys mete to pay.
>   (7245–7250)
> [Another vice is yet to be taken up, which rich men often have, that many a one is so fastidious, and intemperately delicate, that his cook can never prepare his food to his liking.]

Robert's treatment of gluttony concludes with warnings against dining and drinking late Thursday night into Friday's fasting time, and against eating before Mass on Sunday.

Neither Robert Mannyng's sentiments nor his exemplary narratives are impressive for their artistic sophistication or profundity. He does not deal with his subject matter in a consistently logical manner, and much of what he says is digressive and tangential. Yet Robert unquestionably has the "common touch" which relieves most of his stories and much of his moralizing of the dullness which one associates with moral tracts of the genre of *Handlyng Synne*. The stories in the work are structurally subordinate to the discussions, each depending rather closely on the exposition. But the interest of the narrative insertions imparts considerable prominence to them and suggests that the religious summa or confessional manual can provide a suitable frame for a collection of stories wherein the exposition is secondary. Such is the case with John Gower's *Confessio Amantis (Confession of the Lover)*, in which Venus' priest Genius helps the narrator to examine his conscience systematically. Most of the stories which the priest tells ostensibly exemplify one or another of the Seven Deadly Sins, but as a matter of fact the interest of the narratives overshadows that of the discussion.

Confessio Amantis is an important work in its own right and even more than *Handlyng Synne* it is of interest for its relationship to the *Canterbury Tales*. John Gower was Chaucer's friend and contemporary; clear evidence of their closeness is the dedication to Gower (along with Strode, another of Chaucer's London friends) of *Troilus and Criseyde*. In the 1370's Gower had written the first of his three long poems, the *Mirour de l'Omme,* a work in French modeled in great part on the religious summas; and in the 1380's he had composed the long Latin complaint, *Vox Clamantis*. We will refer to both of these in the discussion of the *Canterbury Tales* in the next chapter. In the 1390's, Chaucer's Canterbury period, Gower worked on his own long poem in English, the *Confessio Amantis*. We may well imagine that the two poets discussed with each other their masterworks. Their poems have in common especially that each is an extensive collection of well-known narratives organized by a frame-story into a single poem. Gower as a matter of fact tells in the *Confessio* some of the stories which Chaucer relates in various works: the tale of Seys and Alcyone, several of the stories found in the *Legend of Good Women,* and three of the *Canterbury Tales:* the Man of Law's Tale, the Manciple's Tale, and the Wife of Bath's Tale. The *Confessio* enjoyed popularity comparable, though not equal, to that of the *Canterbury Tales*; forty manuscripts of it survive as compared with the eighty-four of Chaucer's work.

The Prologue of the *Confessio Amantis* ties in only indirectly with the body of the work; it is a lament for the decay of the times. The eight books which follow the Prologue, comprising more than 32,000 lines, are built around the confession of a lover to a priest of Love. Book I begins with the narrator's professing an inability to deal with the matters broached in the Prologue; rather, he says, he wishes to tell one of his love experiences. Not long ago, it seems, Venus appeared to him in answer to his desperate complaining over his lady's treatment of him. Venus said that before she would assist him he would have to be shriven by her priest Genius. The ensuing confession occupies the bulk of the poem. Genius follows the suggested confessional practice by first reviewing with the lover the temptations of the senses and then the Seven Deadly Sins. The treatment of the senses, however, is brief and truncated, whereas each of the Sins provides the major subject for a book. The Seven Sins, then, essentially. are the frame—the basis for organization—of Gower's work, much as they are for summas of the vices and for substantial parts of the religious manuals and penitential literature which we have been discussing. The review of the Sins depicted by Gower is precisely the procedure envisaged in the handbooks, consisting of the priest's enumeration and analysis of the Sins for the benefit of the penitent.

Given this framework, the confessor's discussion should amount to a summa of sin; this is what in effect the Parson, the writer of the *Ancrene Riwle,* and Robert Mannyng provide. Gower's work, however, only superficially provides such a summa, for the lover is confessing sins against Amour to a priest of Venus, whereas the scheme of the Sins which Genius uses is designed to embrace all offenses against morality. As a result, Genius in his lectures seems unable to settle on a point of view; sometimes he discusses morality, sometimes love, and sometimes politics, providing much material on all three of these topics. But he presents no coherent mirror, and the main purpose which the confessional frame serves is to provide occasion for 141 stories.

The uncertain stance of Genius is well exemplified in the sixth book in which gluttony is the subject. Genius opens the book with the commonplace remark that gluttony, the original

sin of Adam, is the source of all the world's woe. He then states
that he will discuss only two species of the sin, drunkenness and
"delicacy" (savoring too many different dishes). Systematic
inclusiveness is thus impaired. The poet, of course, does not
wish to force too far the practices of love into patterns made for
general vice, and not too many species of gluttony are readily
adaptable to the subject of love. The ensuing discussion deals
first with the problem of alcoholic drunkenness; Genius describes the man who, like Langland's Glutton, wakes up after a
night of mad inebriation calling for the bottle:

> That holde I riht a sori feste,
> Whan he that reson understod
> So soudeinliche is woxe wod,
> Or elles lich the dede man,
> Which nouther go ne speke can.
> Thus ofte he is to bedde broght,
> But where he lith yit wot he noght,
> Til he arise upon the morwe;
> And thanne he seith, "O, which a sorwe
> It is a man be drinkeles!"
>
> VI, 48–57

Genius goes on to apply this alcoholic state to that of
love-drunk lovers, and he asks the narrator if he is capable of
such a sin. The narrator readily confessing that he is, Genius
counsels him against the fault while admitting that he probably
cannot help himself.

Genius uses four stories to illustrate the points about
drunkenness which he has made. A story of Bacchus shows how
prayer helped that god to assuage his thirst and by implication
can help a lover. The tale of the love-potion which Tristan and
Isolde drank exemplifies love-drunkenness. Two other stories, of
the Marriage of Pirithous and of Galba and Vitellius, show the
evil consequences of vinous orgies. As with the lecture that
preceded the stories, on the one hand they are about love and
on the other about morals. The exemplums used subsequently
to illustrate the vice of *delicacy* deal only with the food glutton,
not with the love glutton; one story is the Biblical tale of Dives
and Lazarus, which Robert Mannyng also uses in his discussion
of "overdelicious" eating. The remaining half of Gower's Book

VI is taken up with a digression on witchcraft, which contributes little to the ostensible topics but includes some interesting tales.

Gower's stories, drawn mostly from classical sources, are presented in octosyllabic couplets in a forthright and appealing
narrative style. The fact that the stories in themselves are the
chief merit of the *Confessio Amantis* places the work in contrast to
both *Handlyng Synne* and the *Canterbury Tales*. Robert Mannyng's
stories, however charming and loaded with social perception, in
general do not compare in quality with the educated Gower's
masterly "plain style," but his work as a whole possesses an intrinsic unity which the *Confessio* does not have. The section of
the *Handbook* on the vices, inclusive and systematic, makes up a
coherent mirror of one aspect of existence. The mirrors which
the *Confessio Amantis* pretends to, on the other hand, are unor-
ganized and fragmentary. The poem is not a summa of love, for
the framework it uses was made to classify moral vice and only
imperfectly accomodates itself to the subject of love. It is not a
summa of moral vice, for the narrator is confessing his amorous
faults. It actually comes nearest to being a *mirror for princes,* a
kind of treatise in which neither the subject of love nor the Seven
Sins is central. In its other less prominent dimension, as an Allegory of Reason, the *Confessio* makes a more satisfactory whole,
as Russell Peck's Introduction to the work suggests (See Bibliographical Note).

The organizing concept of the *Canterbury Tales,* to be discussed
in the next chapter, likewise suits the subject much better
than that used in the *Confessio.* Chaucer's unifying principle is
not of course the Seven Deadly Sins as some in the past
claimed; it is rather a scheme of social organization which is
clearly related to the tradition of the Three Estates. But this
unifying principle is like the Seven Sins, Peckham's points, the
Four Ages of history and all such encyclopedic schemata in that
it provides a method for dealing with the whole of one aspect of
existence. Chaucer's work, then, like works studied in this chapter, shows how the strong encyclopedic tendencies of medieval
writers were an important source of form and inspiration for
works of appreciable literary value. The writer of the *Ancrene
Riwle* demonstrates that stylistic grace, easy humor, and human

sympathy can inform a treatise with such origins; Robert Mannyng imparts his common touch to another, giving it life and
immediacy; and Gower uses the scheme of the sins in a third
work to display his substantial narrative talent. Chaucer's *Canterbury Tales*, like these, uses a form that is related to didactic
summas, and he makes of it the most important and the most
formally sophisticated of the English literary mirrors.

NOTE TO CHAPTER VI

(The main bibliographical listings for Chaucer's works and for *Piers Plowman* are found in the Note to Chapter II.)

Editions and Translations

Ancrene Riwle. James Morton, ed. *The Ancren Riwle* (Camden Society, 1853), prints the only full edition with variants and glossary to date; it includes a translation into Modern English on facing pages. A more available and accurate edition of Ms. Cotton Nero A xiv, which provides the basis for Morton's text, is that of Mabel Day, *The English Text of the Ancrene Riwle*, EETS 225 (1955). M. B. Salu, *The Ancrene Riwle* (1955), presents a good recent translation; in the Introduction Gerard Sitwell discusses the relationship of the *Riwle* to penitential literature.

Handlyng Synne. F. J. Furnivall's introduction to this treatise, from which I have quoted, is contained in the scarce Roxburghe Club edition (1862). The text alone from Furnivall's edition was later published as *Robert of Brunne's Handlyng Synne*, EETS 119 and 123 (1901–1903); this includes substantial parts of William of Wadington's *Manuel des Péchés* in columns parallel to the English text.

Confessio Amantis. The standard edition of Gower's works—including the French and Latin—is *The Complete Works of John Gower*, ed. G. C. Macaulay, four volumes (1899–1902). An abridged edition of *Confessio Amantis* with a useful introduction has been edited by Russell Peck (1968), and an abridged translation made by Terence Tiller (1963).

The Seven Deadly Sins, Manuals, Mirrors, Exemplums

The authoritative treatment of the seven vices is Morton W. Bloomfield, *The Seven Deadly Sins* (1952). Two recent studies by Siegfried Wenzel have significantly furthered scholarship on the subject: *The Sin of Sloth* (1967), and "The Seven Deadly Sins: Some Problems of Research," *Speculum*, 43 (1968), 1–22. The iconography is dealt with by Adolf Katzenellenbogen, *Allegories of the Virtues and Vices in Medieval Art* (1939).

The religious treatises which proliferated in England in the thirteenth and fourteenth centuries are conveniently discussed and classified by Homer G. Pfander, "Some Medieval Manuals of Religious Instruction in England and Observations on Chaucer's Parson's Tale," *JEGP*, 35 (1936), 243–259. A number of "Manuals for Parish Priests" from Chaucer's century are surveyed by W. A. Pantin, *The English Church in the Fourteenth Century* (1955), pp. 189–218. E. J. Arnould, *Le Manuel des Péchés* (1940), places William of Wadington's work in the context of English religious literature; see Chapter I especially. D. W. Robertson, "The *Manuel des Péchés* and an English Episcopal Decree," *MLN,* 60 (1945), 439–447, shows more explicitly the filiation of the *Manuel* with episcopal activity.

Sister Ritamary Bradley explores the literary tradition of the mirror in two articles: "Backgrounds of the Title *Speculum* in Medieval Literature," *Speculum,* 29 (1954), 110–115; and "The Wife of Bath's Tale and the Mirror Tradition," *JEGP,* 55 (1956), 624–630. Émile Mâle associates the Gothic cathedral with encyclopedic mirrors, particularly Vincent of Beauvais' *Speculums,* in his *Religious Art of the Thirteenth Century* (also entitled *The Gothic Image*). The diverse uses of the reflecting mirror in art throughout history are surveyed and liberally illustrated in G. F. Hartlaub, *Zauber des Spiegels: Geschichte und Bedeutung des Spiegels in der Kunst* (1951).

A standard study of the development and use of the exemplum in English Literature is Joseph A. Mosher, *The Exemplum in the Early Religious and Didactic Literature in England* (1911). See also the chapter on exemplums in Arnould's *Manuel des Péchés,* pp. 107–184.

Criticism of Individual Works

The origins of the Parson's Tale is the subject of Kate O. Petersen's *The Sources of the Parson's Tale* (1901), and of Germaine Dempster's article in *Sources and Analogues of Chaucer's Canterbury Tales* (1941), pp. 723–760. For a general survey of related literature see Pfander's article.

The excellence of the *Ancrene Riwle's* prose style has been generally recognized, most notably in R. W. Chambers, *On the Continuity of English Prose from Alfred to More and His School,* EETS 191a (1932). Chambers' view of the historical development of the style, however, is disputed; see J. A. W. Bennett and G. V. Smithers, *Early Middle English Verse and Prose,* pp. 223–224. D. W. Robertson shows the close relationship of Robert Mannyng's *Handlyng Synne* to confessional manuals in "The Cultural Tradition of *Handlyng Synne,*" *Speculum,* 22 (1947), 162–185. On the *Manuel des Péchés,* Robert's primary source, see studies by Arnould and Robertson referred to above.

John Fisher, *John Gower: Moral Philosopher and Friend of Chaucer* (1964), is the standard treatment of the poet and his works; Mr. Fisher in particular explores the various literary relationships of Gower's works. R. Elfreda Fowler, *Une Source française des poèmes de Gower* (1905), studies at length the relationships of Gower's poems to penitential literature, especially to Friar Lorens' *Somme le Roi* and its tradition; for a caveat to her conclusions see Fisher, p. 140. An important appreciation of the *Confessio Amantis* is contained in C. S. Lewis, *The Allegory of Love,* pp. 198–222.

Chapter VII

The Mirror of Society:
Chaucer's CANTERBURY TALES

Important Works: *Mirour de l'Omme, Sir Pride the Emperor, The Twelve Estates, Dance Macabre,* General Prologue, Shipman's Tale, Summoner's Tale.

The stories in Chaucer's *Canterbury Tales* would glitter in any setting, or without a setting. Indeed, some were composed as separate works before Chaucer conceived the pilgrimage frame. Yet the individual brilliance and self-sufficiency of the stories does not, as one might fear, fragment the Tales; rather, unity and integration of its disparate elements mark the work. This unity and integration is far more profound that that of the works with which the Tales is most often compared, going quite beyond the dramatic unity of Boccaccio's *Decameron,* Sercambi's *Novelle,* and the *Arabian Nights;* and beyond the thematic unity of Chaucer's own *Legend of Good Women* and Monk's Tale and of collections of religious stories like Gautier de Coincy's *Miracles of Our Lady* or the *Golden Legend* of Jacobus de Voragine. Drama and theme certainly contribute importantly to the unity which Chaucer achieves, but these subserve the organizing concept, which is at base that of the summa or mirror. The *Canterbury Tales* is a Mirror of Society. The very center of the work, its keystone, is the General Prologue. The Prologue serves like any other introduction to a series of tales to initiate the narration of the stories, and it serves also through its collection of portraits to introduce and describe the characters who tell the stories and participate in the drama which links them. Its first function,

that of setting the storytelling in motion, is a more or less mechanical one which Chaucer accomplishes with economy and
some admirable poetry. In this aspect the Prologue is allied
with the introductions to the *Decameron* or the *Legend of Good
Women*. The second function, that of presenting the characters
in twenty-one rich sketches, is of more fundamental importance.
These portraits take up the bulk of the Prologue and provide
the basis for the unity of the Tales and for the essential distinction of this work from all other series of narratives.

The Prioress (courtly lady, nun, unmarried) and the Wife of Bath
(bourgeoise, secular, matron) divide the World of Women in the General Prologue. Ellesmere Ms. By permission of the Huntington Library.

Chaucer's portraits are often admired for their realism; this
realism is perhaps more apparent than actual. One way in
which the group of pilgrims clearly defies realistic expectations
is in its total composition. In any group of thirty or so people
who get together for a pilgrimage one would surely expect a
similarity rather than a diversity of occupations and ways of
life. Yet here is a company in which we have conveniently one
of each: one lawyer, one doctor, one merchant, one knight, and

so on. As a matter of fact analysis shows that almost every substantial segment of the populace is represented. Manifestly, this is no accident. The composition of the group betrays Chaucer's intention of mirroring society. The portraits make up the central section of the mirror. The other parts of the *Canterbury Tales* all operate to enlarge this mirror.

For his division of society and many of his character sketches Chaucer was working with traditional materials which may be grouped together under the label "estates literature." As the medieval way of surveying all of vice was through a consideration of the Seven Deadly Sins and their offspring, so the conventional way of dealing with all of society was through a treatment of the Three Estates and their subdivisions. The First Estate is made up of the clergy, led by the pope and including all classes of ecclesiastical personages; the Second Estate is composed of rulers and warriors, most typically of kings and knights; the Third Estate as originally conceived was typified particularly by the peasants, but it came to comprehend all men outside the nobility and clergy—landowner, merchant, peasant, and physician.

The concept of the estates of society is very often used in complaints in medieval literature, particularly in complaints about the decline of the world from an assumed former goodness. In order to show the falling off, the author enumerates the various estates, their subclasses, and their appropriate functions; then he laments in detail the depraved condition of each class. The members of the classes are said either to be lax in their duties or to be disrupting natural order by trying to change their ordained stations in life.

Through the fourteenth century the theme of the estates was much more popular in French and Latin literature than in English. Even the English Gower, while using the theme for the basic organization of his French *Mirour de l'Omme* and Latin *Vox Clamantis,* treats it very cursorily in the English *Confessio Amantis.* In the *Mirour de l'Omme (Mirror of Man),* about 8,000 of 31,000 lines are devoted to a systematic condemnation of the estates. Most of the remainder of the poem is taken up with descriptions of the Seven Deadly Sins with their offspring and of seven offsetting virtues with their progeny. A thread of narrative, accounting for the origin of the vices and virtues and for the corruption of every class by the vices, holds together these summas of vice, virtue, and the estates. Such an alliance of the theme of the Seven Sins with that of the estates was fairly common; oftentimes particular sins were associated with individual classes, as pride and gluttony with the clergy. In this French work of Gower, however, all sins afflict all groups. In his extensive analysis of the estates Gower talks about the various groups of the clergy, beginning with popes and cardinals; he then considers rulers, such as kings and knights; and finally he deals with representatives of the great Third Estate, like lawyers, judges, merchants, artisans, tavern-keepers, bakers, and laborers.

Gower's analysis of the decadence of monks in the *Mirour* (20833–21180) exemplifies his portrayals. He discusses at length the gluttony and envy of monks, then talks particularly about monastic outriders, who take care of the monastery's business with the world. For Gower, as for most estates analysts, "That monk is not a good cloisterer who is made guardian or steward of any outside office. For then he needs saddle and horse to ride over the countryside" (20953–20957). He becomes lordly and greedy, the poet continues, and "Saint Bernard tells us that it is an evil thing to see a steward under a monk's habit" (20974–20976). As in all complaints about the decline of the estates, the ideal which was once realized is contrasted with the actual: "Jerome tells us that the dirt which the monk has in his clothing is an exterior sign that he is without pride and intemperance, and of the cleanness in his heart within, which is white and pure. But our monk at the present day seeks lovely attire for his body and disfigures his soul. Although he wears the frock of sorrow, he has above it the furred cloak of vain honor" (20989–21000).

As he continues, Gower develops further the contrast between the monastic ideal and the reality. Monks of the former time made no woman pregnant, "envy was abolished among them, no prideful offense was in them, silence was not broken by them, no complaint was made in their chapter halls; rather sobriety and continence in unity and patience with powerful charity governed their consciences. Each was respectful of the other and served God in holy life" (21121–21132). Now all of that is changed: "Sir Charity no longer has a refuge, for Sir Envy has killed him, and Sir Hate has usurped and forbidden that Sir Unity should ever come there. Sir Patience is enraged; Sir Obedience is gone whom Sir Pride has taken from us; Sir Murmur has secretly installed Sir Slander who has confounded almost all the order" (21133–21144). The description concludes with an enumeration of the vices which rule in the monastery: Gluttony, Sloth, Vainglory, and Avarice. "Thus Sir Conscience is inactive who used to guard the convent" (21179–21180).

Gower's *Vox Clamantis (Voice of One Crying)*, his long Latin poem composed after the Peasants' Revolt in 1381, is largely a systematic series of complaints presented against the Three Estates. The treatment of them is similar to that in the *Mirour de l'Omme*. Somewhat different approaches to a survey of the estates are exemplified in three shorter works which we will discuss: *Sir Pride the Emperor* and Deschamps' *Lay of the Twelve Estates*, both French, and Lydgate's English *Dance Macabre*.

Sir Pride the Emperor, from the early fourteenth century, is the story of the coronation of Pride as emperor of all the world. Pride derives his support from each segment of society; he sends them instructions on how to behave and they all accord. He writes in turn to pope, king, judges, count, bailiffs, prelates, vavasours (landowners), squires, gentleladies, secular chaplains, ordered religious, farmers, married women, and men of the court. To monks and friars Sir Pride writes in part: "You used to abandon for the love of God your own wills and earthly honor. Now I ask you, for my love, to seek honor. You who have plenty of possessions, do as the rich do." Have nothing to do with the life of Saint Benedict, Saint Dominic, or Saint Francis, he continues, you who are their successors. "Those who are not taken up with care of property may please me in other ways, some by disobedience, others with their learning, others with their singing, others by strong oaths." Again the contrast of the former right customs to the present debased practices is pointed up.

Eustache Deschamps was one of the three contemporary French poets from whose works Chaucer borrowed extensively. His *Lay of the Twelve Estates* sets forth in a variation on the or-

thodox classification a twelvefold division of society, consisting
of the three traditional classes—clerk, knight, and laborer—plus
nine others—judge, artisan, merchant, host, lawyer, notary, physician, priest, and king. He enumerates the duties of the twelve:
the knights should defend the people, the laborers work with
their hands to pay their masters, the clerks teach, the hosts take
care of wayfarers, and so forth. Deschamps finds all of these
classes remiss in their duties, particularly the knights who are
not protecting the people from robbers and marauders. It was
not so in days gone by, says the poet: "The worthies did otherwise, and they have for their deeds perpetual renown, for all
their efforts promoted the virtues. They were not children of the
vices. They wished to make evil suffer and they punished it severely. For this reason they had great power. The world should
heavily lament their passing" (248–258).

An alliance of the theme of the estates with the popular
Dance of Death motif is found in John Lydgate's *Dance Macabre*
(c. 1425), which he adapted from a French original. The Dance
of Death when pictorially portrayed commonly shows a skeletal
Death leading a great chain of dancers, people of all classes and
occupations, across a countryside. The obvious moral of such
depictions is that all mortals are engaged in Death's dance, and
therefore they should have in mind the end of life. As Lydgate
says of his poem,

> In this *mirrour* every wight may finde
> That him bihoveth to goo upon this daunce.
>
> 49–50

The poem consists for the most part of one-stanza speeches by
Death to each of thirty-five people, representing as many walks
of life, and their one-stanza replies. The pope, who is at the
head of the dance, is addressed first; those who follow include
king, abbot, abbess, monk, friar, usurer, physician, squire, gentlewoman, man of law, juggler, laborer, clerk, child, and hermit.

Lydgate's Death is no vitriolic prosecutor of the people whom
he accosts, and Lydgate's poem no lament for the decline of the
estates. Though oftentimes the faults most natural to the individual classes are mentioned, the focus is on the inevitability

of death. Death's address to the monk and the monk's reply are fairly typical:

> *Deeth to the Monke:*
> "Sir monke also with your blak habite
> Ye may no lenger holde here sojour.
> Ther is no thing that may yow here respite
> Ayein my myght yow for to socour.
> Ye mote acounte touching youre labour
> Howe ye have spent it in dede, worde, and thought.
> To erthe and asshes turneth every flour,
> The life of man is but a thing of nought."
> *The Monke answerith:*
> "I hadde levere in the cloistre be
> At my book and studie my service
> Wiche is a place contemplatif to se.
> But I have spent my life in many vice
> Liche as a fool dissolut and nyce.
> God of his mercy graunt me repentance.
> By chere outwards harde is to device;
> Alle be not mery wich that men se daunce."
>
> 377–392

Here the monk, who essentially likes the life of the cloister (in contrast to Chaucer's Monk), admits and repents his faults. In many of the speeches in the poem, such as those of the friar and the child, there is no indication of sinfulness.

In estates literature as it developed it was common to include representative women. Three women participate in the *Dance Macabre:* a lady of great estate, an abbess, and a "gentil womman amerous." All three of these women incline to worldliness. The abbess has luxuriated in physical comforts like fine-furred mantles and soft beds; the lady and the gentlewoman have specialized in coquetry. The gentlewoman laments pitifully:

> O cruel deeth that sparest none estate,
> To old and yonge thou are indifferent.
> To my bewte thou hast yseide chekmate,
> So hasty is thi mortal jugement.
> For in my youthe this was myn entent,
> To my service many a man to have lured.

But she is a fool shortly in sentement
That in hir bewte is to moche assurid.

457–464

Other subclasses of women which appear in estates literature are those of the unmarried maiden, the matron, and the bourgeoise.

In the estates poems that we have considered, three kinds of characterization are at least implicit. Two of these three appear in compliants like Gower's *Mirour, Sir Pride the Emperor,* and Deschamps' *Lay:* first, characters are alluded to who represent the ideal which formerly prevailed in the various estates, like the monks who practiced obedience and poverty; second, present-day figures are shown who have debased the ideal. The third type appears in Lydgate's *Dance Macabre,* where most of the characters neither represent ideals nor are notably perverse debasements of the ideals; they are rather typical figures who possess the skills and faults natural to their ways of life. The three kinds of character and alloys of these kinds—the ideal, the debasement, and the type—appear in Chaucer's General Prologue and throughout the *Canterbury Tales.* Ideal characters coexist with perversely debased persons and with occupational types who are not measured importantly on a moral yardstick.

In the *Tales* the Knight, the Clerk, the Parson, and the Plowman clearly embody ethical perfection in the fulfillment of their duties to society. The Knight, as he should, loves chivalry and is notably successful in his lord's holy wars. The Clerk, in conformity with the proper practice of his calling, gladly learns and gladly teaches. The Parson gives the noble example to his sheep "That first he wroghte, and afterward he taughte" (A, 496–497). His brother the Plowman loves God, assists his neighbor without fee, and pays his tithes willingly. It is interesting that these four figures are the most common literary representatives of the Three Estates: the knight of the nobility, the scholar and the parish priest of the clergy, and the plowman of the laborers.

Other characters on the pilgrimage, by contrast, are exactly what they should not be. Balancing the idealized Parson and Clerk are four churchmen who are diametrical opposites of the ideal: Monk, Friar, Summoner, and Pardoner. On the other hand, though bad knights and bad kings show up in some of the Tales, no debased representative of the Second Estate appears among the pilgrims. In the estate of the commons, the Miller, the Reeve, and the Manciple are to a great extent models of dishonesty in their respective trades.

The remainder of the pilgrims described, though some have been the subject of damning critical analysis, are not definitive examples of improper ethical practices. The burden of their portraits does not call for emphatic condemnation. Though the Shipman cruelly sends home his foes by water and is a thief, his description focusses on his excellent seamanship. In the same way the portrait of the Physician emphasizes his knowledge of his profession rather than his profitable alliance with the pharmacist. And while the Franklin in being overparticular about his "poynaunt sauce" is like Robert Mannyng's gluttonous landowner, his description does not amount to a personification of gluttony. The interest in these men centers on matters that tend to be ethically neutral, much as with the persons portrayed in Lydgate's *Dance Macabre*. Chaucer does not seek with his sketches outright condemnation of the Shipman, Physician, and Franklin, as he seeks condemnation of the Friar and the Monk, but rather he aims to display their typical ways of life. Descriptions of this general variety are also accorded the Squire, Prioress, Merchant, Yeoman, Man of Law, Guildsmen, Cook, and Wife of Bath.

Two of the most interesting portraits of this last sort are those of the Prioress and the Wife of Bath, archetypes, if not ideals in the ordinary sense, of the female. Between them they divide the estate of women: the Prioress is unmarried maiden, gentlewoman, and lady of religion; the Wife is matron, bourgeoise, and woman of the world.

In the General Prologue one is hardly invited to judge the Prioress for her religious practices. Her government of her convent, and her regularity and piety in religious devotions are not mentioned. If her keeping pet dogs and her presence on the pilgrimage indicate an incomplete adherence to the rules, at the same time her mild manner of speaking and properly maintained costume betray no rebel. Actually, the dogs, her dress, and her way of speaking do not function primarily as commentary on her religious habits; they rather point up secular characteristics of the Prioress.

She displays the traits and foibles of both the gentlewoman and the "maiden-lady." Although from the provinces, she imagines herself a lady of high courtly fashion; and although mature (or perhaps because she is mature), she displays the ultrafemininity of the unmarried belle. Both the courtliness and the femininity emerge in her simple smile, the mild exclamations, and the romance-heroine name, Eglentyne. In her nasal singing, pseudo-mastery of French, and delicate table manners she evokes the girl from a finishing school displaying her accomplishments. At the same time her demeanor is that of the serene great lady:

> And sikerly she was of greet desport,
> And ful plesaunt, and amyable of port,
> And peyned hire to countrefete cheere
> Of court, and to been estatlich of manere,
> And to ben holden digne of reverence.
>
> A, 137–141

Both the girl and the old maid in her weep for the trapped mouse and the whipped dogs. Her features and dress are the courtly lady's: straight nose, gray eyes, soft red mouth, broad forehead, carefully pinched wimple, ornate beads of coral and green, and a gold brooch. The focus is on the decorativeness, not the religious implications of the beads, and on the polite tenor as much as the ambiguous content of the motto on the brooch: *Amor vincit omnia.*

Such is the middle-aged courtly maiden whom the Host addresses with such elaborate politeness:

> "My lady Prioresse, by youre leve,
> So that I wiste I sholde yow nat greve,
> I wolde demen that ye tellen sholde
> A tale next, if so were that ye wolde.
> Now wol ye vouche sauf, my lady deere?"
>
> B, 1637–1641

The Host treats the Prioress as the grand lady she strives to appear. When she tells her tale, however, we finally see her in the aspect of woman of religion. And on the evidence of her lyrically pious prologue and her impeccably narrated, if naïve, Miracle of the Virgin, she fills that role quite satisfactorily.

The other half of the female world is amply represented in the General Prologue by the "archwife," the Wife of Bath. It has been said that because she seizes the reins of marriage in her own hands she is an exemplar of the bad wife. However, it is not she who is primarily at fault for this, but rather her delinquent husbands who resign control to her. In medieval terms, if the soul fails to govern the body, the body will tend to follow its natural—often wrong in the larger context, but not unnatural—impulses; likewise, if the husband fails to rule the wife, she will probably act in the willful and physically oriented ways regarded as natural to woman. If the Wife of Bath is fearsome, then so are all matrons *in potentia*; her vices arise from wifeliness unrestrained by her husbands.

The Wife's surpassing skill at clothmaking is a symbol of her sex and station, weaving being the original occupation of wives. As the couplet of medieval levellers has it,

> When Adam delved and *Eve span,*
> Who was then the gentleman?

Her insistent precedence in making her offering in church, the ten-pound hat, and the bold red face all typify her aggressiveness, the female aggressiveness of a mother sow with a litter. Her outliving five husbands exemplifies woman's stubborn endurance, attested to today by insurance statistics. The love of pilgrimages and ability to "laughe and carpe" in fellowship (A, 474) show the easy gregariousness which enable the Wife to provide herself with numerous husbands (not to mention her youthful company). Once she becomes acquainted with a man, she can, in furtherance of her wifely calling, lead him knowledgeably along the paths of love:

> Of remedies of love she knew per chaunce,
> For she koude of that art the olde daunce.
> A, 475–476

The Wife's prologue, her exchanges with the Pardoner and Friar, and her Tale develop a characterization quite consistent with the portrait in the General Prologue. In combination these present a most impressive figure; it is awesome and chastening to recognize in it the eternal wife, undominated and perhaps indomitable.

There can be no doubt that the Clerk's primary reference is to the Wife of Bath when following his tale he addresses "Ye archewives" (E, 1195). And the very label *archwife* indicates the nature of the typal characterizations in the Prologue. The Physician is an arch-physician, the Shipman an arch-sailor, and the Man of Law an arch-lawyer. All of these characters draw the reader's interest because of their full-blooded fulfillment of the types they represent.

The General Prologue is the basis of Chaucer's mirror of society. He builds on this basis in several ways in the ensuing storytelling. In the first place, he adds characterizations of figures who already belong to the pilgrimage or who become part of it. An alchemist and his assistant, in the persons of the Canon and Canon's Yeoman, join the group riding to Canterbury and are depicted by means of the Yeoman's lengthy prologue and revelatory story. The Nun's Priest, the chaplain to the Prioress who is dismissed in a half line in the General Prologue, is portrayed through the Host's banter and his own clever tale of "a cok and hen." The Second Nun is also only a shadow until she reveals her pious and self-effacing personality, especially suitable to a subordinate nun, in her prologue and tale. And the Host, a representative of the important class of inn-keepers, is characterized mostly through his participation in the drama of the pilgrimage.

A second method of broadening the picture of society is through introduction and characterization of additional ranks and segments of society within the various tales. Rulers, the one large element in traditional divisions of estates which is neglected in the General Prologue, are well represented in numerous stories featuring emperors, kings, dukes, popes, and bishops. Other subclasses which gain recognition through characterization in the stories include the apprentice in the Cook's fragment, the widow in the Nun's Priest's Tale, the scholar-magician in the Franklin's Tale, the judge in the Physician's Tale, and the schoolchild in the Prioress's Tale.

But the most important way in which Chaucer enlarges his mirror of society after the General Prologue is through further development of the characters he has already portrayed. For the subjects of his portraits he carefully chose representatives of broad and significant segments of society, and development of these provides an excellent way to extend and animate the mirror. Almost all of the characters portrayed in the Prologue participate and speak revealingly in the links between the tales and characterize themselves in the kind of stories they tell and the way they tell them; and several of them in addition have counterparts in the casts of the Tales. I have discussed somewhat cursorily the Wife of Bath and the Prioress as portrayed in Prologue, link, and Tale. A study in more detail of the figure of the Monk in the whole of the *Canterbury Tales* will point up the several methods by which Chaucer achieved his full characterizations.

The Monk is part of Chaucer's mirror of the First Estate, the Church. Though the fragmentary nature of the *Canterbury Tales* is apparent from the incompleteness of some of the Tales, the lack of many links, and the severe reduction in the number of stories from the proposed scheme, the image of the Church which is presented is remarkably well filled out. Of the twenty-one character sketches in the General Prologue, the six longest are of churchpeople: Friar, Parson, Prioress, Summoner, Pardoner, and Monk. Also notable, though shorter, is the Clerk's portrait. These seven clerics are all prominent in the byplay between the tales; each of them has a prologue which fits admirably into the dramatic scheme of the Tales; and each tells a story well suited to his own personality and to the situation.

Through the development of these characters Chaucer presents a mirror of the Church of his day. Intramural events of the Church do not appear beyond passing glimpses of cell, convent, and chapter. Rather, the ecclesiastics are integrated into, and often dominate, the image of society which the Tales present. The Pardoner sells his indulgences and relics, the Summoner serves his papers, the begging Friar roams his territory, the Clerk reads and teaches, the Monk rides out on the abbey's and his own affairs, and the parish Priest walks through the mire to his parishioners. Their customary appearance and behavior are described in the General Prologue; these are given immediacy in their performances in the links and as storytellers; and in three notable cases the characterizations of churchmen are elaborated in the tales told by other pilgrims: the Summoner has a recognizable counterpart in the Friar's Tale, the Friar in the Summoner's Tale, and the Monk in the Shipman's Tale.

As in estates literature generally, the Monk in Chaucer's analysis of the Church is a very important figure. By Chaucer's time Christian monasteries had existed for more than a millennium, and they were populous, rich, and powerful. In theory the life of study and contemplation which they offered was the closest approach one could make on earth to heavenly existence. When one entered the monastery he was choosing Mary's part, the better part, over Martha's—choosing the contemplative over the active life. Having vowed poverty, the Monk presumably would live on the simplest fare and wear a rough-spun garment; he would properly prize not even the comfort of cleanliness. His activities in the monastery would conduce to contemplation; he would study, observe silence except for limited intervals, pray regularly and frequently in the chapel with his fellows, and always strive to direct his mind toward God. In accordance with his vow of obedience he should docilely follow the rule of his order and commands of his superiors. His third vow, of chastity, would normally present little problem so long as he stayed within the monastery, where young women were not allowed.

Part of the reason for the rise and success of the fraternal orders in the early thirteenth century was the decadence of monastic practices. The acquisition of tremendous riches in the course of centuries had led to widespread corruption. The living conditions became too comfortable, the food too good, the need for productive work too small; perhaps worst of all many of the members had to spend time outside the cloisters taking care of the property and business of their orders. The life of monks outside the monastery inevitably would be secular, a life which would deny the monastic ideal. Thus the monks who were "out-

riders" were objects of particular complaint in estates literature, as we have noted in discussing Gower's *Mirour de l'Omme.*

The qualities of Chaucer's Monk enumerated in the "General
Prologue" are diametrically opposed to those of the ideal monk.
An outrider by occupation and a hunter by avocation, he scoffs
at monastic rules:

> He yaf nat of that text a pulled hen,
> That seith that hunters ben nat hooly men,
> Ne that a monk, whan he is recchelees,
> Is likned til a fisshe that is waterlees,—
> This is to seyn, a monk out of his cloystre.
>
> A, 177–181

The old precepts of Saint Maurus and Saint Benedict which
govern his monastery he thinks old-fashioned. Nor does he believe in wasting his time reading or in working with his hands,
the two occupations most closely identified with monkhood.
Rather than the traditional coarse-woven and grimy robe, he
wears a hood trimmed with fur and an elaborate gold pin (A,
193–196). He is prosperously fat, an admirer of hearty, expen-
sive foods: "A fat swan loved he best of any roost" (A, 206).
No gruel for this proud cleric.

The Monk superficially seems not as objectionable as Friar
Hubert, who is by his contiguous portrait set over against him
in the General Prologue. The Friar's apparently is a much more
virulent venality than the Monk's: by being an easy confessor of
the wealthy, Hubert undermines the parish priest's position and
lines his own pockets; in order to consort with fine folk he ig-
nores the needy; he frequents taverns and corrupts young wom-
en and housewives; and while dressed richly shamelessly begs
from indigent widows. As he shows in his exchange with the
Summoner furthermore, underlying his gentle demeanor is a
nasty and vicious temper. Yet the Monk, for all his apparent
harmlessness in a social sense, merits as low a circle in Hell as
the Friar. For the corrupt activities of the Friar, the Monk
substitutes an indifference to God and man; he has an
imbruted soul.

The Monk's imbrutement and his direct opposition to the
ideal monk, strongly indicated in the portrait, are firmly

verified in the course of the storytelling. We are afforded additional insight into his character in three places: in the links before and after his tale, where the Host and the Knight have revealing exchanges with him; in the series of dull tragedies which he narrates, thereby displaying his shallowness of intellect; and in the Shipman's Tale where Don John the monk acts in ways quite consistent with, and revelatory of, the personality of his pilgrim counterpart.

Despite the fact that no exact equation can be made between the pilgrim Monk and the Shipman's Don John, the latter characterization is quite important in displaying social aspects of the pilgrim. Whether or not characters in the tales are identical with those participating in the pilgrimage is of little significance; in fact, no character in a story can be the same as a person outside a story. It *is* significant that the figures of friar, summoner, miller, and carpenter in various tales are similar enough to pilgrim counterparts to make identification natural. The stories, as a result, make de facto contributions to the characterizations.

Various animosities account for the appearance of stand-ins for the Miller, Reeve, Friar, and Summoner in the tales of their adversaries. The Miller is the natural and particular enemy of the Reeve, as is the Friar of the Summoner. No malicious intention to portray an enemy unfavorably, however, is to be found in the depiction of the Monk in the Shipman's Tale, for the Shipman is given no motive for attacking his fellow pilgrim. Internal evidence, however, strongly favors the association. While it is true that Don John of the Shipman's Tale unlike the pilgrim Monk is a Frenchman, and at age thirty seems somewhat younger than his bald counterpart, they nevertheless have much in common. Both monks are outriders for their abbeys, and Don John's customary gifts of wildfowl (B, 1262) and his use of hunting metaphor (B, 1294–1295) indicate that he shares with the pilgrim a fondness for hunting. Both pursue the chase indoors, too; Don John is obviously a lecher, and the pilgrim's delight in "venery" and "dainty horses" proclaimed in the General Prologue suggests by word-play that he does not always hunt in the woods.

The monks in and out of the tale, furthermore, are handsome

and well-groomed men. The Shipman emphasizes the "fair" face of his monk (B, 1215, 1218), while the Host eulogizes the "ful fair skin" and fine body of the pilgrim, who ought to have been a "tredefowel" (B, 3125–3135). Don John's consciousness and care for his appearance are evidenced by his special barbering for the tryst with the merchant's wife (B, 1499), even as fur-trimmed sleeves show the vanity of the pilgrim. The monks likewise have superficially amiable personalities. When the Host teases the pilgrim he takes "al in pacience" (B, 3155), and he promises to do "al his diligence/ As fer as sowneth into honestee" (B, 3156–3157) to tell his Tale. In the Shipman's Tale Don John not only ingratiates himself with the merchant and his wife, but he also makes himself so popular with the household that they are as glad to see him come as a bird is glad to see the sun rise (B, 1241). But beneath the surface amiability of both figures is an egotism which manifests itself in smug insensitivity to God, friend, and lady-love.

As the Monk is contemptuous of the Benedictine Rule and of Augustine's counsel to monks to work, so Don John spends little time in his cell, preferring the good life, and is sacrilegious in his flaunting of religious propriety. He mixes conversation leading to an assignation with the merchant's wife with the reading of his office. Both he and the wife swear an impure secrecy on his breviary. He pledges to her by God, St. Martin, and St. Denis that his vow of friendship to the merchant is simply a matter of expediency; in other words he swears to the falsity of his oath. Finally, both he and the lady consummate their adulterous plans on a Sunday, the Lord's day.

The arrogance of both monks in ignoring ordinary religious decorum is complemented by their evident feeling that they possess virility superior to that of married men, a feeling both inappropriate and vain. In response to the wife's expression of surprise at Don John's early rising, he replies that five hours sleep ought to suffice any man, except for the

> "old appalled wight,
> As been thise wedded men, that lye and dare
> As in a fourme sit a wery hare."
>
> B, 1292–1294

The Host ascribes to the pilgrim Monk a similar advantage over married men. Religion has taken all the mighty men like the Monk, says the Host, and left only "shrympes" to marry, who are impotent and cause wives (like the merchant's wife) to try out

> "Religious folk, for ye mowe bettre paye
> Of Venus paiementz than mowe we."
>
> B, 3150-3151

The Monk takes no exception to this dubious compliment.

Don John, turning his back on oaths to friends and God, devotes himself to supplying the place of the husband whom he finds rabbit-like. That he is bound to this husband, who is his gracious and generous host, in "eterne alliaunce" (B, 1230) does not prevent John from cheating and cuckolding him, or even from cruel humor when he asks to borrow a hundred francs "for certain beestes that I moste beye" (B, 1462). The beast to be bought is the poor man's wife. Although it may be that the merchant is dominated by a commercial philosophy in regard to his wife, Don John on his side has every reason to respect him. The merchant's reaction to his request for money could not be more handsome. "This is a smal requeste," he says, "My gold is youres" (B, 1473-1474). And not only is he welcome to his gold but also his merchandise: "Take what yow list" (B, 1476), and pay it back only "when it lith in youre ese" (B, 1481). The merchant is more than generous to his sworn brother.

When the merchant returns from Bruges to Paris and goes to see John for friendly reason—"Nat for to axe or borwe of hym moneye" (B, 1528)—he mentions incidentally his current need for money. John perversely interprets the remark as a request for payment, however, and explains that he has already paid the wife. Then he curtly leaves the merchant as if offended (B, 1550-1552). But not content with cuckolding and abusing his benefactor, he concludes the leave-taking with another cold-blooded private joke:

> "Grete wel oure dame, myn owene nece swete,
> And fare wel, deere cosyn, til we meete!"
>
> B, 1553-1554

The merchant, ignorant of his wife's infidelity, cannot recognize the ambiguities here, that he is John's "cosyn" by cozenage and that his wife is the monk's "sweet niece" in the sense of paramour. But he has noticed and mentions to his wife a "manere straungenesse" (B, 1576) between himself and John. He tells her that the monk seemed ill pleased by his mention of business matters (B 1581–1582). Don John leaves the merchant in St. Denis to blame himself or his wife for his disaffection. He has gotten what he came after and has no desire to pay the wife's price out of his own funds. He departs the household, "Farewel, have good day" (B, 1510), with the same unconcern with which the pilgrim Monk refuses to tell a more agreeable Tale after the Knight interrupts his dull chain of tragedies:

> "Nay," quod this Monk, "I have no lust to pleye.
> Now lat another telle, as I have toold."
>
> B, 3996–3997

Don John is not concerned about his friends, and the Monk is untroubled by the reactions of his fellow pilgrims.

In a sense unconcern is proper for monks, since as contemplatives who have left the world their thoughts should be directed away from secular attachments, including those to family and friends. The monks of pilgrimage and tale thus appropriately turn their minds inward, but it is bitter irony that they turn them not to God but to themselves. The selfishness of Don John cannot even be extenuated on the basis of extreme amorousness, the basis on which we tend to excuse lovers like Troilus for their willingness to sacrifice father, brothers, sisters, and country for their sweethearts. John professes to love the wife "specially,/ Aboven alle wommen, sikerly" (B, 1343–1344), but he tricks and leaves her without the slightest hesitation. His night of love is pure self-gratification.

The contrast of the Monk's personality with the Friar's illustrates how the behavior of both is perversely appropriate to their callings. The very name *friar (brother)* signals the brotherly sentiments proper to the calling; the man who follows it should actively associate with people, preaching to them and setting a worthy example. In personality, therefore, he ought to be gregarious and responsive to his fellows. And so Chaucer's Friar is, if not in an edifying way. Hubert's cape is stuffed with knives for gifts to ladies. An expert player on the sociable rote, he frequents taverns where he is well known to the barmaids. And he is "lowly and serviceable" with his benefactors. The fact that he will have nothing to do with lazars denotes a thoroughly unchristian nicety, but not unsociability.

When the pilgrimage gets under way, the Friar shows his gregariousness in commenting unasked on the Wife of Bath's "long preamble of a tale" (D, 831), a remark apparently meant to be genial but which sits well with neither the Wife nor the Summoner. She in reprisal begins her fairy tale with a comment directed against him. Maidens no longer have to worry about elves tempting them, she says, for friars have replaced them all. The Summoner more bluntly states that friars habitually interrupt:

> A flye and eek a frere
> Wol falle in every dyssh and eek mateere.
> B, 835–836

With his acute social sensitivity Hubert is unable to ignore the Summoner's sarcasm and forthwith gets involved in a debate which he seems from the beginning doomed to lose. His story about a summoner is cutting, but the Summoner's about a friar is devastating. Without completely debasing himself the Friar cannot use the churl's terms which are water and air to the Summoner and which give the latter the ultimate advantage. A fine gentleman should never get into an argument with a ruffian; and only very foolish fine gentlemen do. As the Friar becomes embroiled even the Host blushes for him and reminds him of his dignity:

> A! sire, ye sholde be hende
> And curteys, as a man of youre estaat.
> D, 1286–1287

Yet the Friar still has no more sense than to show his pique by breaking into the Summoner's Tale (D, 1761), in so doing virtually admitting that he is the same venal, foolish man who appears in the Tale.

The Summoner depicts his Friar walking around the countryside begging with a fellow brother, who inscribes and soon erases the names of donors, and a servant who carries their loot. Visiting his bedridden benefactor Thomas, this shammendicant drives the cat from the couch and makes himself at home unbidden; right in front of his sick friend he embraces his wife tightly in greeting, then kisses her fondly, chirping "as a sparwe" (D, 1804). When he proceeds to chide and lecture Thomas for the ire which his wife imputes to him, the indivisible gift of fetid air which is his reward seems consummately appropriate. The Friar, however, like his counterpart Hubert, has no sense of his fault or when to give up, and he exposes himself to ridicule on top of contempt when he complains to his influential friend. By telling what has taken place he leaves himself open to the ludicrous suggestion of the squire, and he is thereby subjected to further embarrassment.

In contrast to the indifferent Monk, the Friar of story and pilgrimage is a chronically social person. His gregariousness is quite appropriate to the model of social action provided by Saint Francis, but because the trait is linked with self-seeking, the Friar who should have been a humble brother to man shows himself egregiously venal. So too the Monk's unconcern, which could have led him to the sanctity of Anthony the Hermit, because improperly directed makes him particularly despicable. Both Hubert and the Monk display clearly the consequences of perverting the natural virtues of their respective vocations, and their personalities agree unhappily with their stations in life.

The Summoner's Tale and Shipman's Tale make impressive contributions to the exposition of the Monk's and Friar's personalities, and the ending of each Tale is consistent with the exposition. It is not only because of poetic justice that the Friar of the Summoner's Tale is made a laughingstock by both Thomas and the squire; this consequence is the natural product of the shallow extroversion which is basic to his personality. Neither should the lack of rightful retribution in the Shipman's Tale be interpreted as a fault in the narrative. It is in the interest of consistent characterization and in accord with probability that Don John succeeds, since selfish self-containment conduces to success in taking advantage of people, especially one's friends. Surely his escaping poetic justice does not conduce to immorality on the part of the reader. One does not admire John for his success, but rather on a practical plane he is led—as the Host is—to beware of such men, and on an ethical plane to indignation that such a monk can flourish.

Little doubt can exist that the characterization of the Monk, drawn in Prologue, pilgrimage, and Tale, embodies a general premeditated attack on the monastics of the day, who had to a great extent turned from contemplation of God to contemplation of their own interests. So do three other carefully chosen characterizations of clerics constitute indictments of the particular segments of church organization which they represent. The foolish Friar typifies the decadence of the brotherhoods; the Summoner, as an agent of the diocese, represents episcopal corruption; and the Pardoner, licensed by the Pope, is an instrument of the avarice of Rome. Of the churchmen described in the General Prologue, the holy and impressive figures of the Clerk and the Parson, belonging to classes of churchpeople less involved in the central ecclesiastical organization, remain to show that there is not everywhere in God's Church an opposition between the ideal and the actual.

The indictment of the Church through the damning depiction of four representatives recalls the conventional complaints of estates literature; indeed, the portraits of Chaucer's Monk and Friar are nearly allied to Gower's portraits in the *Mirour de l'Omme*. But in the *Canterbury Tales* Chaucer's main object obviously is not complaint against social corruption. The image of churchmen presented by the Monk, Friar, Pardoner, and Summoner is mitigated by the idealized portraits of the Parson and Clerk, by the piety displayed by the two nuns, and by the unassuming good sense of the Nun's Priest. The attack thus does not focus, as in estates literature, on the corruption of individuals that in turn infects the institutions of society, but rather on the corruption of the institution of the Church, which infects its representatives from the center outward. The fourteenth century was a most difficult one for the Church, and Chaucer was not alone among orthodox Catholic writers to register serious objections to its procedures and practices. Langland and Dante, for example, made more outspoken attacks.

In his portrayal of the other estates Chaucer seems even less interested in indicting the morality of people in general. The Knight is a brave and holy person who participates in the story-telling with good humor and *noblesse oblige*. The Squire too is a noble and refreshingly open young man; the Franklin longs for a son like him. And if there are a few sham knights like January and bad rulers like Nero who appear in the stories, these are more than balanced by exemplary men like Theseus in the Knight's Tale and Arveragus in the Franklin's Tale. The courtesy book for the nobility embedded in the *Tales*—its Mirror for Princes—is thus composed predominantly of good examples.

The estate of the commons in the *Canterbury Tales* is not so admirable on the whole as the class of nobles; but it comprises a much broader and a very interesting group. The representatives of the Third Estate who gain most attention, besides the Wife of Bath, are the churlish and depraved Miller and Reeve. Nevertheless, as we discussed previously, morality is not the central question with most of Chaucer's characterizations of commoners, such as those of the doctor, lawyer, merchant, franklin, wife, and the artisans. These figures are interesting primarily for their fulfillment of occupational archetypes. Thus, despite Chaucer's attention to the rogues, the image of the Third Estate in the *Tales* is not primarily of a corrupt people; it is rather of a people who are skillful, ingenious, and lively, though their morality is typically flawed. Chaucer's Mirror of the Commons, as a consequence, is less closely allied to the estates complaints than is his image of the Church.

Unfortunately, Chaucer's characterizations of the commoners beyond the General Prologue are not generally comparable in extent to his development of the clerics and the Knight and Squire, and it is in the aborted portrayals in this group that the incompleteness of the *Tales* is felt most strongly. Perhaps it is because he was working in newer territory here, with fewer models provided by tradition, that his picture is much more fragmentary.

The *Canterbury Tales* is a mirror in both senses which the word has in medieval literary usage. It is a Mirror of Society first in the sense of comprehensiveness. Working freely with traditional divisions of society inherited from estates literature, Chaucer depicts twenty-one different classes through the portraits in the General Prologue; subsequently in the drama of the storytelling and in the stories themselves, he elaborates on these portraits and also adds to the number of classes represented. In this manner a relatively complete cross-section of society is present-ed, and with much more system than is at first apparent. The *Tales,* furthermore, are a mirror in the sense of presenting ideals or archetypes. Each of the characters in the Prologue is in some way an exemplar of his calling: some, like the Knight and Par-son, embody the ethically charged high ideals of their voca-tions; others, like the Monk and Friar, display such ideals by direct opposition to them in their practices and innate personali-ties. The members of a third group are exemplars of their professions without being remarkably good or bad; representing vocations in which morality or lack of it is not the paramount consideration, they embody the distilled essence of landowner, lawyer, physician, matron, and gentlewoman.

In the past two chapters we have considered mirrors of the vices and of society. In the next chapter chivalric romances will be dealt with as mirrors of knighthood; in most of the better medieval romances the ideal of knighthood is implicit and maintains primary importance throughout. The various knights who participate help to form the mirrors by virtue of their embodiment of the ideal or by their failure to do so. Many romances are mirrors also from the standpoint of their compre-hensiveness, since in the course of works of any extent the por-trait of chivalric life becomes inclusive through sheer accumula-tion of diverse event.

NOTE TO CHAPTER VII

(The main bibliographical listings for Chaucer's works are found in the Note to Chapter II; for Gower's in the Note to Chapter VI.)

Editions

Sir Pride the Emperor. Thomas Wright and James O. Halliwell, eds., *Reliquiae Antiquae*, II, 248–254.

Le Lay des douze estas dou monde. Les *Oeuvres complètes de Eustache Deschamps* have been edited by the Marquis de Queux de Saint-Hilaire and Gaston Raynaud, eleven volumes, SATF (1878–1904); the *Lay* appears in II, 226–235.

Dance Macabre. I have quoted from the text in Eleanor P. Hammond's valuable anthology of fifteenth- and early sixteenth-century poetry, *English Verse Between Chaucer and Surrey* (1927). The EETS has edited the voluminous works of Lydgate in several volumes.

Canterbury Tales. Besides the versions in the collected editions already mentioned, of great importance is John M. Manly and Edith Rickert, eds., *The Text of the Canterbury Tales*, eight volumes (1940), wherein all eighty-four manuscripts are compared; the differences between manuscripts are extensive. The Ellesmere manuscript, generally considered the best, has been reproduced in facsimile, *The Ellesmere Chaucer*, two volumes (1911).

The Three Estates, the Plan of the Canterbury Tales

The standard study of the literature of the Three Estates is Ruth Mohl, *The Three Estates in Medieval and Renaissance Literature* (1933). Treatments in sermons of traditional social divisions, along with pulpit criticisms of individual classes, are discussed and liberally sampled in two works of Gerald R. Owst: *Preaching in Medieval England* (1926), and *Literature and Pulpit in Medieval England* (2nd ed., 1961). Frederick Tupper notes particularly the literary association of the Estates with the Seven Deadly Sins in his *Types of Society in Medieval Literature* (1926).

In a brief but enlightening note, "The Plan of the 'Canterbury Tales,'" *MP*, 13 (1915), 45–48, H. S. V. Jones suggests a basic relationship of the *Tales* to Estates literature. Frederick Tupper was led, by among other things the conventional associations between the Seven Sins and the Estates, to hypothesize that a large portion of the *Tales* was organized around a treatment of the Sins. See particularly his "Chaucer and the Seven Deadly Sins," *PMLA*, 29 (1914), 93–128; and *Types of Society*, cited above. Though Tupper's basic argument was effectively controverted by John L. Lowes, "Chaucer and the Seven Deadly Sins," *PMLA*, 30 (1915), 237–371, the discussions of both men are useful for their insights into the organization of the *Tales* and into the nature and relationships of the characters. A good treatment of the unifying dramatic elements in the *Tales* is Robert M. Lumiansky, *Of Sundry Folk: The Dramatic Principle of the Canterbury Tales* (1955).

Criticism of Individual Works and Pilgrims

Muriel Bowden, *Commentary on the General Prologue of the Canterbury Tales* (1948), is an invaluable companion to any study of the Prologue. Howard R. Patch, "Characters in Medieval Literature," *MLN,* 40 (1925), 1–14, discusses broadly the origins of medieval character study, which are independent of the Theophrastian character. J. R. Hulbert, "Chaucer's Pilgrims," *PMLA,* 64 (1949), 823–828, analyzes Chaucer's methods of characterization in the General Prologue; his classifications are somewhat different from those which I have offered. John M. Manly, *Some New Light on Chaucer* (1926), is an interesting if sometimes misguided attempt to find real-life counterparts to the pilgrims. More important to understanding the bases for Chaucer's portraits is D. W. Robertson, *Preface to Chaucer* (1963), especially his discussion, "Chaucer and the Style of his Period," pp. 241–285.

The affinity of Gower's portraits in his estates writings to Chaucer's in the Prologue, particularly as regards the Friar and the Monk, is treated in Ewald Flügel, "Gower's Mirour de l'Omme und Chaucer's Prolog," *Anglia,* 24 (1901), 437–508; and by John Fisher, *John Gower* (1964), pp. 251–302.

Materials on the Prioress and the Wife of Bath are abundant. Particularly helpful to an initial understanding of the former are John L. Lowes, "Simple and Coy: A Note on Fourteenth Century Poetic Diction," *Anglia,* 33 (1910), 440–451; and the sympathetic analysis of the Nun provided by Sister M. Madeleva in *A Lost Language and Other Essays on Chaucer* (1951), pp. 27–60. Robert A. Pratt, "The Development of the Wife of Bath," in *Studies in Medieval Literature in Honor of Albert Croll Baugh,* ed. MacEdward Leach (1961), pp. 45–79, speculates about the evolution of Chaucer's use of the Wife in the *Canterbury Tales;* in the process a valuable analysis of her central role is provided. Walter C. Curry, *Chaucer and the Medieval Sciences* (rev. ed., 1960), pp. 91–118, casts an interesting horoscope for the Wife based primarily on the birth data enumerated in D, 611–620.

Though critics in general have been too sympathetic with the Monk, some have recognized the extent of his debasement. Robert E. Kaske, "The Knight's Interruption of the Monk's Tale," *ELH,* 24 (1957), 249–267, shows how the Monk is contrasted unfavorably with the Knight throughout the *Tales;* at the same time Kaske points up an additional dimension of the Monk's part in Chaucer's drama. The changes which Chaucer effected in the Shipman's Tale from extant analogues provide an interesting study of his adaptation of a story to fit into the *Tales.* Chaucer, for example, appears to be responsible for making the lover a monk (he is most often a sailor) and for the well-developed characterizations of the wife and the monk; see John W. Spargo in *Sources and Analogues,* pp. 439–446; and Robert A. Pratt, "Chaucer's Shipman's Tale and Sercambi," *MLN,* 55 (1940), 142–145. A study of the imagery of the Tale which provides relevant insights is Janette Richardson, "The Façade of Bawdry: Image Patterns in Chaucer's *Shipman's Tale,*" *ELH,* 32 (1965), 303–313.

That Friar Hubert is thoroughly venal has not been questioned. Valuable studies which explain the use of antifraternal traditions in the *Tales* are Arnold Williams, "Chaucer and the Friars," *Speculum,* 28 (1953), 499–513; and two articles by John V. Fleming: "The Antifraternalism of the Summoner's Tale," *JEGP,* 65 (1966), 688–700; and "The Summoner's Prologue: An Iconographic Adjustment," *Chaucer Review,* 2 (1967), 95–107.

Chapter VIII

The Ideal of Chivalry:
GAWAIN AND LANCELOT

Important Works: Chrétien's *Erec* and *Lancelot;* Wolfram's *Parzival; Sir Gawain and the Green Knight; Sir Gawain and the Carl of Carlyle; The Wedding of Sir Gawain and Dame Ragnell;* Malory's *Morte Darthur.*

When in his letter to Sir Walter Raleigh Edmund Spenser sets forth the "general intention and meaning" of the *Faerie Queene,* he appears to reduce his grand poem to a courtesy book, a guide to conduct for gentlemen: "The generall end therefore of all the book is to fashion a gentleman or noble person in vertuous and gentle discipline." In portraying his hero Arthur as "the image of a brave knight, perfected in the twelve private morall vertues, as Aristotle hath devised," Spenser claims to follow the practice of Homer, Virgil, Ariosto and Tasso. Though he did not complete his scheme, each of the six books which he finished illustrates particularly one virtue: holiness, temperance, chastity, friendship, justice, and courtesy.

Spenser's alliance of his work with ethical treatises is in the final analysis no debasement of its artistry. Chivalric romances, of which the *Faerie Queene* partakes both in subject matter and treatment, are particularly apt to interpretation as courtesy books. Since the leading characters in romance are knights, and the knight's vocation demands exceptionally virtuous conduct both on the battlefield and within the castle, the knight's success usually can be measured according to his fulfillment of the chivalric ideal. As a consequence, the motivation, continui-

ty, and end of the actions are all controlled by the commenda-
bility of the knights' behavior. Ethics enters into the imaginative fabric of romances, and the virtues portrayed become a
function of the aesthetic values produced.

When therefore in his preface to Malory's *Morte Darthur* Caxton emphasizes moral values, he too is not a wholly naïve literary critic:

> And I, accordyng to my copye, have doon sette it in enprynte to
> the entente that noble men may see and lerne the noble actes of
> chyvalrye, the jentyl and vertuous dedes that somme knyghtes
> used in tho dayes, by whyche they came to honour, and how they
> that were vycious were punysshed and ofte put to shame and re-
> buke. . . . For herein may be seen noble chyvalrye, curtosye,
> humanyté, frendlynesse, hardynesse, love, frendshyp, cowardyse,
> murdre, hate, vertue, and synne. Doo after the good and leve the
> evyl, and it shal brynge yow to good fame and renomee.

The romances, especially the best of them, were designed to
exemplify and teach the virtues appropriate to knighthood. In
this chapter we will discuss the romances as mirrors of knightly
behavior; in thus viewing them one may not only learn the
rewards of virtuous action, as Caxton would have it, but he will
also keep his attention on the main arteries of the narrative.

The Squire and the Knight are representatives respectively of the
secular and spiritual spheres of chivalry in the General Prologue. Ellesmere Ms. By permission of the Huntington Library.

Chivalric heroes provided worthy examples for life in the world. In medieval society the knight and the monk stand together as representatives of what Robert Kaske calls "the two great Christian ideals of chivalry and monasticism." As the monk's life realizes the ideal of the contemplative life, so does the knight's of the active life. The virtues of the knight therefore cover the broad range of Christian morals; the ideal indeed was so lofty that the image of Christ as knight was eminently suitable. In *Piers Plowman,* to name but one salient instance, this figure is used several times and developed at some length, as when Faith describes the coming Crucifixion:

> "This Jesus of his gentrice wole juste in Piers armes,
> In his helme and in his haberjoun *humana natura;*
> That Cryst be nought biknowe here for *consummatus deus,*
> In Piers paltok the Plowman this priker shal ryde."
>   B, XVIII, 22–25
> ["This Jesus because of his noble nature will joust in
> Piers' arms, in his helmet and coat of mail, human nature.
> This knight shall ride in Piers Plowman's jacket so that
> Christ shall not be recognized as the perfect God."]

The knightly ideal is a comprehensive and complex set of virtues and aptitudes. The nature of the ideal is dealt with systematically in numerous handbooks for knights produced in the Middle Ages and Renaissance. One of the best-known of such handbooks is Ramon Lull's early fourteenth-century Spanish work which was translated by Caxton into English as *The Book of the Ordre of Chyvalry.* In this work a hermit-knight instructs a squire on the duties and requisites of the knight. The hermit gives the squire a book which he himself has often used to assist his contemplations; it has inspired him to

> remembre or thynke on the grace and bounte that god hath gyven
> and done to me in this world by cause that I honoured and mayn-
> tayned with al my power th'ordre of Chyvalrye. For alle in lyke
> wyse as chyvalrye gyveth to a knyghte alle that to hym apperteyn-
> eth, in lyke wyse a knyght ought to sayve alle his forces for to
> honoure chyvalrye.

The book contains an annotated list of the virtues and duties of the knight (bravery, defense of the weak and helpless, skill in arms, etc.), an account of the process of ordination for the knight, a list of the knight's arms with the spiritual signification of each item (e.g., the spear symbolizes truth), and even a disquisition on the seven vices and seven virtues. According to the treatise, and others like it, the knight's armor is that with which St. Paul equips the Christian (Ephesians, vi, 10–17), and the good knight is the virtuous, zealous Christian.

Chaucer's Knight well satisfies the moral and religious ideal outlined in the *Ordre of Chyvalry*. The Knight has engaged exclusively in holy wars in Eastern Europe and the Mediterranean. He loves chivalry—"trouthe, honour, fredom, and curteisie" (A, 46); he is brave, wise, and humble, and his speech is unexceptionable:

> He nevere yet no vileynye ne sayde
> In al his lyf unto no maner wight.
>
> A, 70–71

Having just arrived home from the campaigns, his first action is to make a pilgrimage to thank God and St. Thomas for his return. By spiritual standards he is the "parfyt" knight; nevertheless, the portrait of the Squire reminds us that there is more to the traditional image of knighthood than the spiritual ideal which the *Ordre of Chyvalry* sets forth and which the Knight embodies.

Chaucer's picture of the Squire brings out familiar secular aspects of the chivalric ideal. The Squire's strength and agility of body, his fresh and gay appearance, and his skill in singing and fluting are emphasized. The battles he had engaged in involve political wars just across the Channel, and his inspiration in battle is "hope to stonden in his lady grace" (A, 88). His accomplishments are those of the successful courtier:

> Wel koude he sitte on hors and faire ryde.
> He koude songes make and wel endite,
> Juste and eek daunce, and weel purtreye and write.
> So hoote he lovede that by nyghtertale
> He sleep namore than dooth a nyghtyngale.
> Curteis he was, lowely, and servysable,
> And carf biforn his fader at the table.
>
> A. 94–100

Though there is no reason to think that the Squire lacks religious virtue, that aspect of his character is not confronted in the portrait.

The ideal set up in romances for knights alternates between, often combines, the Christian ideal exemplified by the Knight and the secular standard fulfilled by the Squire. The ideal also has purely literary aspects relevant rather to fiction than to actual practice. Statements of the knight's duties in the romances may stress obligations, such as that of succoring damsels in distress, which the knight in real life would seldom have occasion to perform. "Literary" duties, for instance, are an important part of the yearly oath of the Arthurian knight reported by Malory:

> [Arthur] charged them never to do outerage nothir morthir, and allwayes to fle treson, and to gyff mercy unto hym that askith mercy, uppon payne of forfiture of their worship and lordship of kynge Arthure for evirmore; and allwayes to do ladyes, damesels, and jantilwomen and wydowes socour: strengthe hem in hir ryghtes, and never to enforce them, uppon payne of dethe. Also, that no man take no batayles in a wrongefull quarell for no love ne for no worldis goodis. So unto thys were all knyghtis sworne of the Table Rounde, both olde and yonge, and every yere so were they sworne at the hygh feste of Pentecoste.

This oath is the most prominent summary statement of the knight's duties in the *Morte Darthur,* and therefore is often quoted. However, Arthur formulates the oath in response to events which have immediately preceded, and it does not have wide application. He institutes it after Gawain on his first adventure as a knight, in the act of refusing mercy to an opponent whom he has conquered, inadvertently beheads a lady, and after Pellenor in his anxiety to fulfill his quest fails to succor a damsel who begs for help; the death of the damsel and her wounded knight is a consequence. The pledge that Arthur requires is better suited to prevent the repetition of such misfortunes and severe breaches of proper conduct than to set up an inclusive ideal.

A more satisfactory statement in romance of a chivalric ideal is found in *Sir Gawain and the Green Knight,* in the analysis of the pentangle that adorns Gawain's shield. To the endless knot which makes up the five-pointed pentangle the poet ascribes a symbolism consisting of five sets of five. First, it signifies that

Gawain is faultless in his "fyve wittes"; that is he guards his senses from temptation. Second, he never fails in his five fingers, which represent fortitude. In the third place, he puts all of his faith in Christ's five wounds, which are the source of redemption. In the fourth place, he derives his strength from the five joys of Mary, whose image is painted on the inside of his shield. Finally, five particular virtues mark his character:

> The fift fyve that I finde that the frek used,
> Wats fraunchyse and felaghschyp forbe al thyng;
> His clannes and his cortaysye croked were never,
> And pite, that passes alle poyntes, thyse pure fyve
> Were harder happed on that hathel then on any other.
>
> 651–655
>
> [The fifth five that this man practiced was generosity
> and fellowship above all things; his purity and courtesy
> were never crooked, and pity, that surpasses all; these perfect
> five were instilled better in this man than any other.]

In sum, he avoids sin, practices the faith with a special devotion to the Virgin Mary, and is strong in both the social and moral virtues especially suitable to the knight at court.

This statement in the poem of the pentangle symbolism expresses many aspects of the chivalric ideal that are implicit in medieval romances. Yet every romance to some extent is a law unto itself and establishes its own standards; the emphases and sometimes the substance of the ideals shift from one to another, as we will see in our consideration of several specific works.

Sir Gawain and the Green Knight, a verse romance written in the late fourteenth century by the poet of *Pearl,* and Thomas Malory's long coherent cycle of prose romances, composed about a century later and entitled the *Morte Darthur* by Caxton, are the two great monuments of Arthurian romance in medieval English literature. The former is a tightly constructed, beautifully patterned narrative of 101 stanzas, made up mostly of alliterative long lines. The latter is a sprawling series of interrelated stories. If the *Canterbury Tales* is a Gothic cathedral, then Malory's work is the labyrinth of Daedalus. Yet like the labyrinth it has a continuity as well as some dead-ends, and it cannot be reduced, as some influential critics would reduce it, to a series of separate stories.

Lancelot is the central figure of the *Morte Darthur,* and Gawain is the hero of *Gawain and the Green Knight.* From the twelfth-century beginnings of Arthurian romance these two knights were the dominant figures in narratives centering on Arthur's court. Gawain is Arthur's nephew and chief counselor; Lancelot is at once Guinevere's lover and the warrior bulwark of Arthur's kingdom. Our subsequent discussion in this chapter will chiefly concern these two knights. We aim thereby at the same time to place the two major English romances in the tradition and to point up the function of the romance heroes of exemplifying—sometimes perversely—chivalric ideals.

Traditionally, the most prominent of Gawain's virtues is his courtesy, his grace in dealing with people. Chaucer's Squire in his tale quite naturally invokes Gawain's name to emphasize the "heigh reverence and obeisaunce" of the messenger knight:

> Gawain, with his *olde curteisye,*
> Though he were comen ayeyn out of Fairye,
> Ne koude hym nat amende with a word.
>
> F, 95–97

The reference is almost automatic, for Gawain was well established as diplomat and peerless model of courteous behavior from the very earliest Arthurian romance which has come down to us, the French *Erec and Énide* of Chrétien de Troyes.

In *Erec,* as in many later romances, the awkwardness and rudeness of Sir Kay provides an excellent foil for Gawain. One incident in particular illustrates the contrasting traits of these two knights. Erec, stunned by his wife Énide's lament for his lost knighthood and intent on proving his courage, happens to ride close by a temporary encampment of King Arthur, but he has no intention of stopping. Kay, however, sees him and insists that he stay the night with the King. Erec refuses; Kay thereupon takes hold of the bridle of Erec's horse and starts pulling him toward the camp. For his trouble Kay then gets a severe blow with the butt-end of Erec's lance, and he goes mournfully to tell Arthur what has happened. Arthur dispatches Gawain. Gawain salutes Erec, and in the best form he requests him for the sake of Arthur and Guinevere to stay the night with them. " 'Sire,' says he, 'King Arthur sends me along this way to encounter you. The Queen and King send you their greeting, and beg you urgently to come and spend some time with them (it may benefit you, and cannot harm), as they are close by.'" When Erec again declines, Gawain quietly sends a messenger off to Arthur telling him to move the camp to a place ahead astride the road while he detains Erec. When Erec eventually discovers the tactic, he can no longer refuse: " 'Ah! Gawain,' he says, 'vour shrewdness has outwitted me. By your great cunning you have kept me here.' "

Chrétien wrote his several romances in the last part of the twelfth century; his Arthurian stories besides *Erec and Énide* are *Cligés, Yvain* or the *Knight of the Lion, Lancelot* or the *Knight of the Cart,* and *Perceval.* These were widely disseminated throughout Europe and were very influential in the development of the Arthurian legends. Particularly important was the *Perceval,* the first grail legend that has survived, which inspired several lengthy sequels and numerous retellings. Wolfram von Eschenbach's *Parzival,* produced in the early thirteenth century during the magnificent flowering of chivalric romance in Germany, is the best of the grail romances.

Gawain has very much the same character in *Parzival* as in *Erec;* indeed, there is a very close analogue in Wolfram's story to the episode related above. Parzival, having ridden close to Arthur's camp, is entranced by some red drops of blood in the snow which remind him of his lady's white and red complexion; noticing him, Kay comes out from the camp and demands that Parzival accompany him. When the bemused lover does not answer, Kay strikes him on the helmet; in return he gets a broken arm. Arthur thereupon dispatches Gawain, who to denote his friendliness goes to Parzival unarmed. Gawain senses that love is causing the knight's trance, so he covers up the drops of blood to get his attention, and then he explains to Parzival what has happened while he has been enraptured. He most courteously entreats him to visit Arthur's camp: "What I ask of you I shall earn by my service. A king is encamped nearby with many knights and many a lady fair. I will bear you company there if you will allow me to ride with you, and I will protect you from any attack." Parzival goes with him willingly.

In Chrétien's and Wolfram's narratives not only does Gawain's courtesy facilitate the movement of the plots, but also his deeds as a warrior are second only to those of the main heroes—of Yvain, Lancelot, or Parzival. His role is of such prominence in the *Yvain* of Chrétien that the Middle English adaptation is entitled *Ywain and Gawain;* and the Gawain subplot in Wolfram's *Parzival* is comparable in length to the main plot. Gawain in these romances is the exemplar of all-around chivalric virtue. The title characters by contrast are better suited to demonstrating the particular points of knightly behavior which bear on the subject at hand. *Erec* is about uxoriousness in knights; Erec, being a worthy but too contented knight, married to a lady of unmatched charm and virtue, is an appropriate hero. The story of *Lancelot* provides a demonstration of the faithfulness required of the knightly lover, best displayed by Guinevere's famous paramour. And the grail legend as conceived by Wolfram deals with the perfectibility of the knight, which could be well shown in the progress of the rude, untutored Parzival.

While Gawain often played a supporting role as a general representative of the virtues pertinent to knights, when courtesy was particularly to be demonstrated he usually was given the leading part. Thus he is the main character in *Sir Gawain and the Green Knight,* the great English romance written almost two centuries after Chrétien's and Wolfram's works. The story of this alliterative poem is designed to prove the compatibility of the spiritual ideal of chastity with the secular ideal of courtesy; and the center of the story is the simultaneous test of Gawain's chastity and courtesy when his host's beautiful wife subjects him to her seductive charms.

Previous to his three private encounters with this lady, Gawain meets challenges to his chivalric virtue which are but typical of the romance. He faces the monstrous Green Knight and lops off his head, only to see him pick up the head and to hear the head, disembodied, promise a return blow the following New Year. Having set out a year later to fulfill his pledge, he braves cruel ice and savage terrain, and climbs rough mountains and fords swift streams, at every stage of the journey finding a foe before him (713–734). These tests of his bravery and fortitude, though severe and in the case of the beheading dramatically shocking, are such as many knights of the Round Table have met before. That which is most clearly to distinguish these adventures of Gawain is yet to come.

The events in the romance following Gawain's wintry trip consist of three days of rest and recreation at Bercilak's castle and then the confrontation of the Green Knight at his "chapel." All through the time at the castle the reader and Gawain together are looking forward to the blow which it seems will inevitably be fatal. But when the second meeting with the Green Knight finally comes, we find that the real test has already taken place at the castle. As the Green Knight himself explains, the three feints with the ax which he makes at Gawain's neck have been governed by Gawain's actions in the three days that the lady tempted him. On the first two days his behavior was blameless, so the first two blows are shunted off; on the third day he culpably accepted the girdle in order to save his life, for which he is given a slight nick in the neck on the third blow. Thus the denouement has depended on the events immediately preceding; the true climax, we see, is found in the lady's visits to Gawain.

Despite the reader's concern about Gawain's head, the artistry of the poet's presentation sufficiently attracts his attention to the bedroom scenes. The several dramatic contrasts—of the magnificent castle with the wild countryside which Gawain has traversed, of the gentle conduct of Bercilak's people with the barbarous behavior of those whom Gawain has just previously encountered, of the beauty of the lady with the ugliness of her companion, and finally of the feminine softness of the chamber with the masculine vigor of the hunting sequences which frame the bedroom scenes—all of these focus our attention on the lady as she approaches Gawain's bed.

Having entered the room furtively, she gazes at Gawain until he opens his eyes, then playfully she puts her hands on his shoulders; holding him on the bed, she demands that he surrender. He gracefully accedes:

> "Me schal worthe at your wille, and that me wel lykes,
> For I yelde me yederly and yeghe after grace,
> And that is the best, be my dome, for me byhoves nede."
>
> 1214–1216

[It will be as you wish, and that pleases me well, for I

> yield willingly and ask for grace. And that is best,
> I think, for I have no choice."]

He says that he could talk with her better if she would let him get up and dress; but she is determined to hold him while she can, she answers, for she wishes to be instructed by his courtesy, which is praised everywhere:

> "And now ye ar here, iwysse, and we bot oure one;
> My lorde and his ledes ar on lenthe faren,
> Other burnes in her bedde, and my burdes als,
> The dor drawen, and dit with a derf haspe;
> And sythen I have in this hous hym that al lykes,
> I schal ware my whyle quyl hit lastes,
> > With tale;
> > Ye ar welcum to my cors,
> > Yowre awen won to wale;
> > Me behoves of fyne force
> > Your servaunt be, and schale."
> > > 1230–1240

> ["And now you are here, and we are alone; my lord and his men have gone far away, other men are in their beds, and my maids also, the door is closed and locked with a strong lock. And since I have him in this house who pleases all, I will spend my time, while it lasts, in conversation. You are welcome to my body to choose your own pleasure. Of strong necessity I must be and shall be your servant."]

When a beautiful lady invites the modern literary picaro to take his liking, he acts without hesitation. But Gawain is of another tradition; as an upholder of the chivalric ideal, he is presented here with a genuine quandary; it is the crucial problem of the story and in a way of the secular-spiritual institution of knighthood as depicted in the romances.

The problem is not whether or not to yield to the lady; it is rather how to refuse courteously. To succumb to the lady's advances would be to sin in chastity against himself, and in charity against her and the trust and hospitality of his host. A forthright rejection of her, on the other hand, would not conform to the courtesy proper to a knight dealing with a noble lady. Kay would have no problem; he would throw her off with violence and abuse. Galahad, not of this world, would ignore her. But Gawain is the prime representative of courtly gentility. The ideal of knighthood which he maintains demands that he respond with courtesy to all as befits their station, and with especial courtesy to a beautiful lady who is his host's wife. Though Christian morality does not demand particular politeness here, romance conventions do. It is as if the poet had posited the problem: Are the Christian virtues of purity, fidelity, and charity compatible with literary courtly standards of behavior? In short, can a knight in a romance be an upright Christian and at the same time a polite courtier? The answer implicit in the events seems to be that it is both possible and highly desirable to be so.

Gawain to the lady's unblushing offer of her body proclaims his unworthiness of such an honor, and he states his readiness to do any service for her which he would merit performing. When she says that by report she knows him worthy of all, he attributes her compliments to kindness and generosity:

> "Madame," quoth the myry mon, "Mary yow yelde,
> For I haf founden, in god fayth, yowre fraunchis nobele;
> And other ful much of other folk fongen hor dedes,
> But the daynte that they delen for my disert nysen;
> Hit is the worchyp of yourelf that noght but wel connes."
> 1263–1266

["Madame," said the merry man, "Mary reward you, for I have found, in good faith, your generosity noble; often people accept the reports of others, but the honor that they ascribe to me exaggerates my desert. That you believe it is to your honor, who know only good."]

Bercilak's lady continues her attempts to compromise Gawain's chastity for three mornings. Not only is he hard put to parry her repartee, but also his physical restraint is sorely tested by the customary kisses which she requires of his courtesy. She makes these charming and alluring:

> Ho comes nerre with that, and caches hym in armes,
> Loutes luflych adoun and the leude kysses.
> 1305–1306

[With that she comes nearer and catches him in her arms,
leans sweetly down and kisses the man.]

Despite such temptations, Gawain unfailingly maintains his
equanimity.

Gawain in a minor way breaks down on the third morning
when he accepts the girdle in the hope that it will save his life.
But the rather small fault involved in his acceptance of the girdle, as in his quite human flinching from the first descent of the
ax, is in his courage. When, in pursuance of his promise to the
lady, he does not reveal the gift to the host, his integrity also is
not enhanced. But neither his courtesy to ladies nor his chastity
is impaired, so that on the whole he demonstrates effectively
that a courteous romance hero can also be an upright Christian
knight. Gawain's native virtue, not the exotic magic of the girdle, preserves his life. His defects in courage and honesty, while
he considers them quite important, show his humanity but do
not seriously stain his achievement.

Though there are many fine touches of humor in *Sir Gawain
and the Green Knight,* the poet nevertheless focuses attention on
chivalric virtue with serious intent. Other less courtly English
romances, though also ostensibly aimed at displaying Gawain's
"olde curteisie," are designed more to entertain than to edify:
among these are *Sir Gawain and the Carl of Carlyle* and the *Wedding of Sir Gawain and Dame Ragnell.* The first presents an analogue to *Sir Gawain and the Green Knight* and the second to the
Wife of Bath's Tale.

Sir Gawain and the Carl of Carlyle concerns a chance visit by
Gawain, Kay, and Bishop Baldwin to the castle of the Carl of
Carlyle, whose title implies roughness rather than nobility. He
is a huge man who has as pets four "whelps"—a boar, a bear, a
lion, and a bull. These fierce beasts run loose around the guests.
We learn later that the Carl and his whelps have killed all the
guests of the castle for the preceding twenty years, but Gawain
fortunately reforms him through courteous performance of all
of his bidding. Since the Carl is his host Gawain accords him
the honor due to a prince. He kneels graciously before him in
greeting. He shelters a colt of the Carl's from the rain under his
own coat, whereas Kay and Baldwin put the colt out in the

cold (and are cuffed by the Carl for doing so). At the Carl's command Gawain embraces and kisses his lovely wife in bed (and would have done the "prevey far" if the Carl had not stopped him). Also on command Gawain throws a spear at his host's head. Having thus proved his "courtesy," Gawain receives many gifts from the Carl, who becomes a knight of the Round Table.

The *Wedding of Sir Gawain and Dame Ragnell* relates a severe test of Gawain's courtesy when he finds himself married to foul old Dame Ragnell, whom the poet delights in describing:

> She had two teethe on every side
> As bores tuskes, I wolle not hide,
> Of lengthe a large handfulle;
> The one tusk went up and the other doun;
> A mouthe full wide and foulle y-grown.
> With grey heris many on,
> Hir lippes laye lumprid on her chin;
> Neck forsothe on her was none y-seen—
> She was a lothly on!
>
> 548–556

Dame Ragnell's rich apparel at the wedding only accentuates her loathsomeness. To make things still worse, at the banquet she greedily eats enough for six, breaking her meat with claw-like fingernails.

Later in bed with her new husband Gawain, she demands that he show her "cortesy in bed." At least kiss me, she asks. Gawain is more than equal to the occasion, and he bravely declares: "I wolle do more then for to kisse☙(638–639). Turning to her upon this declaration, he finds the fairest creature he has ever seen. His courtesy, we may infer, has transformed her. But it takes further noble behavior on his part to make the change permanent. She states that he must choose whether he will have her foul by day and fair by night, or vice versa. After some meditation, he once more decides wisely. He proclaims.

> I put the choise in you.
> Bothe body and goodes, hart, and every dele,
> Is alle your own, for to by and selle.
>
> 681–683

His submission releases her from a spell of necromancy, and she will henceforward be always beautiful.

Though these two popular romances can hardly be set alongside the courtly *Sir Gawain and the Green Knight* as mirrors of chivalry, they nevertheless very clearly reflect the common use of chivalric narratives to display presumed ideals of conduct. As I have mentioned previously, the ideals set forth are not always the same. In the *Carl of Carlyle,* for example, the standards apparently do not include chastity, which is most important in the story of the Green Knight; and courtesy in this same work involves a simpleminded obedience to one's host, hardly appropriate to serious chivalric practice. In the *Wedding of Gawain and Ragnell,* on the other hand, unquestioning submission to one's wife yields the happy outcome, purveying a rather different lesson than that of Chrétien's *Erec* where uxoriousness is destructive. However, it is not only the comic romances in which the standards change shape. We need only to cite Chrétien's *Lancelot,* in which an ethic is exemplified which is quite at variance with Christian standards of chastity that were so important in *Gawain and the Green Knight.*

Chrétien is very careful to state at the outset of *Lancelot* that he is writing at the command of Marie of Champagne, and that she has supplied him with the material and treatment for the story. One infers from this disclaimer that the narrative, which concerns the adulterous love of Lancelot for Guinevere, little suited the poet's moral sensibilities. Nevertheless, he presents the story vividly and entertainingly. The high points of the action are found in Lancelot's failure, then his success, in living up to a rigorous standard of fidelity to his beloved.

The first test of Lancelot comes when he is searching for the abducted Guinevere. He comes upon a dwarf driving a cart, who tells him to climb in the cart if he wishes to find the Queen. Lancelot for a moment is puzzled. If he follows the dwarf's bidding, he will put himself in the position of common criminals who were customarily carted through the towns to advertise their guilt; he is therefore being asked to compromise his honor as a knight. He hesitates just an instant, then jumps on, thereby submitting himself to the jeers of bystanders and subsequent disgrace. Guinevere, however, does not later disdain him for the ride in the cart, nor does she praise him for his fidelity in accepting disgrace in order to find her; rather, she bitterly scorns him for his momentary hesitation. A true lover, she feels, would not pause for any reason in going to his lady's aid.

Lancelot later has a chance to prove that he has learned worthy behavior. At a great tournament, wherein the knightly combatants are the best in the country, and the opportunity to win honor is very great, Guinevere sends him word to do his worst. He immediately agrees, riding forthwith at an opponent and clumsily missing his spear thrust. At the end of the day he has done so badly that when he rides off all ask,

> "What has become of the worst, the most craven and despised of knights? . . . We shall probably never see him again. For he has been driven off by cowardice, with which he is so filled that there is no greater craven in the world than he. . . . Courage never so debased himself as to lodge in his breast or take quarters near him. But cowardice is altogether lodged with him, and she has found a host who will honour her and serve her so faithfully that he is willing to resign his own fair name for hers."

Lancelot disgraces himself for two days till Guinevere commands him to prove once more his valor. Then of course he triumphs.

Chrétien in this poem thus seems to set up an ideal of unhesitating and unquestioning service by the lover to the lady, whatever her whim and whatever the consequences. Other romances purvey similar ideals using similar love situations. But the writers were not always comfortable in depicting idolatrous service in illicit love affairs, and Chrétien's narrative espousal of such amorous fidelity is hardly convincing. One indication of the poet's attitude is shown in Lancelot's thoroughly unchristian attempt at suicide when he thinks Guinevere dead, which is made considerably more ludicrous than pathetic. Perhaps more indicative is an oblique attack on the lovers' adultery and their infidelity to Arthur. When Guievere's bed is found with Lancelot's blood in it, Kay, whose wounds have been bleeding, is accused of having been in bed with the Queen. His response surely amounts to an indictment of Lancelot:

"Let me answer, sire," says Kay, "and I will exonerate myself. May God have no mercy on my soul when I leave this world, if ever I lay with my lady! Indeed, I should rather be dead than ever do my lord [i.e., Arthur] such an ugly wrong, and may God never grant me better health than I have now but rather kill me on the spot, if ever such a thought entered my mind!"

Though Kay is not conscious of the implications for Lancelot in this speech, Chrétien surely is; the words of Kay, more judicious than is his wont, form a just reproach to Lancelot.

Chrétien was a love poet. The stories of *Erec, Cligés,* and *Yvain,* in addition to *Lancelot,* all revolve around the knight's relationship with his lady. And as is common in romance, in these works the knight finds much of his inspiration to noble deeds in his love. But Chrétien lingers little over the sensuous details of the look, the kiss, and the possession of the lady. His characters, like Fénice in *Cligés,* may be bemused by love or even languish because of it, but they do not take permanently to their beds for it. Even in *Lancelot* there is quantitatively small use of the conventions of medieval love poetry such as we discussed in Chapter II. Chrétien, the first and most influential of the romancers, is not notably a celebrator of courtly love, and he is no real patron of illicit love; except for Lancelot, the lovers in his works aspire only to marriage. Of course, as we mentioned in the earlier chapter, even poets who in their stories make great use of the love conventions often tell of married love. Wolfram's *Parzival* and Chaucer's Knight's Tale and Franklin's Tale present outstanding examples of thoroughly chivalric lovers who envision only marriage to their beloveds.

It is true, to be sure, that the best-known lovers of chivalric romance—Lancelot and Guinevere, and Tristan and Isolde—are adulterers; but Chrétien is not the only writer about these lovers to evidence concern over the essential disparity between the knight's relationship to his lady and Christian standards of moral virtue. Medieval writers use various devices to minimize this disparity. For instance, Lancelot's treason to his liege lord Arthur in making love to his Queen is particularly serious in the feudal context. In order to relieve this guilt the romancer of the French prose *Lancelot* has Guinevere rather than Arthur confer knighthood on Lancelot; his fealty thus is owed to her rather than to Arthur. The expedient, of course, lessens but does not remove the moral problem. The still-pernicious nature of their adultery was apparent enough to Dante (and one assumes to most medieval men); it is this *Lancelot* which Paolo and Francesca are reading together, we learn in the *Inferno* (V, 127–128), when the love which sent them to Hell overpowers them.

Despite ennobling effects imputed to courtly-love affairs, and despite often admirable constancy on the part of the lovers, the conflict with Christian morality inherent in the situations was probably always felt by the romancers. Other poets minimize the guilt of their adulterous heroes and heroines in various ways. Tristan and Isolde in all versions of the story are victims of a love potion, and therefore they have little control over their actions. King Mark, Tristan's uncle and ruler, moreover, provides a further extentuating circumstance; he is usually depicted as either old or cowardly (as in Malory), and thus as an unsuitable husband for Isolde. In the story of Troilus and Criseyde, another tale of illicit love told in several romances, Criseyde is a widow; Troilus is therefore not guilty either of adultery or of corrupting a maiden. Chaucer in his treatment of the story more importantly adds the epilogue in which the dead Troilus recognizes the vanity of his earthly attachment.

One could name numerous other instances in which medieval romancers manifest an implicit concern about the paradoxes inherent in the illicit loves of a Christian knight. In the *Morte Darthur,* however, Malory disposes of the paradoxes. He forthrightly presents the extramarital love of Lancelot and Guinevere with no attempt to mitigate their fault or to make the issue of it happy. Lancelot clearly owes his allegiance directly to Arthur, and Arthur is a worthy husband for Guinevere. Thus, though the lovers are presented as admirable people, their sin is manifest, and in Malory's narrative it entails the consequences which must ensue when an ideal is undermined by the persons who should be foremost in upholding it. To Arthur's kingdom, which has been founded on the ideal of chivalry, catastrophe inevitably comes. Arthur's early incontinence which produces the traitorous Mordred; the envy and vengefulness of Gawain and his brothers; and most of all Lancelot's continued adultery with Guinevere precipitate the collapse of the society of the Round Table.

That Lancelot should cause this collapse is particularly tragic in the light of his great virtues. After Merlin in Malory's story ceases to preside over Arthur's fortunes, Lancelot becomes the mainstay of the Round Table and the model which the best of the other knights emulate. When Lancelot lies dead at the end of the narrative, Sir Ector, his brother, summarizes the universal opinion of him:

> "A, Launcelot!" he sayd, "thou were hede of al Crysten knyghtes! And now I dare say," sayd syr Ector, "thou sir Launcelot, there thou lyest, that thou were never matched of erthely knyghtes hande. And thou were the curtest knyght that ever bare shelde! And thou were the truest frende to thy lovar that ever bestrade hors, and thou were the trewest lover of a synful man that ever loved woman, and thou were the kyndest man that ever strake wyth swerde. And thou were the godelyest persone that ever cam emonge prees of knyghtes, and thou was the mekest man and the jentyllest that ever ete in halle emonge ladyes, and thou were the sternest knyght to thy mortal foo that ever put spere in the reeste."

All the fulsome praise is merited; yet even in its speaking the epithets *erthely knyght* and *synful man* undercut it all.

In the denouement of *Morte Darthur,* therefore, the question forcefully obtrudes itself of the worth of earthly glory and happiness. The nearly irreconcilable conflict of secular ambition and love with Christian aims is pointed up in the outcome which produces the deaths of Arthur and Gawain, the retreat by Lancelot and Guinevere to religious lives, and the complete dissolution of the Round Table. The insufficiency of the world to man is shown here in Malory just as surely as it is in the outcome of Chaucer's *Troilus and Criseyde,* when the ghost of the dead Troilus looks down from the eighth sphere

> and fully gan despise
> This wrecched world, and held al vanite
> To respect of the pleyn felicite
> That is in hevene above.
>
> V, 1816–1819

Troilus from an unearthly vantage point has clear insight. But in an earthly court a clear view of the world's vanity is nearly impossible. In the *Morte Darthur* and Chaucer's *Troilus* the secular and the spiritual seem almost incompatible.

In Malory's story not only the disintegration of the whole Arthurian society, but also the contrasting individual fortunes of the exemplars of secular chivalric virtue and of the representatives of spiritual purity point up the essential conflicts of secular endeavor with spiritual virtue. Lancelot ultimately achieves personal success only by leaving worldly battles for the cloister. Tristram and Lamerok, the second and third best of Arthur's knights, despite their nobility meet ignominious deaths as a consequence of adulterous affairs, both stabbed in the back by men whose family interests are affronted by the illicit amours. The path to glory in Malory is not by way of the faithful practices of the lover; it is rather through purity, as is shown by the virtue of the three knights who accomplish the Grail Quest: Galahad, Perceval, and Bors. And the place of glory is not Arthur's court; rather it is in a foreign country with the Grail.

Sir Bors provides the single hope held out by Malory for the reconciliation of the secular and the spiritual. Perceval and Galahad are essentially heavenly knights who only nominally belong to the Round Table. Lancelot and Gawain, the knights most closely identified with the Round Table, fail in the quest because of their sinfulness. Bors, however, a reformed sinner, achieves the heavenly Grail and returns to Arthur to reassume his worldly position. That he is the only one among so many *erthely* knights to achieve the quest indicates how hard it is, at least in terms of the *Morte Darthur,* to conform the secular to the spiritual. In Malory's conception a reconciliation for the whole society is virtually impossible, as the downfall of Arthur's kingdom demonstrates.

The pessimism manifested in Malory's story stands in opposition to the optimistic spirit of most romances of earlier centuries, wherein an ideal is set up, and the knight or knights who are the heroes proceed to exemplify the ideal. Chrétien's Erec eventually achieves the proper subordination of his love for his wife to his practice of chivalry. Yvain, after a misstep, outdoes himself in proving his chivalric fidelity through noble behavior to the lion, to several maidens in distress, to Gawain, and finally to his wife. Lancelot in Chrétien's narrative succeeds in practicing the scrupulous loyalty demanded of the lover. Wolfram's Parzival travels a long road of sin, education, and penitence, but eventually he measures up to his destined position as King of the Grail. In *Gawain and the Green Knight* Gawain demonstrates the compatibility of Christian virtue and romance courtesy. In Malory, however, the brilliant performances and temporary successes of the knights are almost all canceled by eventual failure. The envy and desire for revenge felt by Gawain and his brothers, and the illicit loves of Lancelot, Tristan, and Lamerok all lead to unhappy endings for distinguished chivalric careers. The Round Table itself, founded on chivalric idealism, breaks to pieces on the humanity of its component knights.

The tragedy narrated by Malory nevertheless has in common with other chivalric romances the holding up of an ideal for the gentleman to follow. Though sustaining this ideal is a more difficult and complex matter in *Morte Darthur* than in Chrétien's works, or Wolfram's, or even in *Gawain and the Green Knight,* it is still to be striven for. As Caxton states in his Preface, he prints Malory's works in order that "noble men may see and lerne the noble actes of chyvalrye." Each knight should provide an example to other men and other knights. Galahad tells the newly knighted Melyas, "Sitthyn that ye be com of kynges and quenys, now lokith that knyghthode be well sette in you, for ye ought to be a *myrroure* unto all chevilry." The knight should be a mirror, and the record of his deeds, whether fictional or historical, should likewise provide a mirror.

Jean Froissart, contemporary and associate of Chaucer, in his famous *Chronicles* records many of the battles of the Hundred Years' War, but his eye is not primarily on the destiny of the nations and peoples involved; it rather focuses on the great inheritors of chivalry, Edward III, the Black Prince, and other individual representatives of knighthood. And his main purpose is not to leave a record of the political, economic, and cultural development of this crucial period; it is rather to provide worthy young men with examples of noble conduct. He makes this aim quite clear in his Preface:

Now, therefore, all young gentlemen who wish to advance themselves should have an ardent desire to achieve and be known for valor, by which they will be placed and counted in the number of the worthies; and they should study and consider how their predecessors, from whom they have acquired their inheritances—and perhaps they wear their very armor—are honored and commended by their noble deeds. I am sure, if they will inspect and read this book, that they will find as many great deeds and fine achievements in arms, hard encounters, strong assaults, lofty battles, and all other feats of arms which naturally originate with those who have valor, as they will find in any other history you have heard of, old or new. And this will provide them matter and example to encourage them in noble deeds, since the memory of the good and the record of the valiant rightly encourages and influences the hearts of the young knights who incline and tend to all perfection of honor, of which valor is the principal end and the certain source.

The best of medieval chronicles and romances are designed as mirrors to be held up for the edification and encouragement of gentlemen. Though this courtesy book aspect is not what the modern reader of history and literature is primarily concerned with, recognition of it is an indispensable key to an understanding of the works.

NOTE TO CHAPTER VIII

Editions

Erec, Yvain, Lancelot. These works of Chrétien have been edited by Mario Roques in the series Classiques français du moyen âge: *Erec et Enide* (1954), *Yvain (Le Chevalier au lion,* 1960), *Lancelot (Le Chevalier de la charrette,* 1958). All three, together with *Cligés,* are translated by W. W. Comfort, *Chrétien de Troyes: Arthurian Romance* (1924), from which I have quoted in this chapter.

Parzival. The German text of Wolfram's work has been edited by Albert Leitzmann (rev. ed., 3 vols., 1955–1961), among others. A good translation into English by Helen M. Mustard and Charles E. Passage (1961) is available.

Sir Gawain and the Green Knight. The most up-to-date edition is that of J. R. R. Tolkien and E. V. Gordon, *Sir Gawain and the Green Knight,* rev. by Norman Davis (1967). Of the numerous translations of this poem, two readable versions in verse are those of Marie Borroff (1967) and James L. Rosenberg (1959). The latter has a particularly useful introduction to basic matters by James Kreuzer.

Sir Gawain and the Carl of Carlyle and *The Wedding of Sir Gawain and Dame Rognell.* These works, along with several other popular romances in English such as *Havelok* and *Athelstan* appear in the convenient collection edited by Donald B. Sands, *Middle English Verse Romances* (1966).

Morte Darthur. The authoritative edition is that of Eugène Vinaver, *Malory: Works,* three volumes (1948), with extensive introduction and notes; also in one-volume students' edition (1954) without apparatus and commentary.

Chivalry, Courtesy Literature, and Arthurian Romance

The *Book of the Ordre of Chyvalrye,* translated by William Caxton from the Spanish treatise of Ramon Lull, one of the most popular courtesy books for knights, is edited by Alfred T. Byles, EETS 168 (1926). Among modern studies of chivalry, several are particularly useful to students of Middle English literature. Sidney Painter, *French Chivalry* (1940), analyzes the sometimes contradictory feudal, religious, and amorous aspects of knighthood. A collection of essays edited by Edgar Prestage, *Chivalry* (1928), though now old, has useful articles on a number of topics directly relevant to my discussion, including "Medieval Courtesy Books" and "Chivalry and the Idea of a Gentleman," pp. 183–228. John E. Mason, *Gentlefolk in the Making* (1935) deals primarily with English courtesy literature after 1531; however, Chapter I offers a valuable discussion of its previous history.

Since works of literature comprise a great part of the available documents on knighthood, many studies of the subject depend on literature to a large extent. Léon Gautier's old standard study, *Chivalry,* abridged by Jacques Levron and translated by D. C. Dunning (1965), makes particular use of the twelfth-century epics in its analysis of the institution. A most readable synthesis of the history and literature of chivalry is provided by Henry O. Taylor, *The Medieval Mind* (1925), I, 537–603; II, 3–64. Raymond L. Kilgour, *The Decline of Chivalry* (1937), surveys much French literature of the fourteenth and fifteenth centuries in treating the decay of the institution. Arthur B. Ferguson in his historical study of *The Indian Summer of English Chivalry* (1960) concentrates especially on the ideals of knighthood, making substantial use of English literary texts, including Malory. Two books specifically about the knight in English literature are William H. Schofield, *Chivalry in English Literature: Chaucer, Malory, Spenser, and Shakespeare* (1912); and Charles Moorman, *A Knyght There Was* (1967).

Edmund K. Chambers, *Arthur of Britain* (1927), provides a good brief introduction to Arthurian romance. For further study of the subject two works are basic: James D. Bruce, *The Evolution of Arthurian Romance,* two volumes (2nd ed., 1928), which deals inclusively with the development of the genre; and Roger S. Loomis, ed., *Arthurian Literature in the Middle Ages: A Collaborative History* (1959), which presents a collection of significant essays that survey Arthurian literature of all languages. Tom P. Cross and William A. Nitze, in *Lancelot and Guinevere* (1930), have made a useful study of the literary backgrounds of the Lancelot story. For the traditional character of Gawain, see B. J. Whiting, "Gawain: His Reputation, His Courtesy and His Appearance in Chaucer's *Squire's Tale,*" *Mediaeval Studies,* 9 (1947), 189–234.

Criticism of Individual Works and Writers

Since Chrétien de Troyes wrote the earliest Arthurian romances that have come down to us, his works are important in all histories of the literature, as in Chambers, Bruce, and Loomis, cited above. Two other works on Chrétien might also be singled out: Roger S. Loomis, *Arthurian Tradition and Chrétien de Troyes* (1949), deals especially with the relationships of Celtic materials to Chrétien's Arthurian works; and Gustave Cohen, *Chrétien de Troyes et son oeuvre* (1931; slightly revised, 1948), supplies a good general view of the man and his poetry. Hugh Sacker, *An Introduction to Wolfram's 'Parzival'* (1963), is expressly designed to initiate the student into the study of Wolfram's complex romance. See also the materials on the Perceval legend and *Parzival* in the books already cited (including Otto Springer's essay on Wolfram in Loomis' *Arthurian Literature,* pp. 218–250).

Valuable criticism on *Sir Gawain and the Green Knight* is quite plentiful. George L. Kittredge, *A Study of Gawain and the Green Knight* (1916), offers a comprehensive treatment of the background. Useful discussions of the ethical problems faced by Gawain, though I think the authors stress too much Gawain's failures, are George J. Englehart, "The Predicament of Gawain," *MLQ,* 16 (1958), 218–225; and Richard H. Green, "Gawain's Shield and the Quest for Perfection," *ELH,* 29 (1962),

121–139. Of the several recent book-length studies of the work, Larry D. Benson, *Art and Tradition in Sir Gawain and the Green Knight* (1965), is perhaps the most generally useful. Several important articles (including Green, cited above) are collected in Robert J. Blanch, ed., *Sir Gawain and Pearl: Critical Essays* (1966).

Malory scholarship for the past several years has revolved around the problem of the unity of *Morte Darthur*. Eugène Vinaver's position, that Malory was not concerned with producing a coherent story, is set forth in his Introduction to the three-volume *Works*. The opposing view that the various episodes make a coherent narrative aptly entitled *Morte Darthur*, which is held by numerous critics and students of Malory (including myself), is most notably set forward in the collection of studies, *Malory's Originality*, edited by Robert M. Lumiansky (1964); all contributors to this volume refer extensively to Malory's use of sources. J. A. W. Bennett, ed., *Essays on Malory* (1963), presents seven essays on important aspects of Malory studies. Lancelot's particular role in the work is analyzed by R. T. Davies, "Malory's Lancelot and the Noble Way of the World," *RES*, n.s., 6 (1955), 356–364.

Chapter IX

Conclusion: THE CONCURRENCE
OF THE MODES

Literary mirrors have two major characteristics: they are encyclopedic in scope and they aim to present exemplars or types.
The encyclopedic aspect is typified particularly by the
speculums of Vincent of Beauvais, and by the summas of sin
and of the estates like William Peraldus' *Summa de Vitiis* and
John Gower's *Mirour de l'Omme.* Courtesy books—expository mirrors for children, courtiers, or princes—most characteristically
set up ideals. But narratives too can have the purpose of establishing exemplars. Thus, chivalric romances typically aim to
present models of behavior (or bad examples), and in the Renaissance especially titles for narrative works like *Mirror for Magis-
trates* and *Glass of Government* signal a similar purpose.

Any rigid separation of literary mirrors into two types according to these two characteristics would strain the facts. Medieval writers doubtless thought of these works as at once inclusive and exemplary. And so most of them are in one way or
another, even though one of the two aspects usually predomi-
nates. In discussing the *Canterbury Tales* as a Mirror of Society, I
indicated not only that Chaucer was presenting an inclusive
image of society, but also that implicit in his representation of
the various characters who participate in the pilgrimage are
ideals to be striven after and examples to be shunned. Summas
of sin, too, along with being methodically inclusive generally
present the offsetting virtue of the vice analyzed, and even
when they do not, the virtue—the ideal—is implicit in the
definition of the vice. Encyclopedias of things (and characters)

that are of themselves morally neutral provide exemplars in another way. Vincent expected his *Speculum Naturale*, which characterizes the things of nature as he knew them, to give moral instruction by providing insight into the divine plan. He and his medieval contemporaries viewed the whole world as a book written by God for man's instruction. Explicit moralization, though often appended to contemporary descriptions of natural objects—as in the bestiaries—was not seen as necessary to impart moral content to the descriptions. As they believed, the very structure of natural objects and their organization into hierarchies have profound significance.

As exemplars are inherent in the encyclopedias, so the works in which ideals are set up tend to be encyclopedic. Courtesy books like Caxton's *Book of the Ordre of Chyvalry* are organized by classifications designed to be inclusive. Long narratives, like *Morte Darthur* and *Parzival*, by presenting a great variety of episodes virtually summarize the practices of knighthood. Even in shorter works, such as Chrétien's poems or *Gawain and the Green Knight*, the particular problems which provide the subjects of the stories gain substantial attention in several situations so that the narratives may be thought to provide a kind of inclusiveness.

Medieval literary mirrors, therefore, present images, expositorily or in story, which are intended to be inclusive and to represent the ideal. Their nature contrasts with narrative allegories. Like the representations of painters, literary mirrors show height, breadth, and depth, but they tend to be static, to lack movement in time. With narrative allegories the case is exactly opposite: action, temporal process, is the essence of narrative allegory; it requires movement but no particular spatial extension. The contrast of *Everyman* with the Parson's Tale well displays this difference between the modes. *Everyman* shows minutely the linear process involved in dying; all in the play contributes to this presentation. No pictures are drawn; characterization of the man and his society are completely lacking. These details are not relevant to the process. On the other hand, the analysis of sin in the Parson's Tale lays vice out on display in a series of set-pieces. In one picture the glutton is raising a great tankard to his mouth; in another the proud man is caught in his peacock's pose; and in a third the lecher fumbles with the clothes of a wanton partner. The interest is in the panorama, not in a process. *Everyman* and the Parson's Tale, however, represent relatively pure forms of their respective types; many other works embody both modes to a significant degree.

Works of narrative literature indeed usually have important dimensions of comprehensive description and of forward action. Though we have discussed numerous medieval narrative writings here as either mirrors or narrative allegories, they mostly combine the modes. In Chapter V *Pearl* was shown to be a combination of the modes; the work represents allegorically the process of a man's enlightenment by revelation, and it also provides a mirror of Heaven based on the major Biblical materials. *Pearl* is closely related to Dante's *Comedy,* which effects the most notable combination of the two modes in literature. The subject of his poem, says Dante, is "the state of souls after death." He presents the subject methodically and exhaustively: provision is made in the circles of Hell and their divisions for every kind of damned sinner, in Purgatory every classification of sin has its place of atonement, and in Heaven the spheres provide for each degree of blessedness. The mirror of the afterlife then is inclusive; it also aims to establish exemplars: in Dante's words, "The classification of philosophy under which the work proceeds in the whole and in part is moral activity or ethics, for the whole and the part are devised not for the sake of speculation but of possible action." But of course the *Comedy* does not simply contain an ethical mirror of the afterlife; it also embodies an allegorical action. The story of Dante's tour through the three realms is the story of his own salvation, of his turning his back on sin and facing God. This narrative is an allegory with universal application; it is of the journey of Everyman's soul to God.

Other major works which we have discussed as allegories also have mirror aspects. The *Consolation of Philosophy* is not only an allegory of consolation achieved through reason, but also a philosophical exposition of the state of man in this world; it systematically demonstrates the vanity of earthly things and the care of Providence for all, including man. Alan of Lille's *Anticlaudian* along with its allegory of the creation of a perfect man contains in the descriptions of Nature, Fortune, and Reason, and other abstractions virtually a philosophical mirror of the universe. The immensely influential love allegory, the *Romance of the Rose,* taken as a whole is simultaneously a mirror for lovers and a mirror of the subject love in its broadest sense. Guillaume de Lorris, the author of the first part of the work, states at the beginning that he includes an *art of love* in his romance. He thus allies it with Ovid's and Andreas Capellanus' handbooks for lovers which provide inclusive guides to proper amorous practice. In Jean de Meun's lengthy continuation of Guillaume's poem, the God of Love explicitly designates the whole work a *Mirour aus amoreus.* Furthermore, as Alan Gunn has shown in his study of the poem (called *Mirror of Love*), Jean's work in combination with Guillaume's provides a comprehensive treatment of the whole subject of love; it is then a mirror of love not only for young noblemen, but for all men.

Conversely, the works we have dealt with as mirrors frequently have allegorical actions. The summas of sin and of the estates in Gower's *Mirour de l'Omme* arise in connection with a thin allegorical story line in which the genesis of the sins and virtues and their battle for the souls of man are narrated. The *Confessio Amantis* in addition to an exegesis of the seven sins provides a version of the Allegory of Reason: Venus and Genius play the part of Boethian counselors and lead the poet to acceptance of his incapacity for Venus' service. In the *Canterbury Tales,* though the Mirror of Society is dominant in the whole work, individual stories are allegorical in various ways. Some, like the Franklin's Tale and Merchant's Tale, are allied with love allegories. Others, the *Tale of Melibee* and the Knight's Tale, present versions of the Allegory of Reason. More comprehensively, the whole of the *Canterbury Tales* is a story of the Pilgrimage of Man's Soul. Literally, the narrative which binds the series of stories together is that of a pilgrimage by some thirty people from London to the shrine of St. Thomas at Canterbury; nevertheless, this pilgrimage, like all such religious journeys, figuratively incorporates the story of man's passage from earthly to heavenly Jerusalem. The Parson makes this figure explicit. In his prologue he prays for the "wit"

> "To shewe yow the wey, in this viage,
> Of thilke parfit glorious pilgrimage
> That highte Jerusalem celestial."
>
> I, 49–51

The Parson thus explicitly compares their worldly journey to man's pilgrimage to Heaven. His Tale appropriately is a guide to the Sacrament of Penance; as confession properly comes at the end of one's earthly life, so a guide to it properly consummates the pilgrimage. Though the Mirror of Society is dominant in the *Canterbury Tales,* the pilgrimage which all are making unquestionably provides an important allegorical dimension.

While I have dealt with Arthurian narratives as mirror literature, critics more conventionally speak of the quest as the dominant feature of chivalric romances. The quests usually have allegorical implications. For example, when the knight travels to fairyland and back in pursuit of some special object, spiritual death and rebirth is often implied allegorically. The various Grail quests too present a metaphorical parallel to Christian man's search for salvation. In the narrative of *Parzival,* the callow hero falls into error, then achieves knowledge, repents his sins, does penance, and eventually achieves the Grail; considered in the abstract, the action is a story of sin and redemption. In the *Morte Darthur* there are many quests, but the general success of Arthur's knights in their secular adventures is all but negated by their failure in the quest of the Grail, the symbol of salvation. Salvation for society as a whole is no more possible in Malory than in *Piers Plowman;* each man must find his way alone.

One may object that allegorical meanings are not explicitly assigned to the romances by the writers. This is in general true, though specific allegorizations were not unknown in the romances, as when a hermit in the *Morte Darthur* interprets for Gawain one of his recent adventures:

> "Also I may sey you that the Castell of Maydyns betokenyth the good soulys that were in preson before the Incarnacion of our Lorde Jesu Cryste. And the seven knyghtes betokenyth the seven dedly synnes that regned that tyme in the worlde. And I may lyckyn the good knyght Galahad unto the Sonne of the Hyghe

Fadir that lyght within a maydyn and bought all the soules oute of thralle: so ded sir Galahad delyver all the maydyns oute of the woofull castell."

In most cases interpretations by the writers are lacking; in assigning meanings, nevertheless, one may cite the medieval fondness for allegory, the writers' many statements which indicate its pervasiveness in narratives, and the presence in the stories of common allegorical patterns.

To interpret the romances or any other narratives as personification allegory, of course, at base is simply to find universal applications for the stories. And the location and description of universal forms and patterns is the passion of medieval writers and thinkers. Allegory describes universal processes: death, salvation, falling in love, reasoning. The mirror defines universal categories and characteristics and locates the ideal; it places particular sins, men, or natural objects in their proper classifications with all other similar sins, men, or objects. The sophisticated writer in the Middle Ages finds these modes congenial because he is not usually concerned with idiosyncratic detail. He habitually uses even ostensibly individualizing features for generalizing purposes. For instance, he often employs proper names to classify their bearers: William Langland uses the diminutive Will to make his name stand for the willing faculty, common to all: Malyne in the Reeve's Tale bears a common designation for girls of easy virtue; Bayard in *Troilus* is a usual name for horses; and even in such a name as Harry Baillie, we find identified not only a London tavern-keeper whose historicity is verifiable, but also the officer of the peace for the Canterbury pilgrims—their *bailliff* or *baillie*.

The medieval philosopher commonly speaks of *substance* and *accidents*. The underlying, essential form of any physical object is its substance, while dependent and casual qualities are its accidents. Skin, pulp, seeds, and a certain characterizing shape comprise the substance of an apple; individualizing size, color, freckles, and flaws, and the location in time and place of the particular apple are its accidents. The way of thinking which analyzes physical things in such a dichotomy is extended in the medieval writers' approach to all sorts of classifiable phenomena. Though a monk might have red hair or a glutton possess great learning, these likely will be seen as accidental and not substantive manifestations of their characters and will probably not be remarked by the writer. But the glutton's fat and the monk's introversion (whether beneficent or maleficent) are matters of substance, integral to their special characters and the depiction of them. At the same time in processes such as dying or falling in love, it is of only casual significancè whether one man dies of leprosy or apoplexy or another woos his lady with candy or with flowers. Specification is not important. Either of the diseases provides the essential to dying, an immediate cause, and either candy or flowers supplies the gift which is often an important step in the love affair. The allegorist will direct the reader's attention to the constants rather than to these particularizing matters.

Both allegory and mirror represent the writers' attempts to locate and express the universal, unchanging substance of the life, objects, and actions of the world. Both modes are directed to "oure doctrine" in an all-encompassing quest of the essential. A sensitivity to them provides a ready route of access to the best of Middle English literature.

Index

of Medieval Authors and Works

All works, except for anonymous writings, are listed by author. Page references to Bibliographical Notes are italicized.

Alan of Lille, *Anticlaudian,* 28, 102–104, 105, 106, 109, 110, 113, *114, 115,* 117, 120, 128, 130, *217–218; Complaint of Nature,* 102

Albertan of Brescia, *Book of Consolation and Counsel,* 102, 104–105, *114*

Alcuin, 18

Alfred the Great, 93, 103–104, 105

Ancrene Riwle, 30, 140, 144–148, 156, 158–159, *160, 161*

Andreas Capellanus, *De Amore,* 63, 65, 69, 87, *88,* 218

Bede, Venerable, 18

Blow, Northren Wind, 41–42, 56, *58, 59*

Boccaccio, Giovanni, 65; *Decameron,* 163, 164; *Filostrato,* 71

Boethius, *Consolation of Philosophy,* vii, 22, 28, 57, 91–105, 110, 111, 113, *114, 115,* 117–131 *passim,* 217

Cassiodorus, *Institutes,* 29

Caxton, William, 195; Preface to *Morte Darthur,* 191, 210; *Book of the Ordre of Chyvalry* (translation of Lull), 192–193, 216

Chaucer, Geoffrey, vii, 18, 31, *32, 34,* 61–62, 93; *Anelida and Arcite,* 74; *Book of the Duchess,* 23, 37, 39, 46, 65–87 *passim, 89,* 102, 139, 155; *Canterbury Tales,* viii, 17, 22, 30, 139, 140, 158, 159, 163–186, *187–189,* 191–195 *passim,* 215, 218, 219, 220; Cook's Tale, 174; Franklin's Tale, 63, 86, 175, 218; Friar's Tale, 176; Knight's Tale, 85, 86, 102, 218; Man of Law's Tale, 155; Manciple's Tale, 155, Merchant's Tale, 83, 84–86, *90,* 218; Miller's Tale, 83, 85; Monk's Tale, 163, 178; Nun's Priest's Tale, 23, 83, 174; Parson's Tale, 30, 37, 140, 142–145, 156, 216–217, 218–219; Physician's Tale, 175; Prioress's Tale, 175; Reeve's Tale, 83, 220; Shipman's Tale, 83, 176, 178–181, 183, *188–189;* Summoner's Tale, 176, 182–183; *Tale of Melibee,* 102, 104, 107, 113, 218; Wife of Bath's Prologue and Tale, 28, 83, 86, 102, 155, 174, 182; "Former Age,"

94; "Fortune," 94; "Gentilesse,"
94; *House of Fame,* 17, 42–45,
46, 51, 56, 57, *58, 59,* 98–100,
113; *Legend of Good Women,*
124, 155, 163, 164; *Parliament
of Fowls,* 46, 86; *Troilus and
Criseyde,* viii, 22, 28, 65–87
passim, 88, 89–90, 94, 100–102,
113, *115–116,* 155, 208–209,
220; "Truth," 94
Chrétien de Troyes, vii, 210, *212,
213,* 216; *Cligés,* 197, 206; *Erec
and Énide,* 196–197, 198, 206;
Lancelot, 197, 198, 204–206;
Perceval, 197; *Yvain,* 197, 198,
206

Dante Alighieri, 18, 65, 71, 93,
94; *Convivio,* 25–26, *34,* 121;
Divine Comedy, vii, 23–25, 27–
28, *34–35,* 86, 117, 119–133
passim, 134, 135, 137, 138, 140,
147, 184, 207, 217
Deguilleville, Guillaume, *Pilgrimage of the Life of Man,* 108,
138
Deschamps, Eustache, *Lay of the
Twelve Estates,* 167–168, 170,
187

Everyman, 28, 46–49, 51, 56, 57,
58, 59, 64, 216–217

Froissart, Jean, 96; *Chronicles,*
210–211

Gautier de Coincy, *Miracles of
Our Lady,* 163
Gawain Poet. See Pearl Poet
Geoffrey of Vinsauf, *Poetria Nova,*
20, 74
Gerson, Jean, *Consolation of The-
ology,* 126–127, *134*
Giraldus Cambrensis, 30
Gower, John, *161–162; Confessio
Amantis,* 30, 140, 155–159, *160,*

165, 218; *Mirour de l'Omme,* 147,
155, 165–167, 170, 177, 184,
188, 215, 218; *Vox Clamantis,*
155, 165, 167
Gregory the Great, 18, 143, 152
Guillaume de Lorris, *Romance of
the Rose,* vii, 20, 22, 28, 37–38,
40–41, 42, 45, 57, *58,* 61–87,
88, 89, 95, 98, 100, 113, 218.
See also Jean de Meun

Hoccleve, Thomas, 30

Isidore of Seville, *Etymologies,* 29

Jacobus de Voragine, *Golden Legend,* 163
Jean de Meun, 18; *Romance of the
Rose,* 21, 64–65, 78, *88, 89,* 93,
94, 98, 137, 218. See also Guillaume de Lorris
John of Salisbury, 30

Kingis Quair, 95, *114*

Lancelot, French prose version,
206–207
Langland, William, *Piers Plowman,* vii, viii, 17, 18, 22, 23, 28,
31, 36, 42, 46, 49–57, *58, 59–60,*
64, 98, 102, 105–113, 117, 125,
128–130, *136,* 139, 140, 148–
150, 157, 184, 192, 219, 220
Lorens, Friar, *Somme le Roy,* 141
Lull, Ramon. See Caxton
Lydgate, John, *Dance Macabre,*
167, 168–170, 171, *187*

Machaut, Guillaume de, 65; *Fountain of Love,* 77; *Remedy of Fortune,* 77, 95
Malory, Sir Thomas, *Morte Darthur,* vii, 31, 86–87, 191, 194,
195–196, 207–210, *212, 214,*
216, 219–220
Mannyng, Robert, *Handlyng Synne,*

30, 140, 150–159, *160, 161,*
171
Marguerite poetry, 124–125, *136*
Martianus Capella, *Marriage of
Mercury and Philology,* 29

Nigel Wireker, *Speculum Stultorum,*
138

Pearl Poet, vii, 31; *Patience,* 122;
Pearl, 23, 28, 117, 119, 122–128,
130–133, *134, 135–136,* 138,
217; *Purity,* 122; *Sir Gawain and
the Green Knight,* 17, 122, 194–
196, 198–202, 204, 210, *212,
213–214,* 216
Peraldus, William, *Summa de Vitiis*
141, 143, 215
Petrarch, Francis, 71

Revelation of St. Bridget, 119

Sercambi, Giovanni, *Novelle,* 163
Sir Gawain and the Carl of Carlyle,

202–203, *212*
Sir Pride the Emperor, 167, 170,
187

Thomas Aquinas, 26; *Summa
Theologica,* 29, 140
Trivet, Nicholas, 93, 97

Usk, Thomas, *Testament of Love,*
95, *114,* 124–125

Vincent of Beauvais, *Speculum
Maius,* 22, 138, 215, 216

*Wedding of Sir Gawain and Dame
Ragnell,* 202, 203–204, *212*
William of Wadington, *Manuel
des Péchés,* 141, 150
Wolfram von Eschenbach, *Parzival,* 63–64, 197–198, 210, *212,
213,* 216, 219

Ywain and Gawain, 198